THE COUNTRY HOUSES OF ENGLAND
1948–1998

THE COUNTRY HOUSES OF ENGLAND

1948 – 1998

John Cornforth

CONSTABLE · LONDON

First published in Great Britain 1998
by Constable and Company Ltd
3 The Lanchesters, 162 Fulham Palace Road
London W6 9ER
Copyright © 1998 John Cornforth
ISBN 0 09 479150 3
The right of John Cornforth to be identified as the author of this work has been
asserted by him in accordance with the Copyright, Designs and Patents Act 1998
Set in Monotype Garamond 12pt by
Servis Filmsetting Ltd, Manchester
Printed in Great Britain by BAS Printers Ltd

A CIP catalogue record for this book
is available from the British Library

CONTENTS

ILLUSTRATIONS

between pages 144 and 145

Author's note

The author thanks all those who have provided him with illustrations and plans, in particular Francesca Scoones at the National Trust and Camilla Costello and Olive Waller at *Country Life*.

ACKNOWLEDGEMENTS

A study of this kind is in part a giant patchwork pieced together from conversations and through correspondence with many people who have been kind enough to spare the time to answer questions, make suggestions and observations and haul me back on course. Some are people I have known through work over many years and with whom I have discussed related matters before or with whom it has been a pleasure to renew contact after a number of years. I am particularly grateful to all those owners and their wives or husbands who have received me and discussed aspects of the situation as they see it today. I have found it especially interesting to revisit houses after many years, sometimes not since I wrote about them in *Country Life* in the time of their predecessors. A number of people have taken the trouble to read drafts or sections of my text at different stages and made comments, which have been enormously helpful to me. To all those whose names follow I offer my thanks.

Dana Arnold, The Earl of Arundel, Mr and Mrs Hal Bagot, Mrs Elizabeth Bankes, Lord Barnard, Gareth Binns, Lady Braye and Lieut-Colonel Edward Aubrey-Fletcher, Edmund Brudenell, The Duke of Buccleuch and Queensberry, Mrs William Bulwer-Long, Neil Burton, Sir Richard Carew Pole, Frank Carr, The Dowager Countess Cawdor, Dame Elizabeth Chesterton, John Chichester-Constable, The Marquess of Cholmondeley, R.E.J. Compton, The Hon. Mrs Cunliffe-Lister, The Duke and Duchess of Devonshire, Martin Drury, Robert Dufton, Mrs A. Dundas-Bekker, Terry Empson, Jane Fellars, Alan Frost, Mr and Mrs Peter Frost-Pennington, The Knight of Glin, Quentin Goggs, Mrs Patrick Gordon-Duff-Pennington, Sir James and Lady Graham, The Duke of Grafton K.G., Michael Hall, Max Hanna, John Harris, Mr James and The Hon. Mrs Hervey-Bathurst, the late Lady Mary Hesketh, Robert Fleetwood Hesketh, John Hodgson, James Holloway, Norman Hudson, Captain J.D.W. Husband, Sir Thomas Ingilby, Lord and Lady Inglewood, David Innes, Donald Insall, Peter Inskip, Antony Jarvis, Dame Jennifer Jenkins, Simon Jervis, Charles King-Farlow, Tim Knox, Mrs Sheila Landi, Mrs Isobel Lattimore, Lady Victoria Leatham, Sir Charles Legard, The Earl of Leicester, Donald Lockhart, Todd Longstaff-Gowan, John MacLachlan, Lorna McRobey, Rodney Melville, the late Sir Arscott Molesworth St Aubyn and Lady Molesworth St Aubyn, Lord Montagu of Beaulieu, John Neale, Mrs John Nutting, Oliver Pearcey, John Popham, Peter Prideaux-Brune, Richard Reynolds, Colin Richards, Mark Roper, James Rothwell, Christopher Rowell, Matthew Saunders, Martin Shaw, Simon Seligman, The Earl of Shelburne, Sir Tatton Sykes, Owen Tebbs, Henry Tempest, Commander and Mrs Michael Saunders Watson, Nicholas Thompson, Michael Wade, Merlin Waterson, Lord Walpole, Paul Walshe, John Warde, Anthony Wells-Cole, Paul White, Colonel Anthony Wilson, Heather Wilson, Giles Worsley.

One name sadly missing through ill health is that of Jeremy Benson, who with Michael Saunders-Watson was one of the key musketeers in the mid 1970s and early 1980s, as members of the Joint Committee of the Amenity Societies, the HHA and Members of Parliament will remember.

That list does not include those most closely involved with the pulling of the text into shape over the past 11 months. Here, first, comes William Proby, who has had quite enough to do as President of the Historic Houses Association without steering this particular ship. With his wife, Meredyth, he has responded at all stages of its voyage, even when it was still far too early to see where I was heading. They have been a great support.

Richard Wilkin, the Director General of the HHA, has made many useful suggestions, while Peter Sinclair and Geraldine Jones must have hoped it was not me ringing up yet again with a question; and Peter's dog, Molly, a key member of the Chester Street staff, has not bitten me when I have threatened to give the photocopier another attack of indigestion.

Deidre Chappell, an old *Country Life* colleague, has helped with the tying up of many loose ends that occur within the script.

Andrew Best has been an unusually active technical midwife, making all the arrangements between me, the HHA and the publishers to turn an idea into a book as well as being my agent.

FOREWORD

There were several reasons why the Historic Houses Association have supported this publication. First, it seemed right to commemorate our twenty fifth anniversary with a serious study of country houses. Secondly, by coincidence, it is fifty years since the publication of the Gowers report, which, for the first time recognised the role of the private owner in the maintenance of historic houses. Thirdly it is nearly twenty-five years since the dark days of the proposed wealth tax and the exhibition at the Victoria & Albert museum entitled 'The Destruction of the Country House'. Lastly, although a great deal has been written about country houses these publications have tended to be either of glossy magazine format or to be essentially historical perspectives tracing the origins of country houses in their heyday. Very little has been published about the fate of country houses since the last war or attempted to look at their current role in society.

John Cornforth is supremely qualified to write this book. For thirty years he has dedicated himself to the study of country houses. His work with the National Trust and *Country Life* have given him an intimate knowledge of country houses in the round. He probably knows more about individual houses than any other living commentator and he is uniquely equipped to consider changing attitudes in both the private and public sector. His interest and knowledge of interiors also give him a much wider perspective of country houses than pure architecture.

Although the book covers much familiar ground there are many interesting new ideas. Most importantly John Cornforth shows how interest in country houses has developed from a narrow architectural viewpoint to where it is now the entity of house, garden, park, contents, archives, surrounding buildings and estate which is seen as the real jewel and the unique contribution of country houses to British culture. Also, he shows how attitudes within and outside the National Trust have developed so that the Trust are now tending to preserve country houses as accurate records of taste in years gone by, whilst it is the private owner that, through family occupation, provides a continuous and evolving pattern of ownership which links the past with the present. This recognition of the different roles of the National Trust and the private owner, both vital in their own way, makes the survival of the private owner even more important and emphasises how fortunate we are in this country that the private owner has survived, often against the odds, and now provides a very significant part of the national heritage and a vital pillar of both the tourist industry and the economy.

An encouraging feature of the book is that John Cornforth found the modern owner far more optimistic than his or her counterpart twenty-five years ago. This is in part a tribute to the resourcefulness of individual owners who have been able to adapt in an extraordinary way to the greatly changed social and economic circumstances of the late twentieth century but it also reflects a much more enlightened and sup-portive attitude from Government and the public generally as millions of people over the past twenty-five years have been able to visit and enjoy country houses and their settings. Despite this, as John Cornforth points out, the survival of the private owner is still delicately balanced and the entities for which owners are responsible are as fragile as ever. This can be seen all too clearly in the area of taxation where apparently minor and inconsequential changes to the legislation can have a devas-tating effect on the survival of individual properties. Indeed it must be anomalous that, unlike a number of other European countries, this country still provides very little incentive through the tax system for owners to maintain their houses, even if relief from capital taxes are available. Although most of the great treasure houses may be secure either in private or public ownership there are many lesser known prop-erties, each gems in their own particular way, that could easily slip away unrecorded as indeed they did in the disastrous years after the war. John Cornforth shows convincingly that these entities once lost cannot be recreated and are gone for ever.

Above all the book shows the emerging consensus that private owners should be encouraged, a consensus that would have been unthinkable a generation ago. This reflects the views of millions of people who visit these houses and enjoy their settings every year. This

consensus is entirely in keeping with a partnership approach, long advo-
cated by the Historic Houses Association, between owner and
Government, on the basis that the private owner is needed to maintain
this part of our cultural heritage and the owner needs some help from
Government to carry out this responsibility. There are compelling
financial reasons to assist the private owner since the cost of bringing
even one of these houses into the public sector is usually many millions
of pounds. The challenge is for private owner and Government to work
out a comprehensive and long lasting strategy for the survival of the
country house that is fair to both the owner and the public. If this could
be done we could at last move away from the crisis management that
has tended to characterise recent years to the great benefit of all. As
John Cornforth concludes, this is really no more than the recognition
of the old adage 'a stitch in time'.

   That our ideas for a joint exhibition and publication have been trans-
lated into reality is entirely due to the generosity of our sponsors – Aon
Risk Services and ITT London & Edinburgh – without their support
none of this would have been possible.

William Proby
September 1998

PREFACE

During the time I was writing this report I realised that it could not be described as wholly independent. While the views are mine, and not necessarily those of the Historic Houses Association or its members, it is only right to say that I have become aware of how much I have been influenced by writing about country houses and allied subjects in *Country Life* since 1961. It was through *Country Life* and more particularly Christopher Hussey that I became involved with the National Trust in 1965; and I have been a member of committees ever since. Later, after Christopher Hussey's death in 1970, I succeeded him as a member of the Historic Buildings Council for England and continued to serve until 1985. Between 1972 and 1974 I wrote my *Country Houses of Britain: Can They Survive?* and after that worked with the Tax Group of the Joint Committee of the Amenity Societies on their case against the proposed Wealth and Capital Transfer Taxes.

I have visited fewer great houses than might be expected, partly because of time; but also I thought it important to devote more attention to those that are less obvious. Moreover I am particularly aware of the lack of chapters on Scotland, Wales and Northern Ireland. Hence the title of the book.

Where I remain independent is that after 38 years in London I have no desire for even the smallest cottage or garden in the country, let alone any yearnings for acres of land or roof.

The Country House and the Development of Preservation Thinking 1945–1998

The millennium naturally prompts thinking about both the future and the past, and if we are to consider the present and future of country houses, we have to think about their recent past as well. And there is a case for taking that look 14 months early, in November 1998, because then the Historic Houses Association celebrates its first 25 years of work. The year 1998 is also the 50th anniversary of the appointment of the Committee chaired by Sir Ernest Gowers to consider the problems and future of houses of outstanding historic or architectural interest in Britain.

While it is the HHA's anniversary that prompted this study, it needs to be seen in the longer perspective of 50 years for the achievements and the disappointments of recent years as well as new threats to be understood and to appreciate the extraordinary and increasingly rapid developments in thinking that make it such a positive story. So much has happened in both the expansion of the field and the deepening of every aspect of it in the last 30 years that there is much to digest, much more, indeed, than I appreciated when I began. So what follows will, I hope, provide a foundation from which to look forward at the future of country houses in the next century and the next millennium.

One of the phenomena of post-war Britain has been the growth of popular as well as specialist interest in country houses, gardens and parks and the way that they have come to be appreciated as one of the greatest British contributions to European civilisation. How and why that has happened is not widely understood: indeed, the more one thinks about it and the deeper one digs, particularly in books like Martin J. Wiener's *English Culture and the Decline of the Industrial Spirit 1850–1980* (1981) and provocative essays in Raphael Samuel's *Theatres of Memory* (1994), the more unanswered questions pop up. Nevertheless not only are country houses one of the most important elements in the tourist industry with some 15 million visitors to privately owned houses and an estimated 45 million visitors to their gardens, parks and landscapes, but they are significant providers of employment in rural areas and both direct and indirect contributors to local economies and local life. Also they make a valuable but still not fully developed contribution to education at all levels. So in 1998 it is worth attempting to look back at developments in attitudes and see how they have influenced step-by-step advances in legislation. As Peter Mandler wrote in his *The Fall and Rise of the Stately Home* (1997), 'The story of the country house's rise to prominence after 1974 is an absorbing one and deserves a book on its own.' Also it is essential to consider how to move forward, bearing in mind that family attitudes and circumstances and the economic situation of country houses and estates will go on changing, while the broader perception of them will continue to develop and the political framework will change. Indeed the Finance Act 1998 included alterations to the system of exemption of works of art that could have a damaging effect on collections in historic houses that was clearly not the intention of the legislation, while the proposed abolition of the 'one estate election' could have a drastic effect on the funding of country houses that are part of agricultural estates. These could undermine the private and public partnerships that have been built up round country houses and supported through legislation and government agencies, in particular English Heritage.

During the past 50 years the significance of country houses in Britain has come to be seen as both broader and deeper in a great many ways, some of which will be considered here. However, as in so many fields of knowledge, the detail has become so overwhelming that it is increasingly difficult to form a balanced overview. Yet one of the most important developments has been in the very overview of them, in the concept, derived from planning thinking, of those houses being part of entities that are worthy of preservation: these entities consist not just of the fabric of houses, but their contents, gardens, parks and settings, their ancillary buildings and also their estates, which can be effective agencies for good planning, embracing agriculture, forestry, nature conservation and archaeology as well as the conservation of groups of buildings, sometimes even whole villages, and the wider landscape.

Here owners' attitudes, particularly those of the younger generation, may have changed too. Twenty-five years ago almost all owners regarded the land rather than the house as the key to their thinking and giving point to their lives, making the work and the worry worthwhile. It was the land that provided the way of life; and they were landowners who had inherited country houses, not house owners who had inherited land. Today some owners see the balance differently, because running an estate has to be a business involving rethinking the traditional balances between agriculture and other activities, developing new enterprises and creating new income, rather than providing a way of life; and in many cases it no longer supports a family. They see the house and land as part of an indivisible whole, with the estate having little point without the house, and the house providing the point and reward for all the effort that they have to put into keeping the place going so that it can be handed on to the next generation.

How many country houses and historic houses are there; and what is the difference between them as the words are used here? I use 'country houses' to mean houses that have kept their historically associated contents, gardens and parks, and often their estates, while 'historic houses' is used for the much larger category of houses that do not have historically associated contents and not necessarily gardens and parks or supporting land. Despite all the listing and cataloguing that has gone on in the past 25 years, it is still impossible to say how many there are in either category, because all the time little-known manor houses with historic contents are coming to light. By December 1996 there were 363,049 listed buildings, 8947 of which were Grade 1, and 19,909 Grade 2*. Thus it would be reasonable to guess that there are probably about 1500 country houses that are still fairly complete entities in private ownership. The Gowers Committee thought that there were probably not less than 2000 houses. In 1974 I thought that there were probably about 1500 left, which was clearly an underestimate while Michael Sayer in his *Disintegration of a Heritage: Country Houses and their Collections 1979–1992* considered in the mid-1970s that there were more than 2000 seats in the United Kingdom, with the number dropping to 1400 by 1992.

Despite the growth of the National Trust and the National Trust for Scotland and the holding of country houses by many other organisations, including a growing number of individual trusts, the majority of the most important houses and collections still remain in private hands. So are a high proportion of historic buildings and monuments open to the public: in 1997, of the 2013 open, 44% were privately owned, 25% belonged to local authorities, 19% to the Government or its agencies and 12% to the National Trust. Moreover, perhaps surprisingly, none of the most important country houses in England have been lost during the past 25 years (if Mentmore, the mid-19th century Rothschild house and collection in Buckinghamshire, is not included, and I am sure most people would castigate me for not doing so): Warwick Castle and Kedleston, in Derbyshire, are the only ones to have passed out of private ownership, the former with some of its contents to Madame Tussaud's, and the latter to the National Trust.

On the other hand there have been a number of crises over important individual country houses, and costs of devising futures for them have continued to spiral in an alarming way, with almost £80 million spent on rescue packages since 1981 by the National Heritage Memorial Fund and the Heritage Lottery Fund. The creaming off of star objects as well as the draining of outstanding and interesting historically associated contents continues from a very wide range of houses. Moreover a considerable number of houses have been sold and all their historic contents dispersed. Thus all the time the overall holding of houses with historically associated contents is being slimmed down. Contrary to what is sometimes said, it is not being replaced by new owners: a number of houses find well-endowed purchasers, who may spend a great deal on initial restoration, but few stay long; and even fewer develop into interesting entities.

All this helps to explain the increasing value placed on the houses that have survived intact, bearing in mind that losses in the future, as in the past, are bound to happen for a host of reasons that are beyond the reach of systems of preservation devised by legislation.

While there is much to worry about and it is hard to know how many houses are in low water financially or heading towards it, the situation is very different from the dire conditions in 1948 or 1974: almost all the owners I talked to were more optimistic than I expected them to be. Thus it would be wrong not to recognise the remarkable achievement of owners, the contribution of bodies like the National Trust and the National Trust for Scotland, private trusts and public bodies as well as government support through legislation and funding. Houses face the future with a sense of appreciation and concern that is quite remarkable to anyone who remembers the 1940s and 1950s.

[4]

The establishment of the Historic Houses Association in 1973 was one natural and essential step in the process of development, because it was clear that the privately owned houses needed their own organisation to help each other, work with other bodies, inform the public and make their case to Government. However, when it was being planned, no one could have foreseen how it, and, indeed, the whole amenity movement, would soon become involved in a campaign opposing the new Labour Government's proposal to introduce a Wealth Tax and replace Estate Duty by Capital Transfer Tax in the Finance Act 1975, which threatened to wipe out the private sector of what quickly came to be called the National Heritage, a phrase hardly used in the 1960s. The new Association had been preparing for European Architectual Heritage Year (EAHY), which was to be held in 1975.

Indeed that was what had prompted the HHA's godfather, the Historic Houses Committee of the British Tourist Authority, to commission my *Country Houses of Britain: Can They Survive?* for publication in October 1974. I had been asked to go to the BTA Committee, and the day before I attended a press conference announcing the programme for European Architectural Heritage Year. I had not expected its purely urban thrust, and I said to the Committee that unless they made their own shout in 1975 they would be squeezed out. Their response was to ask me to make it. Later I told Roy Strong, who was appointed Director of the Victoria and Albert Museum in 1974, about what I was doing, and that gave him the idea to hold what became *The Destruction of the Country House 1875–1975* exhibition, which thanks to the support of Jack and Drue Heinz also opened in the autumn of 1974. So it was just chance that the BTA publication and the exhibition conceived in relation to EAHY coincided with the new Labour Government's tax proposals. A reading of John Harris's *No Voice From The Hall* (1998) will confirm that the exhibition was about buildings, not about owners, and was not some kind of aristocratic plot as some have tried to make out.

The most striking aspect of the exhibition grew out of John Harris's passion for demolished houses that started in 1946 when he was 15 and developed as part of his work as an architectural historian in the late 1950s and 1960s. For the first time he and others attempted to work out what had been lost not only since 1945 but since 1870; and almost everyone was astounded and shocked at the results. According to the list in *Save Tomorrow's Ruins* there were 431 country houses demolished in England, with 17 more in ruins and 28 burned and demolished; 175 demolished in Scotland, with 10 in ruins and 18 burned and demolished; and 23 demolished in Wales and 10 in ruins. The total came to 712. But as a result of work since then the list at the end of *The Destruction of the Country House* book could probably be increased by 50%.

An important second aspect of the exhibition was the attention it gave to gardens and landscapes, and this was a reflection of John Harris's and Marcus Binney's own growing concerns. A third was Marcus Binney's unsuspected talent for publicity. It was as if the exhibition opened the lid of a box for him, and like Jack he popped out. He saw that there was a way of getting publicity for the exhibition by feeding local newspapers with information about houses in their areas. As a result of that he set up Save Britain's Heritage, which has been a leading campaigner for threatened buildings ever since.

During 1975 the Government in effect abandoned its proposal of a Wealth Tax, but in the Finance Act that year it replaced Estate Duty with Capital Transfer Tax, which came into force from March 1974. With it also came the first novel proposal for the exemption of outstanding buildings and their protecting land.

How that proposal and those for maintenance funds that followed were eventually modified and constructive legislation came out of them will be discussed later; but the way the crisis was handled by the amenity movement, the press and the owners, and met with an unprecedented degree of public support, immediately transformed the subject of the country house and its future from being a matter of concern to a limited circle of owners, public bodies and individuals to one of wide public fervour and support. That has included a gradual appreciation of the point of country houses and their estates by many officers of local authorities. They have been influenced by a combination of conservation thinking, an increasing awareness of their historical and cultural significance and of their role in garden and landscape history in the 1980s and '90s, and a recognition of the contribution houses and estates make to the economic success of tourism and the provision of employment in their areas. In some cases their interest has been stirred by threats to historic gardens and parks, and in others by negotiations over Capital Transfer and Inheritance Tax exemptions, but it has happened step by step: a pattern of interest and concern has developed empirically and unevenly, almost without anyone being clearly aware of what has been happening, and certainly without any grand theories.

The years 1975 to 1982 saw real progress in legislation, in relation both to taxation, as will be explained, and, as a result of the furore over the Government's handling of Mentmore, to the establishment of the National Heritage Memorial Fund in 1980. That in turn led to the desire to prove that it could save historic houses, with Canons Ashby (Fig. 24), in Northamptonshire, as the immediate test case.

It was inevitable that all the campaigning for country houses and the heritage should have stirred up a reaction along the way; and it would be wrong to overlook it here, because of its influence on the broader climate of opinion, in particular the writing of many journalists about houses, political concerns for the Heritage and how the National Heritage Memorial Fund and the Heritage Lottery Fund are viewed by the Government. Here two books of the mid-1980s stand out, Patrick Wright's *On Living in an Old Country* (1985) and Robert Hewison's *The Heritage Industry* (1987). In 1991 Patrick Wright brought out *A Journey through the Ruins*. It is these books and the writings of David Cannadine, now on the other side of the Atlantic, that have prepared the way for the much broader sweep of Raphael Samuel's *Theatres of Memory* (1994) explaining why history matters so much to many people today.

The reaction of the mid-1980s did not affect the flurries of activity over a number of individual houses whose futures became uncertain for a variety of reasons – Calke Abbey and Kedleston, both in Derbyshire, Belton House, in Lincolnshire, and Weston Park, in Shropshire – and required special action for their preservation. But Dame Jennifer Jenkins, who as chairman of the Historic Buildings Council for England from 1975 to 1985 knew as much as anyone about the overall situation of country houses, was almost certainly right in deciding to concentrate on the countryside rather than country houses when she became chairman of the National Trust in 1986. As she wrote in *From Acorn to Oak Tree* (1994): 'Everywhere I went I was asked about the Trust's great houses, seldom about the coast or the countryside or even the Lake District. One of the aims I set myself was somewhat to redress this imbalance. This was not because I was uninterested in the houses but – at least in part – because I thought that threats to the countryside had become more pressing than threats to historic houses.'

1979 saw the coming in of the Conservative Government under Mrs Thatcher and the first reversal of tax policy since the Second World

War, with the comprehensive reduction of income and capital tax rates. Thus whereas in 1973–74 the top rate of income tax was 75% over £20,000, and 83% over £24,000 in 1978–79, that dropped to 60% over £25,000 in 1979–80 and to 40% over £19,300 in 1988–89.

Similarly Capital Transfer Tax in 1975–77 was levied at the top rate of 75% on estates over £2 million, with 60% in the bracket of £150,000 to £500,000. By 1984–85 it had dropped to a top rate of 60% on estates over £285,000. And when CTT was replaced by Inheritance Tax in 1986–87, the top rate was 60% on estates over £317,000; and that was dropped to 40% on those over £100,000 in 1988, with the threshold being raised to £215,000 in the year 1997–98.

In the late 1980s and early 1990 there was a lull in public consciousness about country houses, and a false sense that all was well with them for the time being. That was reflected in a feeling fanned by Nicholas Ridley, when he was Secretary of State for the Environment in 1986–89: he showed no sympathy for the difficulties of those who had inherited houses and said that there were plenty of would-be owners to take on what appeared on the market. So it may not be just coincidence that in those years English Heritage began to direct grant aid away from country houses in private ownership. At the same time a great deal was going on in the sphere of historic gardens and parks expanding into broader landscapes: there, thinking was developing very fast, not least in the scope of exemptions from capital tax. Also there were a number of important initiatives by the two National Trusts, with a number of schemes being landscape-led in a quite new way.

However, what is just as important is the number of conditional exemptions of land relating to outstanding buildings that have gone through, and also the number of maintenance funds set up that have involved land. No list of cases is published, but there have been 326 cases of conditional exemption and over 100 maintenance funds set up. It is reasonable to assume that most of those places would not have survived without those provisions, and the possibility of exemption has given many other owners the confidence to soldier on. Without those provisions there would have been many more crises, and the country house scene today would look very much thinner. Moreover the benefits in terms of conservation planning have been infinitely greater than was conceived when the legislation was being pressed for in 1974–76.

The tax changes during the years of Conservative Government gave most owners a new confidence and optimism and that was, perhaps surprisingly, not altered by the results of the election in May 1997. That was partly because the new Labour Government did not appear to have the same social and economic priorities and objectives as its predecessor in 1974.

Certainly the rich, and so by implication country house owners, have not been seen as targets for attack from the new Government as they had been 23 years earlier. Indeed on a debate on the Lottery in 1996 the Labour Party reiterated its support for private ownership of houses as being the best and most economical way of looking after them. Mark Fisher, then Minister for the Arts, came out strongly in favour of them: 'The historic houses have a good story to tell. They are important not just for their architecture, but also for the works of art they contain and for their gardens. Together they represent a contribution to our cultural heritage which few countries can match. The private owner is a most effective guardian of this heritage. It is the Government's role to ensure that historic houses remain in secure private ownership so that future generations can enjoy that which we currently treasure.' However, so far the Government has shown disappointingly little sense of commitment to the heritage or any of the arts and its approach to access and exemption of works of art is a crude simplification of an exceedingly complicated situation which could produce results that are the opposite of what is intended, leading to the sale of objects and the closure of houses rather than making more places more available.

Indeed its strongly populist approach to all the arts and the heritage, with a greater and probably simplistic approach to access, may well upset balances carefully built up over many years. That emphasis is likely to influence conditions attached to repair grants, exemptions as well as in lieu *in situ* deals; and could lead to seriously damaging sales of contents as well as owners' decisions to sell up completely. The populist approach is also apparent in the Government's continued running down of the National Heritage Memorial Fund, which concentrates on places and things for the long term rather than on immediate benefits for people. So when important country houses get into difficulties, it is going to be much more difficult to work out solutions for them than in the 1980s and early 1990s when the National Heritage Memorial Fund was better funded.

So despite the improvements in the economic situation and the legislative system, country houses still seem to be involved in a steeple-chase – and the course tends to change all the time through new hazards appearing. Losses on Lloyd's caused undisclosed, and so uncertain, damage which people are reluctant to talk about, but it would appear to have caused fewer sales of country houses than was at one time feared and most families seem to have been able to rearrange their affairs so that they have survived. But, of course, it is impossible to know what else has had to be sold to meet losses, and how many country houses have a permanently reduced capital base. Now there are all the uncertainties surrounding the future of agriculture.

Moreover it has been largely a matter of luck, or bad luck, whether country houses have fallen at one or more tax jumps or have had a clear round in the past 30 years. It has to be remembered that almost all have had nasty falls at one or more death duty jumps in the years before 1945 and these have cut away at their supporting assets. So in looking at any country house today it is essential to ask what has happened over the past 100 years and particularly how it got through the years of Capital Transfer Tax. No one can presume that the steeple chase is over and constant changes to tax law make forward planning difficult, if not impossible. Inheritance Tax has given many owners an opportunity to look ahead, but not all are able to take advantage of that, and when there is an unexpected death, there can still be disaster.

Despite the publication of studies commissioned by the Historic Houses Association and Mandler's book, I became increasingly concerned that the whole subject of the country house needed a fresh and different kind of look that turned away from statistics to ideas, attitudes and influences. This was partly because the establishment of the Heritage Lottery Fund in 1995 raised totally new possibilities of aid, although it was far from clear what – if anything – the HLF should do for privately owned houses. Also I felt that the time had come to take stock and see how far we had come since 1948 in order to look forward.

While working on this book I have been constantly struck by the different kinds of conversation I have with owners and with those involved with houses through working in museums or the National Trust or as writers, but without owners' priorities, responsibilities or problems: indeed these conversations are carried out in almost different languages, with the same names but other vocabularies and grammars. Despite that, the views of non-owners, and particularly of those involved with houses in other ownerships, are essential buttresses to the survival of the private sector in a changing world: through concentrating on places almost to the exclusion of people, they are constantly developing thinking about houses and so are essential to the vitality of the continuing cause of country houses.

What does not come out here is the vital contribution of individuals outside the circle of owners, because it is not easy to write about those who make official systems work at local as well as national levels and get them to change, develop and expand. Indeed it would be possible to write a completely different book around all those who have made key contributions to the solutions of problems and improvements in the system in the last 30 years. It is their good will and enthusiasm that help develop wider understanding and pleasure and so public support.

The limited time available to me and the scale of this publication meant that I have approached the subject differently. In 1974 I was concerned with trying to suggest the scale of the problem, finding out how many houses still survived, how many had gone since 1945 and how the economics of houses worked, in particular how their future was bound up with fluctuations in the prosperity of estates and the contribution they made to tourism and tourism made to them. Many of the themes, with the exception of demolitions, which, happily, now are insignificant, continue to be as relevant today as they were in 1974, and much more familiar. But given the increase in the number of buildings regarded as outstanding by English Heritage to 28,000, and changes in pressures on government expenditure in general and in attitudes to support for the arts, education and so on, it seemed more helpful to turn away from taxation as the main theme, to the country house as an entity involving contents and setting.

That in turn raises again the argument for maintenance funds and considering their current strengths and weaknesses, which are discussed. However taxation is a difficult, indeed dangerous, subject for a layman to write about, especially in a study that is written largely in historical terms, because it is unrealistic to consider individual taxes: it is the total package and how individual taxes interlock and affect all the elements of an entity that have to be understood. That is a highly technical field and best left for professional bodies such as the Historic Houses Association to discuss with Government.

On the other hand this study says more than many might have expected on houses in other forms of ownership, particularly the

National Trust. There are several reasons for this. First the National Trust has become a stronger, more professional, owner of houses and gardens in the past 25 years, opening 27 country houses as well as other buildings, gardens and landscapes. Also it is important to be able to relate the positions of private owners and the National Trust and to understand the influences it has come to have on the private sector. It is necessary to understand what the Trust can and cannot do; and to realise that it is not some kind of corporate ogre with a master list of desirable places for which it is ready to make sudden take-over bids. Indeed it is not widely appreciated that the Trust happens not to have taken on any country houses since 1991 but continues to see itself as a refuge of last resort. On the other hand it has taken on several historic landscapes, which have involved less heavy costs and smaller endowments.

Also it needs to be understood how and why the Trust now provides an alternative way of showing houses to those pursued by private owners. Although most of the families continue to live in the houses that they have given to the Trust, the Trust no longer pretends that rooms are still lived in when they aren't. Thus privately owned houses and those belonging to the Trust have taken two different routes and are coming to represent two different kinds of history almost without people realising it, even those involved with or close to the Trust. In the 1950s and '60s the Trust imitated private owners, trying to make its houses looked lived in, as if the owners had just gone out for the afternoon. Since the mid-1970s the Trust's houses and gardens have continued to evolve, and so have had an increasingly positive history of their own; but, unless donors' families continue to live fully in them, the houses no longer reflect those families' ongoing history: instead they reflect changing attitudes and interpretations of the past. Privately owned houses, on the other hand, continue to lay more emphasis on family lives and fortunes, and so the balance between present and past is different; and so is the concern for the future. How and why this duality has developed will be considered at different stages in the study, because it is crucial to understanding the situation today and why the privately owned houses are so important for the future.

Visitors tend to have different attitudes to houses that are privately owned and those owned by the Trust and other bodies. Clearly they prefer the former, perhaps because they find it easier to approach the past through people, and owners represent a living past. The houses owned by the Trust they regard as less human, and they thus tend to be more critical of them.

While the strengthening of the National Trust has been enormously valuable and it has had a variety of influences on the houses in private ownership, it in no way reduces the value of those houses. On the contrary it increases it: however well the Trust presents a house – and it is now subject to considerable pressures that will be explained – it knows it can never capture the essence or the thrill of a private house that is well kept up or has preserved a magic from the past.

Thus today, as in 1948 and 1973, happily the privately owned houses still represent the most important section and have the finest collections, and on the whole they appear to be in much better heart than they were a generation and two generations ago. That is an enormous and often unrealised achievement. While much of the credit is due to owners and their wives and also to their advisers, it has also depended on the interrelationships of the private and public sectors as they have built up over the years, on the legislative framework that has grown up step by step and on the support of government bodies and agencies that make the systems work and develop. Much of this has happened in a piecemeal fashion, particularly in the development of such spheres as exemptions from capital taxation and the growth of repair grants, but it is based on the realisation that public interest and benefit is best served through private management, and that the systems have to make it possible for private management not only to survive but to flourish.

The situations that individual families face are so varied and so changing that at any one time very little is known about the real financial position of country houses. However, it is clear that more needs to be done to sustain the achievement and also more thought given to how to help the weaker brethren and strengthen them before it is too late. Increasingly official preservation action is driven to fighting in the last ditch and forgets the old adage about 'a stitch in time'.

PART I

I

◆

The First Steps Towards the Preservation of Houses, Gardens and Parks 1896–1945

The idea that English country houses have been open to visitors since the days of Elizabeth I is an appealing one, as it is to see late 20th century tourists as the successors to the redoubtable Celia Fiennes who rode about England in the years around 1700, or to those who stayed in the early 18th century inns built for travellers anxious to see Castle Howard or Houghton, who flocked to Chatsworth in the mid-19th century when the 6th Duke of Devonshire ordered that the fountains should be played for them, or who went to Eastnor Castle (Figs 2, 27 and Plate X) in Herefordshire from Malvern in a horse-drawn brake organised by Lady Henry Somerset for those who did not have their own carriages.

The tradition of country house visiting is an old one; but there is another side that was ignored or overlooked until Peter Mandler's *Fall and Rise of the Stately Home* drew attention to it: the lack of interest in country houses in the second half of the last century and in the first four decades of this century on the part of some of their owners and the public.

At the same time the enthusiasm for old houses goes back a very long way, certainly as far as the early 17th century and even into the 16th century; but even if only the last 150 years are considered, the roots are various. On the one hand there was the craze for restoring manor houses that started well before the 1880s when a number in the West Country, which had sunk into being farmhouses on larger estates, began to be sold off and attract new purchasers who restored them and laid out good gardens round them. A great many houses in that region were described in *Country Life* in the 1920s and '30s, and later several were left to the National Trust by their saviours, among them Great Chalfield, in Wiltshire, restored in 1905–12 and left to the Trust in 1943,

[17]

Lytes Cary, in Somerset, restored after 1907 and bequeathed in 1948, Westwood Manor, Wiltshire, restored a few years later and bequeathed in 1956. Another was Hidcote, in Gloucestershire, which is now thought of just as a garden, and which was the first 20th century garden to come to the Trust in 1948. One of the last houses in this group is Sissinghurst Castle in Kent, which was acquired by Harold Nicolson and Vita Sackville-West in 1930 and transferred to the Trust in 1968.

Some members of the Souls were drawn to old houses, among them Lord and Lady Plymouth who restored St Fagan's Castle, near Cardiff, as well as building a huge Jacobean Revival pile at Hewell in Worcestershire, and Lady Elcho, the eldest daughter of Percy and Madeline Wyndham, for whom Philip Webb built Clouds, in Wiltshire, and the wife of the future 11th Earl of Wemyss, who lived at Stanway, in Gloucestershire. To what extent Lord Curzon's involvement with the preservation of buildings in England and India can be linked with his friendships among the Souls is a moot point, but it was he who in 1911 saved Tattershall Castle, in Lincolnshire, and then acquired and restored Bodiam Castle, in Sussex, both of which he bequeathed to the National Trust. And as well as inheriting Kedleston, he rented both Montacute, in Somerset, and Hackwood, in Hampshire.

However, it is necessary to provide some form of framework in order to understand why England lagged behind most European countries in developing a policy for preserving historic buildings; and also how the way for what happened after the Second World War, in particular the Historic Buildings and Ancient Monuments Act (1953), was prepared over the previous 71 years. It took nine years for the first and very limited Ancient Monuments Protection Act (1882) to reach the statute book. It was promoted by Sir John Lubbock, later 1st Lord Avebury, who bought the key prehistoric sites at Avebury, Silbury Hill and West Kennett Farm. Neither that act nor its successor, the Ancient Monuments Protection act (1900), which was drafted by Sir Robert Hunter, one of the three founders of the National Trust and Solicitor to the Post Office, were concerned with occupied buildings or overrode owners' freedom of action. It was only with the Ancient Monuments Consolidation and Amendment Act (1913) that the concept of listing ancient monuments was introduced; and that an owner was required to seek permission to alter or demolish a listed ancient monument.

Even if there were no effective controls over occupied buildings before the First World War, perhaps surprisingly, the kernel of the idea of protecting collections of works of art had been planted. They had first come under threat as a result of the agricultural slump of the 1870s and the legislation that allowed for sales from settled estates, with the great sales from Blenheim Palace and Hamilton Palace in the early 1880s paving the way for much that was to follow.

When death duties were introduced in 1894, with a top rate of 8%, that seemed a fatal blow to many of those with inherited houses and collections. Thus Walpurga Lady Paget, the German wife of a diplomat and an ardent country house guest when in England, wrote after a visit to Hatfield in 1895 or 1896: 'Lady Salisbury told me that Lord Salisbury [the 3rd Marquess who was Prime Minister in the 1890s and died in 1903] had made over Hatfield and everything else to Lord Cranborne on account of the fearful death duties. In the meanwhile all the works of art are going to America and Russia.'

However, in the Finance Act 1896 the principle of exemption of works of art was introduced, the qualification being objects of 'such national or historic interest that they would be purchased or accepted as a bequest by one of the national collections'. That was redefined in the Finance Act 1930 and the revised rule applied until 1969. What had happened in 1896 appears to be explained by the future Lady Sackville (the wife of the 3rd Baron, the heir to Knole and the mother of Vita Sackville-West) in her diary for 17 April that year: 'Last night Sir Michael Hicks Beach proposed in his budget to abolish death duties on pictures and heirlooms. This will save Knole. He has written to me telling that it was I, who made him understand the injustice of the law, when we met at the Wimbornes.'

To what extent the idea of exemption was inspired by a desire to protect historic collections *in situ* or keep works of art off the market where they could not be afforded by British institutions and so go abroad is not clear; but the presumption must be that the second was the more powerful argument. Certainly it was the latter concern that led to the establishment of the National Art Collections Fund in 1902.

Between the two World Wars there were only two pieces of legislation, the Ancient Monuments Act (1931) and the Town and Country Planning Act (1932). Neither of them were concerned with historic houses, but they introduced two important principles: preservation was seen as being a part of planning, and a historic building did not have to be uninhabited. The first act was designed to enable local authorities to protect monuments and their settings from unsuitable developments, while the second permitted local authorities to serve preservation orders on buildings of architectural or historic interest; but, of course, there were no lists of historic buildings worthy of preservation to guide them.

It would be interesting to know more about the growth of the idea of planning embracing preservation, but it was certainly in the mind of Clough Williams-Ellis from as early as 1921 when the sale of Stowe (Fig. 35), in Buckinghamshire, was announced. In a letter to *The Spectator* in the issue of 23 July, he wrote: 'There are few places better worth preserving or better suited for public delight and education. Properly arranged and wisely administered Stowe might become a great cultural centre . . .' In 1922 the house and gardens were purchased for the newly founded school.

Five years later in *England and the Octopus* he devoted the ninth chapter to *The Great House: Its Conservation and Conversion*. There he wrote: 'It is unthinkable that the great houses of England should be allowed to perish away – the really great houses, that is – those that are great in their architecture, their associations and the beauty of their settings and not merely great in size – We need to differentiate between the honest-to-God Stately Homes of England and the considerable tail of merely large or pretentious houses with no better claim to the title than auctioneers' say-so . . . It would be well if some impartial, authoritative and really critical commission could sit on our Country Seats and make a list of those which really deserve protection as national monuments and as characteristic and precious parts of England.'

A growing awareness of the threat emerges in leaders in *Country Life* in the late 1920s and early 1930s. They were probably mostly written by Christopher Hussey, who had known Clough Williams-Ellis since before 1926. The subjects give a sense of the thinking in the magazine: on 4 April 1925 there was one on *The Importance of the Landowner*, and on 29 May 1926, on *The Peril of the Countryside* in which occurs the observation: 'The great estates might have exercised some control in certain districts, and, no doubt, did for a time, but they are fast breaking up, if they have not already done so.' There were, however, no leaders on country houses as such until one in the issue of 4 February 1928, entitled *Such as Knole*, written on the death of the 3rd Lord Sackville: 'Knole is one of a group of great and historic houses that are kept up by their owners as much for the benefit of the public as for themselves. The house is open most days of the week, and the park is always open to wander in wherever the visitor wishes. It is exceedingly unjust and short-sighted that one who inherits such a place should pay Death Duties on a house and park which is regarded even by him as national property . . . Such houses, their contents and parks, should be entirely relieved from Death Duties, local rates and taxes, and be recognised for what they are: priceless national possessions in which the continuity of life must be preserved, even at the cost of a few thousand pounds to the Exchequer.'

Almost two years later, in the issue of 25 January 1930, under the prophetic title of *The National Heritage*, the same line was taken: 'That our great country houses, with their treasures of art, their wide-spreading parks and delightful gardens, have now come to be considered as national and not merely personal heritages we owe to the generosity and practical spirit of the landowners of today . . . we may well ask whether the Government will not do something practical to prevent the constant breaking up of beautiful properties into ugly building estates and the dispersal abroad of well-nigh priceless collections . . .'

A few months later, in June 1930, Christopher Hussey wrote about Blickling Hall, Norfolk, one of the houses belonging to the new 11th Marquess of Lothian, the former Philip Kerr, who had inherited, in March 1930, five houses as well as massive death duties. At that time Blickling was let, but Hussey presumably discussed the articles with him.

That suggests that Lord Lothian was aware of the growing concern of *Country Life* about the problems of country houses in the years immediately before he made his now famous speech at the National Trust's annual meeting in 1934 that led to the formation of the National Trust's Country Houses Scheme. The speech was not a bolt from the blue as used to be supposed, but the result of careful preparation of the ground. At the National Trust's annual dinner in 1933 Professor W.G. Constable, the first head of the Courtauld Institute, spoke of houses at risk. Early in 1934 Lord Lothian asked Donald Matheson, the Trust's newly appointed Secretary, whom he knew through his Round Table, whether the Trust might take up the country house question; and Matheson, having discussed the matter with Lord Zetland, the chairman of the Trust, got his agreement to invite Lord Lothian to speak. Also Lothian obtained a list of notable country houses from *Country Life*, which came to 639 houses with a sub-division of 57 'big' houses such as Knole, Hatfield and Haddon.

That must have been drawn up by Hussey, and, indeed, the speech, which deserves to be reprinted, reflects Hussey's thinking and writing on the need for the extension of exemption to houses and gardens. That was to apply even if they were sold intact with their contents for preservation as a whole, with death duties only being levied if the property was broken up. He also wanted the Treasury to 'permit inclusion in maintenance claims of all sums spent on upkeep or restoration or embellishment of such houses'. In return he envisaged public access from time to time. 'Such action (by the Treasury),' he said, 'is a natural part of that new order of planned private enterprise which is increasingly coming to replace both the unrestricted individualism of the early capitalistic era and the universal socialization of early Socialist thinkers.'

In 1935 the 5th Earl of Onslow, the owner of Clandon Park, near Guildford, sent a birthday message to *Country Life*: '. . . It has among other services rendered one in particular, namely, the description in minute detail of all the great Country Houses of England as they were actually lived in as the houses of their owners. Perhaps in twenty years' time none will exist in that condition.'

Who else took up the idea of tax exemption at that time is now hard to discover, but one was Roger Hesketh, a friend of John Summerson and Christopher Hussey, and later, after the Second World War, a Member of Parliament and amateur architect who in the 1960s designed for himself what is arguably the most successful country house built in Britain since the Second World War, Meols Hall, near Southport (Fig. 61). At the end of 1930 he took over *The Master Builder*, a trade paper for the building industry, and tried to make it into an alternative to *The Architectural Review*. While he did not attempt to introduce country houses into it, he was interested in developing concepts of town and country planning and the role of parks in regional planning. Private parks had been named in certain regional plans, and in his editorial for January 1932, he suggested that any park scheduled under a regional planning scheme as worthy of preservation should be exempt from death duties and rated at the same level as agricultural land: he was arguing for what he regarded as works of art on planning grounds, an approach that anticipates positive action by some 45 years.

If tax relief was a new idea, so was the enthusiasm for 18th century architecture and particularly country houses. The taste for 18th century English pictures and furniture was developed first by architects and painters in the 1860s, but that for early Palladian interiors was only just getting going in the years before the First World War. Then the kind of spirit that inspired Albert Richardson's *Monumental Classic Architecture*, which came out in 1912, was nipped in the bud by the war. The war also delayed a number of books that were to be influential between the wars and even after. They include Bolton's two folio volumes on *The Architecture of Robert and James Adam*, which appeared in 1922, Percy Macquoid and Ralph Edwards's *The Dictionary of English Furniture*, which appeared in three folio volumes in 1924–25, and the nine folio volumes of *English Homes* started by H. Avray Tipping in 1914, but which stopped short of the Regency period. It was only between the wars that people began to write about the late 18th and early 19th centuries, with Bolton writing his first book about *The Works of Sir John Soane* in 1924 and John Summerson writing his first edition of *John Nash* 10 years later, the same year that Margaret Jourdain wrote *Regency Furniture 1795–1820*.

This broadening appreciation of classical architecture and country houses brought with it a growing awareness of the threat, and it is significant that 1937 saw the foundation of the Georgian Group as an offshoot of William Morris's Society for the Protection of Ancient Buildings. The immediate stimulus to that was the destruction of 18th century buildings in London and in particular the threat to Carlton House Terrace, but some of its founding members were interested in country houses. Thus it is worth bearing in mind the parallelism between the enthusiasm of writers about architecture, in particular Christopher Hussey, the fashion for the 18th century that is expressed in books like John Steegman's *The Rule of Taste* published in 1936, and those circles interested in the National Trust and the Georgian Group. It was the thinking and writing of these small interlocking circles that was to be so influential after the Second World War and into the 1980s. They had a strong and clear aesthetic canon encapsulated in the title of Steegman's book. In a recent lecture Michael Hall, the present Architectural Editor of *Country Life*, emphasised how that kind of taste was pioneered by architects, designers and decorators and how it became a new aesthetic ideal: 'What had happened,' he suggested,' is that the architecture of authority had been replaced by an architecture of the authority of taste. Country houses now aspired to embody not power, but civilization.'

By the time of Lord Lothian's speech the Trust had become involved with country houses almost by accident. In 1931 Mr E.E. Cook had

1. The Great Hall at Montacute, Somerset, about 1935. Montacute was the first large house opened to the public by the National Trust and was virtually unfurnished.

given the Society for the Protection of Ancient Buildings a substantial sum of money to buy historic buildings for preservation. The Secretary, A.R. Powys, had a personal interest in Montacute, in Somerset, and he knew that the Phelips family, who had let the house since 1911, were trying to sell it without success. Indeed in 1931 Gerard Phelips put it for sale for £5882 'for Scrap'. However at that time the SPAB was not empowered to hold buildings, and so Mr Cook agreed that the house should be purchased and given to the National Trust.

The Trust did not know what it was letting itself in for by accepting a supremely beautiful Elizabethan house but one which was virtually empty of contents and without any endowment (Fig. 1). The supposition was that the Trust would continue to find a tenant for it, a usual practice at the time, and that, provided it was put in order, it would bring in £1500 a year in rent and only need £500 a year spending on it. Alternatively it could be opened to visitors and earn £100 a year. Thus it was that Montacute came to be the first large house that the Trust opened to the public.

Not surprisingly, however, by 1936 it had become 'an empty and rather embarrassing white elephant', as James Lees-Milne, the first secretary of the newly formed Country Houses Committee, described it many years later.

Round about that time Sir Charles Trevelyan, the elder brother of G.M. Trevelyan, the historian and a great supporter of the National Trust, was beginning to think about the future of Wallington and its estate in Northumberland. Indeed in 1936 he announced it was his intention to bequeath it to the Trust. He in turn inspired Sir Geoffrey Mander, who with his wife stayed at Wallington in 1936, to give Wightwick Manor, a late 19th century house on the outskirts of Wolverhampton, to the Trust, a gift that went through in 1937. Many years later Sir Charles's eldest daughter, Mrs Dower, wrote: 'My father considered Wallington not so much *owned* by him as entrusted to him by inheritance to use for the benefit of the public . . . He felt that, however public spirited any future owner might be, or anxious to share the beauty and interest of Wallington with others, there could be no guarantee that the place would remain in private hands in an uncertain post-war world. He therefore decided to give Wallington . . . outright to the National Trust as the best way of ensuring that it would be cared for in perpetuity as a place for the public, and of preserving its close relationship with the community of the estate.'

The National Trust Act of 1937 permitted the Trust to acquire and hold land and investments for the endowment of properties. The first place to come with an endowment was Old Devonshire House in London WC1, which was given by Major Benton Fletcher in July that year, but it was destroyed by bombing in 1941. That Act enabled the Trust to accept its first bequest of a major house and estate in 1940, Blickling, in Norfolk, which came under the terms of the will of Lord Lothian. It has never been fully explained why Lord Lothian chose to do that rather than leave it to his successor, because in his 1934 speech he had spoken against the idea of houses as museums and it seems he had a vision of such a house finding a new life as a place for people meeting under the eye of a well-disposed tenant.

After James Lees-Milne was invalided out of the army, he returned to the Trust in 1941, and he remained the dominant influence on the Country Houses Scheme until he retired as part-time Architectural Adviser in 1966. In 1951 he was succeeded as Historic Buildings Secretary by Robin Fedden, who ran the department with drive and energy until he retired in 1974, but Jim Lees-Milne remained the inspiration in a way that is quite hard to understand 50 years later. As I wrote in 1981, 'Although he always belittles his work, it was James Lees-Milne more than any other single person who gave shape to the Country Houses Scheme in its first 15 years, providing it with its particular appreciation of history, seeing houses as the embodiment of so much of our past, both local and national, and only after that as representative of architectural styles and the setting for collections of works of art. It is an approach that is strongly literary as well as visual, and considerably broader than that encouraged by the specialisation of art history; it is also warmer in its feeling for the individuality of people and places past and present. In all this, James Lees-Milne gave form and direction to the perhaps not altogether clear instinct of the leaders of the Trust in 1936.' Not only did he actively encourage owners to offer their houses to the Trust, but he also persuaded the Trust to accept them.

However, as he wrote in the mid-1970s, 'It cannot be claimed that the Country Houses Scheme started with a bang,' and, as Peter Mandler put it less kindly, 'On the superficial level the National Trust's Country Houses Scheme was a failure in these early years.' 'However,' Mandler continued, 'the Scheme did bring discussion of the country house, its status and its future, into public awareness in a way that was not so even a few years earlier when Hussey was almost alone in promoting it.'

The effects of the Second World War on country houses and perceptions of them were complex. As John Martin Robinson showed in *The Country House at War* (1989) and John Harris has explained in his memoirs of passionate country house snooping from the age of 15 in 1946, *No Voice From the Hall* (1998). 'It is extraordinary to realise that, away from the flow of armies between Russia and Normandy, the war might not have existed for many chateaux and schlosses. In Britain it was different, and the difference can be seen as a by-product of the 'Dunkirk' spirit, for after Dunkirk nearly every country house had some role to play in the war effort, either through compulsory requisition or as a result of its owner offering it for patriotic uses . . . by 1945 nearly every country house of any considerable size had been requisitioned by compulsory order. The exact number has never been ascertained, but must have approached two thousand at least.'

He goes on to describe the extraordinary state of the abandoned houses that he sought out and explored. So it is not surprising that so many were never reoccupied by their owners, who saw no future for them and decided to cut their losses, sell the contents and gut or demolish them. And, of course, in a number of cases their owners or their heirs had been killed during the war. At Castle Howard, which had been seriously damaged by a fire in 1940, the trustees, believing that the family would never move back if and when peace came, sold many pictures, having been advised by a leading auctioneer that the prices of pictures would never be higher than they were in 1944; and they would have sold the house to the school evacuated there if they could have agreed a price. It was only after Mark Howard, who had inherited in 1935 at the age of 17 and was killed in 1944, was succeeded by his brother, George, later Lord Henderskelfe, that the latter stopped the process of dispersal. He opened the house in 1952, and eight years later successfully rebuilt the dome.

Yet at the same time the destruction caused by the war made people more aware of what had survived and encouraged a patriotic view of the British tradition in architecture, with a heightened appreciation of houses of the past, and a new enthusiasm for recent and contemporary painting. Those two threads came together in the work of John Piper, who as well as being commissioned to paint the ruins of Coventry Cathedral in November 1940, and the bombed churches of Bristol in February 1941, was commissioned by the Queen to do two sets of views of Windsor Castle, the first set commissioned in 1941 and the second set completed in 1944. As a preparation for them he painted Vanbrugh's thrilling pile at Seaton Delaval in Northumberland. However his main wartime country house series was that of Renishaw Hall, in Derbyshire, commissioned by Sir Osbert Sitwell and used by him as illustrations in his autobiography.

The new spirit can also be seen in books like V. Sackville-West's short *English Country Houses* in Collins' patriotic Britain in Pictures series (1941 and republished in 1996). The book opens with her well-known hymn in praise of English houses: 'There is nothing quite like the English country house anywhere else in the world. France has her chateaux, Italy her historic villas, Spain her gardens like the Generalife hooked on to the hillside, Germany her robber castles, but the exact equivalent of what we mean by the English country house is not to be found elsewhere.'

However, what seems curious today is Vita Sackville-West's lack of appreciation of grand 18th-century architecture. In that she was rather old-fashioned for her time, being rooted in her own upbringing at

Knole. She was intensely pessimistic about the future: 'Even before the war the prospect was dark enough, but with war taxation and the present rate of death duties it seems improbable that any family fortune will long suffice to retain such homes in private ownership . . . The only hope for these houses seems to be that they should pass into the good keeping of the National Trust.'

A second and more influential book was G.M. Trevelyan's *English Social History*, which finally appeared in Britain in 1944. It was phenomenally successful, and, although later scorned by most professional historians, it struck a deep chord with readers over a long period. As David Cannadine has written in his life of Trevelyan: 'Throughout the book, Trevelyan wrote with more feeling then ever before about what now seemed to him the mortally endangered fabric of English life: landscape and locality, flora and fauna, places and people . . . For Trevelyan, this pastoral civilization reached its apogee during the eighteenth century . . .

'Everywhere', wrote Trevelyan 'the England of Elizabeth was becoming *par excellence* the land of manor-houses, bewilderingly different from one another in size, material and style of architecture, but all testifying to the peace and economic prosperity of the age, its delight in display, in beauty and in the glory of man's life on earth.' And on the following page there is surely a sign of the Trust's influence on him: 'Montacute in its glory of dull gold – just a country gentleman's house in a remote district of Somerset, built in the local stone, yet certainly one of the most beautiful and magnificent homes in the world.' And later: 'Everywhere that perfectly beautiful equilibrium between man and nature, which marked the Eighteenth Century landscape, was in process of being established.' Comforting and inspiring words to read in 1944.

How close that book was to the National Trust ethos before and after the war can be gathered from Trevelyan's leading role in the Trust from 1928, when he became chairman of the Estates Committee and vice-chairman of the Executive Committee, offices he was to hold until 1949 and 1946.

1944 also saw the publication of Sacheverell Sitwell's *British Architects and Craftsmen*, covering the period 1600–1830 and arguably the most moving book ever written about the arts in England. Although, like Trevelyan's, scorned by professionals, it was immensely successful, going through four editions by 1948; moreover it had a profound influence on a younger generation who entered the world of architecture and preservation in the late 1950s and early 1960s. In his Introduction Sitwell wrote: 'Now the perils of our modern times weigh heavier on architecture than on the other arts. Not only in war; for the hand of the destroyer has been little less dangerous in times of peace. Yet our old buildings are more loved and valued by more of the population than ever before. This is the contradiction.' And later: 'But, so far as Englishmen are concerned themselves, an increasing number of men and women, as the years pass by, go to our old architecture for their pleasure and recreation.'

The increased awareness of the architectural and artistic patrimony of the country was accompanied by a new consciousness of the need for improved planning when peace came, and in this historic buildings and preservation were to play a new part. The first step towards this was the establishment in 1941 of the National Buildings Record to compile mainly photographic evidence about buildings that might be destroyed; and out of that grew the principle of listing enshrined in the Town and Country Planning Act of 1944. That entrusted the new Ministry of Town and Country Planning with the task of listing buildings of special historic and architectural interest, both inhabited and uninhabited. It was intended to put a marker on damaged buildings that might be restored when peace came and on buildings that might be bombed, and as a guide to local authorities in assuming new planning responsibilities.

Owners, generally of a younger generation, who had inherited during the war or immediately after and who had fought in the war, returned determined to reopen their houses, but 53 years later it is hard to visualise what they faced. That was brought home to me back 30 years ago when writing an article about Longford Castle, near Salisbury, when the late Lady Radnor took me up on to the roof to look out over the gardens: she recalled standing by their beacon fire on VE night in 1945: 'We were telling ourselves that the miracle had happened; we were all alive, the house had not been bombed, the troops in it were British and not German, we had won the war. Nevertheless in all the rejoicing my husband, speaking as the owner of a country house, said to me, "Now our personal problems begin."'

2

◆

The Recovery of Country Houses: Private Initiatives and Public Support 1945–1973

(a) *The Return of the Owners*

In the late 1990s it is even more difficult than in the early 1970s to envisage what owners of country houses faced after the war. Very few large houses had not been taken over for some wartime purpose – for military purposes, schools, government offices and agencies, convalescent homes, museum storage and so on – and, when they were returned to their owners in 1945–47, many were shabby and down-at-heel, if not actually heading towards dereliction.

Most of those who had remained in their houses were living in great discomfort. James More-Molyneux, writing in *The Loseley Challenge* (1995) of the hardness of his parents' situation at Loseley, near Guildford, in Surrey, remembered: 'Electricity had not yet been laid on, there was no heating, as the boilers were out of commission, so there was no piped hot water: if you wanted a bath you put the kettle on the kitchen stove and carried it up to the bathroom. Many friends had urged mother and father to move out of that cold, uncomfortable house . . . My father refused to consider it: he knew, he told me later, that if they had moved out Loseley would not have survived . . .'

Not only were funds tight, but there were shortages of building materials and restrictions on their use. Estates were even more run down and in need of investment than the houses that they were supposed to support; and only in the 1950s did agriculture start to be modernised and become profitable, sustained by the 1947 Agriculture Act. Also it is forgotten how puritanical many people were in their attitudes to comfort and convenience and how used to austerity they had become. One owner remembers his mother going to the kitchen in 1939, picking up a dish cloth and saying that she had never done the washing up before, but now she expected to do it for the rest of her life.

Virtually all the staff who had kept houses going before the war had disappeared, and those who remained found it even harder than their employers to adjust to the new conditions that had destroyed their own hierarchy. Younger people rejected domestic work as being demeaning, and modern equipment was scarcely known, so heating systems, even if they existed, were out of date, and kitchens were usually remote, quite often on a different floor to the dining room, and ill equipped. And a surprising number of great houses still lacked electricity.

When the 6th Marquess of Exeter inherited Burghley House in 1956, not only was the estate run down, the house in need of repairs and there were death duties at 80% to pay, but there was still no electricity. So he introduced a lead from the back door to his dressing room to work his razor and a second to the television set. The house was still lit by gas. Electricity did not reach the top storey until 1982.

So it is not surprising that many owners, particularly those who had been in the saddle before the war and were used to running houses with staff, decided that the struggle was not worth it in the new Socialist Britain and packed it in. In his *Ancestral Voices* (1975) James Lees-Milne encountered a number of them, and his account written in 1943 of the 3rd Lord Newton (born 1888, died 1960), the owner of Lyme Park, a vast, deeply romantic but also daunting house with Stockport and Greater Manchester at its park gates, can stand for others: 'The world is too much for him, and no wonder. He does not know what he can do, ought to do or wants to do. He just throws up his hands in despair. The only thing he is sure about is that his descendants will never live at Lyme after an unbroken residence of 600 years.'

The situation was particularly hard for elderly couples and for those who had lost sons in the war. In May 1947 James Lees-Milne went to see Lord and Lady Mount Edgcumbe at Cotehele, their second house up the River Tamar, and some miles from Mount Edgcumbe, which had been severely damaged in the war. There as he described in *Caves of Ice* (1983) he found 'Lord Mount Edgcumbe [the 6th Earl who inherited from a cousin in 1944 at the age of 71 and died in 1965] is in bed with a temperature, but his Countess, a little, gentle, sweet and pathetic old lady, was about. Their story is a tragic one. They inherited during the war, and their only son was killed at Dunkirk. They are now packing up to leave Cotehele, which since the thirteenth century has been in their family . . . The splendid Mt Es, having lost their son and heir are taking to live with them their unknown heir and his wife, who come from New Zealand.' Cotehele, one of the most romantic medieval houses in the West of England, was the first house to be accepted in lieu of tax through the Land Fund and transferred to the National Trust.

When James Lees-Milne went to dinner at Holkham in June 1947, he wrote in his diary: 'I sat next to Lord Leicester [the 4th Earl, 1880–1949] who said how disappointed he was that the family entail prevented him handing over Holkham. His last words to me were: "If you can find any means whereby the Trust can take over this house and its contents, I shall be prepared to leave it, should my not staying on make the transfer easier . . . Lady Leicester is away, staying in Silvia's house, with a nervous breakdown brought about by anxiety and the worry of keeping up Holkham with practically no servants. What these wretched landowners have to go through! Yet Holkham is superbly kept up, all the steel grates, for instance, shining brightly, the work of one devoted daily."

Today Lord Leicester's position is difficult to grasp, but what brings it into sharp focus is the realisation that his average rents per acre were considerably less than they had been nearly 200 years earlier. In 1776, in Coke of Norfolk's time, they stood at 8s 6d per acre: in the 1930s they were about 5s an acre. By 1960 they had reached about £4.60.

On the whole it was the younger owners who had inherited during the war or soon after who felt able to take up the challenge, or at least have a go, but for almost all the going was very hard. The late Mrs Hervey-Bathurst inherited Eastnor Castle, in Herefordshire (Figs. 2 and 27), in 1944 from her father, who said to her that she should not feel that she had to take it on – 'it might be too much'. It nearly was in the 1950s when she considered demolishing it, but she and her husband battled on, as she explained in a matter-of-fact, uncomplaining way in a lecture to a local society in the mid-1970s: 'We do have a major problem if there is a lot of snow and frost. The battlements are built about 7 foot off the lead walkways so it is virtually impossible to shovel snow off the roof, the drains which are like street drains run down the inside of the walls into the cellars, I try to keep them clear of leaves etc, but if the snow thaws and freezes which it often does, they block up with ice, then when there is a sudden thaw we flood. My son came back from a party one winter about 2 a.m. and heard me on the roof

2. Eastnor Castle, Herefordshire, in 1971. An aerial view suggesting the scale of Smirke's building and the complexity of the roofs to maintain and repair.

trying to clear the drains, my husband being away rather wisely . . .'

A first sign of recovery was the opening and reopening of houses to the public, but whereas before the war there was usually no charge or a small one that went to charity, now the opening was for the places themselves. In many cases owners were very tentative. That can be gathered from the introduction that the late Marcus Wickham-Boynton wrote to a later edition of the guidebook to Burton Agnes, in Yorkshire: 'During the early Spring of 1949 I decided, not without a good deal of uneasiness, to try the experiment of opening my home, Burton Agnes Hall, to the public every Thursday afternoon during the summer months. One doubted whether the general public would be interested in seeing over somebody else's home, even if it were a beautiful Elizabethan house built over three hundred and fifty years ago . . . It was very soon clear that visitors realised they were in fact guests, although paying guests, and that they were prepared to treat my home as if it were their own.'

James More-Molyneux has written of Loseley that it was a tremendous feat on his wife's part 'to have got the House from its dereliction in 1946 to be ready for public viewing in 1950. We opened four afternoons a week from June until 30 September at two shillings a head. The first year we had around a thousand visitors, but the decision to get the House in order and open to the public was much more significant than we realised at the time. The House was now transformed from a slumbering grubby geriatric, unkempt, to a beautiful much-loved creature, friendly, steeped in peace, that people loved to visit. There was no going back.'

The National Trust opened 11 houses in 1946 and 19 in 1947. The first private houses were Arundel Castle, Burghley and Holkham in 1946. Burghley opened on Easter Sunday thanks to the support of a band of volunteers, and 1700 people came, with 1400 going round the house; and so Lady Exeter was able to send a cheque for £151 to the County Nursing Association. These three houses were followed by Haddon Hall and Penshurst Place in 1947. Newby and Parham opened in 1948; Chatsworth, Burton Agnes, Hatfield and Longleat in 1949. Castle Howard opened in 1952. By 1951 there were enough houses open for *Country Life* to produce the first edition of a pictorial introduction *Country Houses Open to the Public*.

However what drew attention to this movement were the highly publicised openings organised by Lord Bath at Longleat, Lord Montagu at Beaulieu in 1952 and the Duke of Bedford at Woburn in 1954. It was they who turned a low-key tradition into an up-to-date business that provided days out for families and made the idea of house and garden visiting into a popular activity.

Some would not have been able to return to their houses without financial assistance with repairs, which began in 1953 as a result of the Gowers Report and the establishment of the Historic Buildings Council. The dire situation facing owners and the novelty of giving

Government money to privately owned buildings is hard to grasp to-day, but the Duke of Grafton, the only surviving member of the original Council, recalls pessimists saying in its first full year, 1954–55, when its expenditure only came to about £100,000, 'well, you'll never be able to do anything with that.' Repair grants also played an important part in the opening of houses to the public, because from the beginning public access was one of the conditions of receiving a grant.

Today what owners did and the difficulties they overcame are taken for granted, and certainly it is forgotten how many of them had to overcome the opposition of their trustees who wanted to get rid of houses that they saw as liabilities. Thus when the late Marquess of Hertford, who had succeeded in 1940 at the age of 10, came into Ragley in 1951, he received a letter from his lawyer saying that the trustees proposed to sell the house to demolition contractors for £5000. He was determined to save the house and move back into it: he had spent the war there, when it was mostly occupied by a hospital, but in 1947 his mother had told him that they could not afford to go on living there and in 1950 they moved out into a farmhouse on the estate, leaving the house empty and decaying. It was only when Lord Hertford married in 1956 that he moved back into Ragley and began to put it in order, being ready to open it to the public for the first time in 1958, with 50,000 visitors coming the first season. The costs, however, proved too great, and by 1963 he thought that he might have to give up. The situation was then saved by a grant recommended by the HBC, as can be gathered from its report for 1964: 'One historic house which has attracted a good deal of attention this year is Ragley Hall. The cost of keeping up this great house has for some time been a considerable burden on the resources of its owner, Lord Hertford, who in 1963 approached us for advice and assistance as he feared that he might be compelled to abandon it. It appeared to us unthinkable that a house of the grandeur and importance of Ragley – visited as it is by upwards of 50,000 people each year – should be allowed to disappear, the more so since grants totalling £15,470 had already been made on our recommendation towards the cost of repairs. We therefore recommended a further grant to cover the whole cost of the more urgent repairs, as well as a grant of £2000 a year for five years to contribute towards the cost of upkeep . . .'

In 1955 Mario Praz, the Italian scholar, went to Chatsworth, an experience he recorded later in his *House of Life* (1964): 'I managed to obtain special permission to visit the house, not now inhabited by the Duke of Devonshire who is reduced to living in a more modest house in the neighbouring town of Bakewell, as being more practical and more economical – reasons which can well be appreciated in the austere atmosphere of present-day England. . . . And even as one entered the house by a service door . . . one was struck by a feeling of extreme melancholy for things vanished and remote . . . The enormous rooms and corridors and galleries of the house were icy.'

Although Praz did not recognise it, 1955 was to be a turning point for Chatsworth, because it was then that the agent suggested to the present Duke and Duchess that they should live in the house. The Duke's father, the 10th Duke, who had succeeded in 1938, had moved into the house straight away, but when war was declared in September 1939, the family moved out and the house was dismantled in 11 days so that Penrhos College could move in. In 1944 the Duke's eldest son, the Marquess of Hartington, was killed on active service in Belgium, and that was a blow from which he never really recovered. Also it meant that no plans for the hand-over of the property to his second son, Lord Andrew Cavendish, could begin until he came out of the army in 1946. That year the College moved out, and two years later the Duke decided to reopen Chatsworth to the public, although he himself did not move back into what was an uninhabitable house. Opening took place at Easter 1949 and, despite petrol rationing, 75,000 visited the house in the first year.

The following year the 10th Duke died unexpectedly, not quite five complete years after the hand-over to his son had taken place, and so the estate was hit by death duties at the rate of 80%. Thus in the harsh conditions of the times it seemed likely that the family would never move back into the house and that some museum use might be the only answer. So the idea developed of the house becoming a Victoria and Albert Museum of the North, an idea that owed a good deal to the imagination and ambition of Sir Leigh Ashton, the dynamic first post-war Director of the Museum who had already persuaded the Government to buy the contents of Osterley and Ham and had taken on Apsley House. Also it coincided with Socialist views on cultural planning. By July 1953 the principles of the scheme were agreed, but it proved impossible to agree a basis for valuations, and so in 1955 the negotiations came to an end.

It was then clear that the estate would have to maintain Chatsworth anyway, so the agent suggested to the Duke and Duchess that they should consider moving back. However, because of the amount of work involved in restoring and modernising the private side of the house (happily there was no dry rot), the final decision to do so was not taken until 1958; and the family moved in in November 1959. While the scale of Chatsworth means that its story cannot be taken as typical, the post-war period of 14 years from 1945 to 1959 could be paralleled in many places.

By 1970, as a result of the Duchess's rearrangement of the house and the Duke and Duchess's improvements in the gardens, it had never looked more splendid. However, it is surprising now that the Duke was far from confident about either its future or family occupation. He real-ised that the remaining agricultural estate could not permanently sustain so large a house and garden, but he could not embark on making a positive plan for it, which eventually became a charitable trust, until after 1974 when the estate duty and interest was finally settled. Throughout that time he felt that it was probably an Indian summer for the place, with his generation probably being the last one to live in the house.

At other places it took even longer for the house to recover and be reoccupied. At Newburgh Priory, in Yorkshire (Fig. 3), Captain Wombwell, who had inherited in 1913, had moved out in 1939, leasing the house for 21 years to a school and never imaginging that he would ever return. The school left after the war, before the lease was up; then there was a bad fire; and that was followed by rampaging dry rot. In 1953 the Wombwells asked Sir Martyn Beckett to do a plan for them to move back into part of the house, but that seemed beyond them, and by the early 1960s the vast building looked doomed. Then it was sug-gested that they should apply to the Historic Buildings Council for a grant, and in 1965, the year after one was offered, work got under way; but it had to be accepted that the whole gallery range would be left as a shell, and it was not practicable to completely restore the fire-damaged central block. Without the HBC the job would have never started, but without the enthusiasm and support of Mrs Wombwell it could have never been seen through.

At Heydon, in Norfolk (Figs 4 and 5), the house was not restored until the 1970s. Indeed the whole recent history of the place is a most surprising one and not only represents a remarkable achieve-ment on the part of the late Captain W.H.B. Bulwer-Long and his

3. Newburgh Priory, Yorkshire, from the air. The gutting of the Gallery wing on the left had to be accepted as part of the saving of the house by Captain and Mrs Malcolm Wombwell in the years after 1965.

wife, but, as will be seen later, it shows how thinking has developed.

The house had been let in 1932 by Captain Long's maternal grandmother, Mrs Granville-Duff, and when she died in 1949, she left instructions that the contents of the Hall, except for the portraits, should be sold. No doubt she never envisaged that the family would ever live there again. In 1966 Captain Long came out of the army and returned to Heydon to farm 160 acres that were in hand, and obviously he and his wife wondered what they would do if and when the Hall ever became free.

When it did in 1970, his trustees advised him to demolish it, sell the land and move to Virginia Water. So the first thing was to reject that advice and, encouraged by their neighbour and a former member of the Historic Buildings Council, Sir Charles Mott-Radclyffe of Barningham Hall, who said that they could not abandon it but must move in and do the work gradually, the Longs decided to do just that. But they had to

4. and 5. Heydon Hall, Norfolk, in 1923 and 1982. Most of the 19th century additions were removed in 1973 when the house was reduced to its original Elizabethan form and restored by the Bulwer-Longs, who re-occupied the house after a break of 40 years. An aerial view and the village are illustrated in Figs 62 and 63

rationalise the house by reducing it by almost half to more or less its original size and also get a grant from the HBC for the repair of the Elizabethan building. In 1973 they got the HBC's approval for both as well as planning permission to reduce the building. The Longs moved in in 1975 – with the builders – and a week later Mrs Long had a baby; and for the next two years they shared the house with the builders.

As the restoration and opening of the houses gathered pace, it made a growing contribution to tourism, but it was only in the mid-1960s that there began to be official recognition of the importance of historic houses in the expanding tourist industry. In 1966, as Lord Montagu records in *The Gilt and the Gingerbread*, there were 599 houses open and they attracted 16 million visitors, with 7 million going to those privately owned, which earned £1 million as a result; and the tourist industry was growing three times as fast as the country's physical exports. Thus, as a result of a novel conference the British Tourist Authority held for Historic House Owners, it established in 1966 its Historic Houses Committee, the forerunner of the Historic Houses Association in 1973. The BTA's support was a recognition of the significance of houses that helped to prepare the way for the events of the early 1970s, while the growth in the habit of house visiting helps to explain the scale of support for the cause when it was threatened by proposed tax changes.

By the late 1960s most of the great houses were open, even if only on one afternoon a week. But there were a few houses that enthusiasts other than those with specialist reasons had difficulty in visiting. So when a younger generation of owners took over, they felt that they had a duty to open their houses and give others the pleasure of their collections. Thus, when the late Marquess of Cholmondeley succeeded his father in 1968, he decided to open Houghton, in Norfolk. The Duke of Buccleuch, who succeeded in 1973, decided to open Boughton, in Northamptonshire, Bowhill at Selkirk and Drumlanrig in Dumfriesshire, partly because he had already become interested in extra-mural education when an MP for Edinburgh. The Duke of Wellington, who succeeded in 1972, decided to open Stratfield Saye in Hampshire.

While the attitudes of younger owners were changing, public opinion, or at least the small section concerned with architectural preservation, was also becoming more active and more militant in the late 1960s and early 1970s.

That happened over the sale of Heveningham Hall, in Suffolk (Fig.

6), in 1969, when a campaign had to be organised to persuade the Government to acquire the place through the Land Fund. One element in that was the interest of Marcus Binney in the architecture of Sir Robert Taylor; he had read the History of Art at Cambridge and had written a short thesis on Taylor's villas.

Three years later the great European neo-classical exhibition at the Victoria and Albert Museum provided a wider context for English architectural historians specialising in the period to draw attention to the uncertain future of several key neo-classical houses, in particular The Grange, in Hampshire, remodelled by William Wilkins in 1804, and Belsay Castle, in Northumberland. In 1964 the Barings bought back The Grange estate, which the family had owned from 1817 to 1934, with the house in a very poor condition, and in 1970 they were granted permission to demolish it. However, demolition did not go ahead straight away, and the exhibition stimulated a campaign to save it. That eventually ended with the building being taken into guardianship and Belsay being acquired by the D.o.E. in 1982.

Another influential and long drawn out but ultimately successful campaign was waged over Barlaston Hall in Staffordshire, a villa attributed to Sir Robert Taylor that stands so splendidly looking out over its former estate on which Wedgwood had built its factory between the Wars and which had also figured in Marcus Binney's thesis. By the late 1960s not only was it showing signs of neglect, but it was threatened by coal mining and by standing on a fault, so in 1968 Wedgwood said that it would seek permission to demolish it. That led to two public enquiries, in 1975, when it was strongly opposed by Save Britain's Heritage, and in 1981. At the second Wedgwood offered the house to Save for £1 on condition that they restored it within five years, but it took great persistence to get British Coal to pay the compensation that the Coal Board had offered at the enquiry and provide the concrete raft for the house to stand on. Despite the contractors going bankrupt during the recession, the structural repairs were completed thanks to support from English Heritage, the NHMF and the Manifold Trust, but there were insufficient funds to complete the interior. However in 1992 Mr and Mrs James Hall bought the shell for £300,000 and since then they have completed the house, as can be seen from the article in *Country Life* on July 30, 1998.

Taken together these cases demonstrated a new more militant attitude on the part of preservationists and the press, with an increasingly well-directed artillery that could be fired at the Government, public bodies, companies or owners who appeared to be failing in their duties to look after buildings. It was the counterpart to the increasing anger about bad planning and the destruction of historic towns, which first appears in *The Architectural Review* in the mid-1950s with Ian Nairn's *Outrage*, which began as an occasional contribution in the autumn of 1955. That, and in particular the destruction of Bath, stirred up public opinion and was fanned by the press as conservation became a political matter of increasingly widespread concern. Planning and preservation legislation was toughened up and the Town and Country Planning Act of 1968 gave stronger protection to listed buildings, punishment for demolition without consent and neglect, and also introduced spot listing.

So it is not chance that people involved with this change of mood were the moving spirits in *The Destruction of the Country House* exhibition.

(b) *The Establishment and Uses of the National Land Fund 1946–1972*

Today the National Land Fund is probably most widely remembered because the Government would not use it to save Mentmore, the Rothschild house and collection in Buckinghamshire, in the mid-1970s. And it is all too easy to give a negative account of it, concentrating on the way it was run by the Treasury and its failure to fulfil the idea of Dr Hugh Dalton, the Chancellor of the Exchequer, who, when he established it in 1946 with £50 million raised from the sale of surplus war materials, saw it as 'a thank offering for victory, and a war memorial'.

Great use was made of those phrases in the parliamentary debates of the late 1970s, but it should be remembered that Dalton was, as his biographer, Ben Pimlott, has written, 'the most Socialist Chancellor of the Exchequer Britain has ever had'; and that in his budgets he 'launched a broadside against wealth.' He saw the Land Fund as being a way of acquiring real estate for National Parks and the National Trust that would have to be sold by private owners. However, it was only because the purposes of the Fund were broadened by later legislative amendments that it was to achieve so much for houses and works of art.

The first point was that Dr Dalton dealt with the weakness in the Finance Act 1910 which had introduced the idea of the acceptance of land in satisfaction of tax but had virtually nullified it by making no provision for compensating the Inland Revenue for tax foregone. He arranged for the Land Fund to be used for compensating the Revenue; and this was the basis of many acquisitions of houses, as will be explained.

As far as houses were concerned, the Fund got under way to a slow start, but that is less surprising when it is remembered that Dr Dalton's main interest was in land. Thus Cotehele in Cornwall was the only major house accepted in lieu of tax and given to the National Trust between 1946 and 1950. Penrhyn Castle, in North Wales, followed in 1951–52. It was courageous to accept Thomas Hopper's Norman Revival masterpiece of the 1820s at the time, given current attitudes to 19th century buildings; but what was seen as more important was its estate of 40,000 acres of upland and mountain land with 60 farms stretching up into Snowdonia.

What else was offered and rejected has not yet been revealed, but there were two problems. One was to do with the Treasury's refusal to provide endowments with the places offered to the Trust. The power to endow had been introduced only as a result of a private member's amendment; at the time a government spokesman made it clear that there was no intention of making use of it, and subsequent Governments stuck to that.

Instead the deficits including repairs incurred by the National Trust on the six houses which had been accepted in lieu of tax or bought through the Land Fund and which were unendowed (Dyrham, Hardwick, Saltram, Beningborough, Sudbury and Cragside) were intended to be met (and continue to be met) out of the allocations to the Historic Buildings Council for repair grants (and since 1985 English Heritage). And in the case of Hardwick they never covered the work on the estate and buildings such as the stables. This was doubly unsatisfactory. The Trust found it had to argue for settlement after it carried out the work and incurred the charges. And the HBC found an increasing proportion of its allocation for repairs being committed to meeting running costs over which it had little control.

The second weakness was that, as first set up, the Fund could be used to acquire property but not works of art and the contents of houses. That first emerged over Ham House and Osterley, two houses close to

[43]

London on offer to the National Trust, where it could not be used to buy their contents, and the Government had to find another way to get round the problem. That led the National Trust to press the Gowers Committee to recommend that the legislation should be amended, but it refused. So after the Committee's report was published in 1950, Lord Crawford, as chairman of the Trust, wrote to *The Times* on 27 June 1950: 'The trust regrets that the report has not adopted its proposal that "chattels" might be accepted by the Treasury in payment of death duties, as land may now be accepted. The report recognizes that a house with its contents frequently forms a single unity of the highest importance; the trust agrees that the finest of these should remain permanently in their traditional surroundings; and the Government have already accepted this proposal by purchasing the contents of Ham House. In the opinion of the trust, the preservation of the contents of these houses would be greatly facilitated by the adoption of its recommendation.'

That point was dealt with in the Finance Act 1953 when the purposes of the Fund were broadened to cover the acceptance of chattels and works of art associated with houses in 'certain ownerships' including government agencies and the National Trust (but not private ownership). That amendment, it now turns out, was made primarily to deal with the Government's dilemma over how to acquire contents at Chatsworth to be offered in lieu of tax if and when it became a national museum.

At the same time there was a similar problem at Petworth, in Sussex, where the house had been given to the National Trust in 1947 by the 3rd Lord Leconfield, but the contents had remained his property. Heavy duties had arisen on his death in 1952, and the only reasonable way to settle them was to offer works of art at Petworth and for them to remain *in situ* in the house.

More will be said in a later section about Petworth, but that amendment led to the saving of many other houses together with, in many cases, at least part of their contents – Ickworth, in Suffolk, Berrington, in Herefordshire, Saltram, in Devon, Beningbrough, in Yorkshire, Hardwick, in Derbyshire, Brodick, on the Isle of Arran, Farnborough, in Warwickshire, Melford, in Suffolk, Clevedon, in Avon, Shugborough, in Staffordshire, Sissinghurst, in Kent, Sudbury, in Derbyshire; and some contents in many other houses including The Vyne, in Hampshire, Culzean, in Ayrshire, Hatchlands, in Surrey, Powis, in

Powys, Hanbury, in Worcestershire, Waddesdon, in Buckinghamshire, Knole, in Kent, Uppark, in Sussex, Chartwell, in Kent, Ascott, in Buckinghamshire, Clandon, in Surrey, Ashdown, in Berkshire, the temples of Rievaulx in Yorkshire.

A second important amendment to the Land Fund was incorporated in the Historic Buildings and Ancient Monuments Act 1953, which permitted the Fund to be used to reimburse the Minister of Works and his successors, and relevant colleagues in Scotland and Wales, for their costs in acquiring property of outstanding historic and architectural interest, its setting and its contents, and to reimburse them for the costs of management and repair. That enabled Dyrham in Gloucestershire, and Heveningham, in Suffolk, to be acquired and also contents to be bought for Hatchlands and Clandon in Surrey, Beningbrough, in Yorkshire, Coughton, in Warwickshire, Uppark, in Sussex, and Audley End, in Essex. That provision was also used for Iver Grove, Buckinghamshire (a small house then attributed to Vanbrugh and subsequently sold as a private house), Cobham Hall, Kent (now an independent school) and Rushton, in Northamptonshire (now a school for the blind). Also money was produced so that the National Trust could buy Croft Castle, in Herefordshire, and the National Trust for Scotland could acquire Kellie, in Fife.

As it turned out, the amendment to the Land Fund in the Finance Act 1953 did not solve the Government's problems over Chatsworth, because when the negotiations broke down over how to value the contents of the house, the scheme to make it a national museum was abandoned. That left the trustees of the Chatsworth Settlement with the need to sell on the open market what at first seemed likely to be a considerable number of major works of art to meet the tax bill, with the near certainty that they would go abroad because British institutions would be unable to buy them in the face of foreign competition.

Therefore in the Finance Act 1956 the purposes of the Land Fund were enlarged once more to cover the acceptance of works of art pre-eminent for their aesthetic merit or historic value, and not necessarily associated with a particular building. That enabled works of art to be accepted and to be allotted to public institutions. In fact the first case dealt with in this way was the Van der Weyden *Pieta* from Powis Castle in 1956–57. That was followed by eight major works of art from Chatsworth, a smaller number than was first feared.

The private treaty sale mechanism was introduced in 1930 but was not widely used until after 1953 and then often alongside the Land Fund. Since it was recognised that taxation was usually the main reason for a sale, a special arrangement was introduced whereby the owner benefited from a remission of a quarter of the tax payable and so received a higher nett price for an object, while the receiving institution paid a lower price that took the remitted tax into account; and the loss of tax was borne by the Government. The rate of remission is not written into legislation and is negotiable, but since 1970 25% has been the presumed figure. This has been an enormously important arrangement as can be gathered from *Christie's Sales to the Nation 1956–1972*. Some of the more recent cases are mentioned on p. 182.

Those transfers have been followed by a great many more offers in lieu and private treaty sales to public collections, among them the Panshanger and Knowsley Rembrandts to the National Gallery and the Brocklesby Bernini *Neptune* and the Hovingham Giovanni de Bologna *Samson and the Philistine* to the Victoria and Albert Museum. The claims and needs of regional galleries also became recognised in 1965 with some objects from the Spencer-Churchill collection at Northwick Park, Gloucestershire, being sold after his death by private treaty to various institutions in London, Edinburgh, Birmingham, Oxford and Cambridge.

The failure to endow properties given to the National Trust and the problems that the Trust and the HBC faced in dealing with the deficits out of the repair grant allocations led the National Trust to explore alternative arrangements with local authorities. In fact these had been anticipated in two North Country houses, Speke Hall, near Liverpool, which was accepted by the Trust in 1944 and leased to Liverpool City Council, being later run by the Museums Department of Merseyside County Council until 1986 when the Trust took over direct management supported by an annual grant from Merseyside, and Lyme Park, in Cheshire, which was given by Lord Newton without endowment in 1946 and leased to Stockport Corporation. They provided precedents for the way that Tatton Park, in Cheshire, was handled. It was left to the Trust by the 4th and last Lord Egerton of Tatton on his death in 1958, with the park being accepted in lieu of tax: since then it has been financed and administered by Cheshire County Council. After that came Shugborough in Staffordshire, which was accepted by the Government in lieu of tax in 1960, transferred to the National Trust and maintained and administered by Staffordshire County Council. The last of these was Sudbury Hall, in Derbyshire, which was accepted in lieu of tax in 1967 on the death of the 9th Lord Vernon and run in conjunction with Derbyshire County Council until about 1994.

Since the original Land Fund did not cover Northern Ireland, in 1949 a separate Ulster Land Fund was established. Not only was that given the power to provide endowments, which was done on several occasions for houses passed to the National Trust, but it was used to accept places in lieu of tax and also to purchase them. Thus Castle Coole, in Co. Fermanagh, was taken in 1951; Castle Ward in 1953; and when Florence Court was given to the Trust by Viscount Enniskillen in 1954 it was endowed by the Ulster Land Fund.

Less used was made of the Land Fund in the late 1940s and 1950s than Dr Dalton had anticipated, as he explained in 1957. Then the Conservative Government, taking note that only a little over £900,000 had been spent between 1947 and 1954, raided it, reducing its capital from £50 million to £10 million, saying: 'This will for a number of years suffice to meet all demands on the Fund under present policies which we mean to continue.'

The first real crisis involving a country house and the Land Fund did not come until 1969, when Heveningham Hall, in Suffolk (Fig. 6), came on the market. As a result of public pressure the house and its original contents made for the rooms decorated by James Wyatt, together with the park, were bought by the Government in 1970 through the Land Fund as a holding operation. Having acquired the house, the Government was faced by a difficult situation, because the National Trust had become disillusioned with the deficit funding of other places accepted in lieu of tax or acquired by the Government and said that it would not take on any more; and the Government refused to use the Land Fund for endowment. However, the Trust did agree to run the house on behalf of the Government on an agency basis and did so from 1970 until 1978, but finally gave up because the D.o.E. would not provide the money required for repairs, nor would the Government produce an endowment fund.

So in 1981, by which time a satisfactory arrangement might have been worked out with the National Trust through the support of the National Heritage Memorial Fund, the Government, against all advice, decided that the house should be sold to a private buyer, choosing a Swiss holding company of Mr Al-Ghazzi, which paid £726,000. However, since there was no way in which the contents could be tied to

6. The Hall at Heveningham Hall, Suffolk, in 1925. In 1969 a campaign had to be organised to persuade the Government to acquire it through the Land Fund, but no permanent solution was found for the house; and in 1981 the Government decided to sell it. Sold again since then, it is now in private ownership but without its original Wyatt furniture and not open to the public.

the building, the Government retained them and left them on loan in the house. Repairs were begun, but in 1984 the house was badly damaged by a fire and afterwards two of the principal chimneypieces were stolen; and when the upper storeys of the east wing were repaired, they were remodelled rather than restored; the restoration was still not complete at the time of Mr Al Ghazzi's death in 1991.

The only encouraging official step was the planning brief produced by the Suffolk Coastal District Council as a guide for any prospective purchaser, which was in effect a strong warning showing how little alteration would be acceptable either to the fabric of the house or to its setting, and pointing out the obstacles to subdivision and any new building in the landscape as well as the objection to constructing a golf course in the park.

On Mr Al Ghazzi's death the United Bank of Kuwait, acting through Coopers and Lybrand as receivers, gave the Government the option to buy the house back, which was one of the terms of the 1981 sale. When that was not taken up, the receivers put the house on the market in 1993 at a price of £4.5 million. Thus again the Government refused to act responsibly.

The failures of successive Governments have meant that the interior of Heveningham, with the only Wyatt rooms to have survived intact with their furniture, has suffered very severely and has now lost its original furniture, which remains in the Government's possession, but without a home. The house has a new private owner, who is restoring it and its setting, but it is no longer open to the public, even by appointment.

It is a tale as sorry as it is long, and it leads on to the disaster of Mentmore and the Land Fund in the mid-1970s, which is considered in a later chapter.

(c) *The Gowers Committee and its Report*

1998 marks not only the 25th anniversary of the HHA but the 50th anniversary of the appointment of the Gowers Committee, whose report *Houses of Outstanding Historic or Architectural Interest* published in 1950 was, and remains, the foundation stone of government policy for historic houses.

Here it is surely remarkable that the country had as two Chancellors of the Exchequer in succession Dr Dalton, who set up the Land Fund, and then Sir Stafford Cripps, who was concerned about the country house problem and wanted to know what to do about it. However, what is so striking about Cripps's appointment of the Gowers Committee on 10 December 1948 was the presumption of the importance of the houses and lack of need to explain or justify it: its brief was 'To consider and report what general arrangements might be made by the Government for the preservation, maintenance and use of houses of outstanding historic or architectural interest which might otherwise not be preserved, including, where desirable, the preservation of a house and its contents as a unity.'

The Chancellor had announced the Committee's appointment in a written reply that was reported in *The Times* on 11 December 1948: 'Sir Stafford Cripps states that on more than one occasion in the last year or so it has been necessary to make special provision from public funds in order to secure for the nation certain houses of national importance which might otherwise have been in danger. The Government think that it is unsatisfactory to have to deal with such cases in a piecemeal way, and that it is necessary to work out a general policy.'

Ham and Osterley are the obvious houses, but there were at least three others, Audley End, in Essex, Harewood House, Yorkshire and Charlecote Park, in Warwickshire. In the case of Audley End the 9th Lord Braybrooke was faced by death duties arising from the deaths of his two predecessors in 1941 and 1943, and in 1946 the National Trust tried to arouse the Government's interest through Mrs Dalton. Two years later the house was acquired by the Ministry of Works. In the case of Harewood, which had been used as a hospital during the war, heavy death duties arose on the death of the 6th Earl of Harewood in 1947; and, according to James Lees-Milne's diaries, Cripps was 'quite ready to ask Parliament to buy the contents of both Harewood and Osterley, and indeed realized he would have to do this sort of thing increasingly in the future. He proposed having a list drawn up of the 100 greatest houses with collections.' Charlecote could have been another, because when the National Trust agreed to accept it without endowment after the war and launched an appeal, Dr Dalton promised to provide a pound for every pound subscribed by the public.

When the Gowers Committee's report was published in 1950, it was clearly not what Cripps and his colleagues had expected. The first paragraph, in *Part A: The Present Position. The Case for Preservation* opened with the words: 'What our terms of reference require us to consider is not whether houses of outstanding historical or architectural interest should be preserved, but how this is to be done. This suggests, as does the very fact of our appointment, that the case for taking all reasonable measures to save them is required, and that we need not argue it at length.'

That statement is surely most remarkable, first because of the way it assumes the historical and aesthetic importance of houses can be taken for granted; then in presuming both national responsibility for them and that preservation is a part of planning. It shows that these ideas were reflecting the thinking of a Labour Government three years after the end of the war; and also it indicates how far thinking had developed since Lord Lothian's speech in 1934, partly as a result of the National Trust's attempts to get its Country House Scheme off the ground but also because of the heightened awareness of the significance of all the arts that had developed during and after the war.

Paragraph 8 continues: 'We believe it to be wholly mistaken to suppose that these considerations concern only the few. A broadening of interest in the arts in this country is a striking phenomenon of recent years . . . We have no doubt that fine architecture and craftsmanship, placed in settings of outstanding beauty and rich with historic interest, make their appeal far beyond a limited circle of experts; and especially perhaps to those in whose daily life beauty can normally play but little part.'

The main weakness of both the Government's understanding and the Committee's report was in their underestimate of the importance of contents and their vulnerability; this was understandable given the low level of the art market at the time, but it has led to some of the most insoluble problems relating to houses. While both recognised the significance of contents in the unity, and the report recommended listing, but without going into any detail of what it might cover and who might carry it out, paragraph 160 said: 'The number of houses is comparatively small in which this matter of unity of house and con-tents is really important. The danger of dispersal is slight: the owners, who, by hypothesis, are still living there, may be expected to be as jealous of their treasures as any Council would be. So far as the danger exists, we think that the right way to guard against it is for [the proposed Historic Buildings Council] in granting any financial assistance, to impose a condition that no listed chattels will be sold without the Council's approval . . .'

The Committee was on firmer ground in considering gardens, parks, designed landscapes and garden buildings as part of the concept of the house. However, it did not comment on the relation between houses and estates.

What it did stress was the value of private ownership, quoting Christopher Hussey, who told them that these houses 'remain a living element in the social fabric of the nation, uniting visibly the present with national history.' Paragraph 123 said: 'let us consider first the house that is still the family home, for to preserve it in that form is best, if it can be done,' and it went on to quote the Pilgrim Trust's evidence that 'They are not merely beautiful structures, but possess an indefinable atmosphere as the centres of a highly civilised home life. To convert them into mere 'show-places' or to institutionalise them as museums . . . would deprive them of their intrinsic character and rob them of their "soul".' In its Summary of Recommendations it stated as 'Policy XIII That designated houses should, so far as possible, be reserved as private residences occupied preferably by the families connected with them.'

In praising the National Trust's Country Houses Scheme it said: 'The Trust is the only public body capable of preserving a country house as a home, and of holding and administering it as an entity with its art collections, furnishings, gardens, parks and agricultural estates.'

It was this aspect of the house as a home and representing the continuity of history that led the Committee to consider whether the best course was not to help the owner: 'If today the representative of the family cannot live in the ancestral home this is probably because he cannot afford it. The problem is whether some proper means can be found of giving him financial help.' This thinking led to the Committee's two main recommendations: one was to establish Historic Buildings Councils in England, Scotland and Wales whose duties would include providing repair grants. The second, as a corollary to that, was to introduce a tax claim in respect of repairs.

The Councils were set up under the terms of the Historic Buildings and Ancient Monuments Act 1953, but they were not given all the functions recommended by the Committee and their roles were purely advisory: they could not give grants, only recommend them to the Minister; and sometimes he needed persuasion or even rejected their advice. Recognising the weaknesses of the statutory listing system as established in 1944 and extended in 1947, the Committee wanted the Councils to compile a special list of designated houses that it deemed worthy of preservation, which could be used as a basis for a tax claim. That was never done.

At that time the rates of taxation were such that no one could have more than £5000 a year, and only 70 taxpayers in the country were left with more than £6000, which represented a gross income of £100,000 a year. On the other hand the Committee noted that 'Many great houses now need not less than £5000 a year, some as much as £10,000 to maintain them, not on any luxury standard, but on the minimum necessary to preserve them and their contents from deterioration.' That explained the attraction of the National Trust Country Houses Scheme: 'A taxpayer who pays 19s 16d in the pound on the top slice of his income may be able, by forgoing only £125 a year of his spendable income, to put £5000 a year into the hands of the Trust for the upkeep of his house.'

(d) *The Contribution of the Historic Buildings Council for England*

'But we could not ignore the fact that the lead on our roof was becoming more and more a sieve – tin and china baths were less and less able to contain the raindrops – you could smell the mushrooms even through the tobacco smoke in the Tower, and one day looking up at the dome of the Grand Stairs we saw mushrooms growing down as well as up, while little worm casts littered the floor in the Chinese Room. Our friend, relative and architect, Hugh Creighton, said we must call in the Historic Buildings Council and the experts started to arrive and shake their heads.' (From Sir Ralph Verney's introduction to the Claydon guidebook.)

The experts may have shaken their heads, but in 1955 the Historic Buildings Council recommended a grant of £24,000, which at that time was a very large sum of money: indeed it was the largest it had yet offered. Forty years on such figures are hard to see in perspective – on a straight cost of living index comparison, £24,000 in 1955 is the equivalent of £360,000 today – and a list of grant figures of that time might seem tedious and irrelevant, but the reports for the years 1953 to 1973 provide a valuable perspective on the history of country houses and developing attitudes to historic buildings in general in that period.

In 1953 the whole concept of grant aid for privately owned buildings was so new and unfamiliar that it took time to get the system going. The word had to be spread, and owners needed to be sure that they were not putting their heads in some noose of Socialist devising. Thus in the early years *Country Life* regularly published illustrated articles to show where the money was going; but probably much more important was the role of the Duke of Grafton, then Earl of Euston, who knew, or at least was known to, a wide circle of people through his work for the Society for the Protection of Ancient Buildings and the National Trust. A remarkable number of repair stories and saves of places seem to start with requests to him for advice or help, many more than he recalls to-day.

In its first half-year only £10,656 spread over five grants was offered, including one of £6000 to Doddington Hall, Lincolnshire (Figs 50 and 52), and £3000 to Lydiard Park, Wiltshire, which belonged to the local authority. However in 1954 the total went up to £254,304, and among the grants were three modest ones to Burghley House, Lincolnshire, including one of £570 a year for five years for maintenance; one of £5400 for Chastleton, Oxfordshire; £1400 to Croome Court, Worcestershire, for garden architecture; and £10,000 for Holkham, Norfolk. In 1955 the total went up to £370,756 in 139 grants. Among them were Broughton Castle, Oxfordshire (£7500); Browsholme Hall, Lancashire (£2500); Doddington (another £4000), Holkham (£8000); Knole, Kent (£5000); and Shugborough, Staffordshire, for garden architecture (£3500).

If Claydon was offered £24,000 and Clandon £20,000 that year, £7000 for Stanford Hall, Leicestershire (Figs 7 and 46), might not sound remarkable, but it was enough to encourage the 7th Lord Braye and his wife to move back into the house. His father had moved out in 1939, presuming that he would never return, and he let the house, first, happily, to a convent school, and then to a less satisfactory institution that left in 1950. The house then stood empty for eight years, but not long after the 6th Lord Braye died in 1952, Sir Gyles Isham, who had gone back to Lamport Hall, Northamptonshire and had close connection with the preservation world, told his successor of the new possibility of grant aid. As a result Lord Braye approached the HBC in 1954. A grant was offered the following year, and repairs went ahead, so Lord and Lady Braye were able to move back into the house; and in 1958 they opened it to the public for the first time. Since then a series of repair grants offered to Lord Braye, and during the last 13 years to his daugh-

7. Stanford Hall, Leicestershire. An early repair grant in 1955 was crucial to the return of Lord and Lady Braye to the house, its restoration and opening to the public. Since then there have been a series of repair grants to the house.

ter, the present Lady Braye, have been crucial to the survival of the house (just as grants to the church have been essential to that).

Naturally any account of the grant system concentrates on what the Government has contributed, and, because percentages of grant are never published, it is often forgotten how much the recipients had to contribute. For the first 25 years grants to individual owners were generally on a 50–50 basis, but that glosses over the difficulties owners invariably had in raising their share, forcing them to sell land or contents from the house, or having to decline the grant because of their inability to raise their contribution. So all the time successes (and struggles) like that for Stanford need to be set against failures to get work on buildings started so that eventually a great deal more work has had to be done at a higher cost.

Soon after it started work the Council became aware of other categories of buildings that required support. In 1954, for instance, it offered its first grants for garden buildings and began to consider terraces in towns, suggesting to Bath City Council the establishment of a joint scheme for the repair of the Georgian terraces there. That led it in its 1955 report to comment on the thorny subject of the great variety of local authorities' attitudes to historic buildings. Two years later Duncan Sandys formed the Civic Trust to encourage a greater awareness of the problems of town planning facing local authorities and private developers. These growing concerns met with some response in 1962 with the Local Authorities (Historic Buildings) Act, which empowered them to make repair grants, and which was also to strengthen the Town Schemes which the HBC had been keen to develop.

While these expansions of the Council's work might at first sight seem irrelevant to country houses, it was the broadening of the work that the Council was entrusted to do that enabled it to do so much for historic houses over a period of 30 years: they were seen as part of a broader company of individually outstanding historic buildings.

In 1963 the Council looked back over its first 10 years: 'However a few remarks on the general state of historic buildings in 1963 compared with 1953 is instructive and, we believe, though with some reservations, encouraging. In 1953 it is no exaggeration to say that the prevalent attitude, at any rate among owners of large houses, was one of despair. Staffing problems, caused by full employment and high taxation, linked with high maintenance costs, seemed to indicate that even the prospect of grants towards the cost of major structural repairs opened up by the Historic Buildings and Ancient Monuments Act of that year, would be insufficient to stem the flight from the big house and the sale of its contents . . . In 1963 the position is very different, and, while there is no room for complacency, the dominant note is no longer one of despair. Many owners have been encouraged by the financial help available to continue living in their house – and, we believe, have not regretted the sacrifices which they themselves have had to make in the process.'

The HBC could well have blown its trumpet rather louder, but Christopher Hussey did so in the *Country Life Annual* for 1964: 'Looking back on the decade, the most notable achievements can be sorted in four main categories: first, houses that grants have saved from almost certain abandonment and probable destruction; second, architectural repairs consequent or enabling new uses (some houses in this group could equally be classified under the first heading); third, extensive restorations that grants alone made possible; and fourth, grants for thorough repair of houses offered or belonging to the National Trust.'

And he went on to give examples. Among the saves from demolition were Rushton Hall, Northamptonshire, which was eventually acquired by the Land Fund and became a school run by the Royal National Institute for Blind Children, and Cobham Hall, Kent, which was also saved by the Land Fund and became an independent school. Among saves through co-operation with private owners he cited Ragley Hall, Warwickshire, Croft Castle, Herefordshire, Wotton House, Buckinghamshire, Heath Hall, near Wakefield, and Mawley Hall, Shropshire, which was saved from demolition by the use of a Building Preservation Order and finding someone to take it on; among institutional uses he cited Kimbolton Castle, Huntingdonshire, Milton Abbey, Dorset, Prior Park, Bath and Farnham Castle, Surrey. As far as the National Trust was concerned Dunsland, in Devon, and Claydon and Clandon in 1955 and Benthall Hall, in Shropshire, in 1957, were all taken on with the help of the HBC. And it is likely that certain in lieu deals, like that over Shugborough in 1960, were influenced by the support that the HBC had already given to the place before the tax debt occurred.

Indeed it is arguable that the Trust's Country Houses Scheme would have collapsed without the support of the HBC and withered without the support of the Land Fund.

However, the problems of country houses could still be daunting, as with Burton Constable in East Yorkshire (Figs 8 and 32). When Mr John Chichester-Constable inherited it, as a gift in marriage in 1963, the challenge seemed overwhelming because there were only four acres in hand and £700 in the capital account. So he wrote to Lord Euston, who recommended he consult as an architect for repairs Francis Johnson of Bridlington who in turn recommended Donald Insall. The latter produced what at that time was a novel kind of report that showed everything that needed to be done and what it would cost. The estimate came to almost £300,000, which represented two-thirds of the HBC's total allocation for the year. Mr Chichester-Constable applied to the HBC for a grant towards the first phase costed at £112,650 and was offered the then very large sum of £65,000, but he could not find his 50%. Talks were held with the National Trust at the Government's suggestion, but they too came to nothing. In fact grant-aided work on the house was not agreed until 1972–3, when the Minister finally approved the offer. By then land had been sold for development, so there was some money for repairs, but even so financial enquiries revealed that a grant at a higher rate than 50% was justified.

8. Burton Constable, Yorkshire. It took almost 10 years for John Chichester-Constable to get agreement for grant-aided repairs to begin in 1972–73. In 1991–92 a charitable trust for the house was set up through the initiative and support of the National Heritage Memorial Fund.

Part of the problem was that the HBC's allocation was virtually frozen throughout the 1960s, and yet all the time repair costs were rising. By 1958 offers of grant had risen to £548,597, but in 1959 a ceiling of £400,000 was set and by 1969 that had only been increased to £575,000, which, because of rising costs, was actually worth less than £400,000 in 1959. It was only in 1970 that the allocation was increased to £1 million and in 1973–74 to £1.5 million.

For my 1974 report I worked out that about a third of the total allocated for grants had gone to country houses, with 40 out of 102 new grants going to them in 1958, 38 out of 140 in 1968 and 40 out of 175 in 1970. Up to the end of March 1973, £2.65 million had gone to privately owned houses, £0.7 million to institutions and £1.95 million to the National Trust (a figure that covered the five houses taken on at the request of the Government).

In the late 1990s it sometimes appears as if there was a great deal of special pleading for country houses in the first 15–20 years after the Second World War and that they were helped at the expense of other kinds of building and particularly buildings in towns. In fact what is surprising is the lack of appreciation of historic towns and buildings in them at every level. Little was written about them, except for The Old Towns Revisited series in *Country Life*. And the amenity societies, although they campaigned for individual buildings, lacked the political skill and weight to have much effect either locally or nationally. Thus towns and cities suffered from the pro-country and anti-urban current of English thinking that only began to be reversed in the 1960s after the Civic Trust was established. Indeed it was only in the late 1970s that television thought that historic towns were worthy of attention in the series of programmes made by Alec Clifton Taylor and first shown in 1978.

By the mid-1960s, however, it had become clear that the problems of historic towns were even more serious than those facing historic houses, and new initiatives were required. That led to the commissioning in 1966 of the reports to the Minister of Housing and Local Government and their local authorities on Bath, Chester, Chichester and York which were published in 1968 and were to be the basis of the expansion of urban conservation policy in the following years.

The growing concern about towns led to the creation in 1970 of the Department of the Environment and so the bringing together of the Ministries of Housing and Local Government, Public Building and Works, and Transport and Planning. That prepared the way for a much more integrated approach, the development of preservation into conservation, and historic buildings including country houses entering the political arena.

(e) *The Expansion of the National Trust's Country Houses Scheme*

The scale of the National Trust's thinking after the war can be seen in its reopening of Montacute (Figs 1 and 9). In December 1944, even before the Trust regained possession of the house after its wartime use by the Victoria and Albert Museum, Eardley Knollys, the first Regional Representative, decided that the house must be furnished, and so a special Montacute Committee was set up, with Eardley Knollys and James Lees-Milne doing the physical work. They had such limited funds that once they could not afford £3 10s to pay for a van to come over

[59]

9. The Great Hall at Montacute as refurnished as a country house for reopening by the National Trust in 1946.

from Stourhead with a load of furniture; and Eardley Knollys and Vita Sackville-West did the planting in the garden themselves so the house could open in July 1946. Probably no one at the time realised how difficult it was going to be to refurnish the house as a convincing country house, or as Sir Malcolm Steuart expressed it in his will in 1951 when he left his collection 'for the adornment of Montacute House in order that it may re-assume its former character as the stately home of an English gentleman as distinct from the aspect of a museum.'

In the first five years of its Country Houses Scheme, 1937 to 1941, the Trust received five places, and then between 1942 and 1946 13 more, all as gifts or bequests. Between 1946 and 1956 it received 38, of which four were HBC grant or in lieu cases, and between 1957 and 1961 another 12, nine being grant or estate duty cases. After that the pace reduced with only two places between 1962 and 1966 (one estate duty) and three in the years 1967 to 1971 (one estate duty); and then five between 1972 and 1976.

The Trust opened 11 houses in 1946 and 19 more in 1947. That year its houses were visited by 120,000 people and by 433,000 in 1949.

The growth in these years owes a great deal to the remarkable authority and drive of Robin Fedden. He had joined the Trust in 1946 as the curator at Polesden Lacey, in Surrey, and succeeded James Lees-Milne as Historic Buildings Secretary in 1951, holding the post until he retired in 1974. Unlike Lees-Milne, he was not deeply rooted in the history and romance of ancient English places, in particular manor houses and the houses of squires, because he had spent much of his early life abroad, but he absorbed Lees-Milne's approach and added to it a remarkable eye for an unusually wide range of works of art and a gift for making rooms and houses look agreeable, convincing and lively to visitors as well writing readable guidebooks about them. He was also very effective in establishing good relations with the HBC. However he was also an outdoors man, who enjoyed mountaineering, walking, canoeing and skiing; and that added to his standing both within the Trust and outside.

He was very definitely an anti-museum man, and, as he explained in an early BBC talk about Polesden Lacey: 'The objective that the Trust kept before them therefore in setting out the varied contents was to create not only the appearance of a large country house of 1910, but the illusion of a house still lived in . . . We had, it was to be hoped, created an Edwardian interior and atmosphere, but how were they to be kept alive? I became painfully aware that the life of a house tends all too surely to depart with the owner, and that "museum" and "mausoleum" might not only *sound* alike.'

Here allowance has to be made for the hideousness of most museums at that time, the Fitzwilliam Museum at Cambridge with its furniture and carpets being the exception. The post-war Primary Galleries at the Victoria and Albert Museum (Fig. 10) opened in 1947 were thought progressive at the time, if stark to us, and at Temple Newsam at Leeds Philip Hendy ruthlessly unpicked many of the lesser 18th century rooms, ripping out chimney pieces and laying cork floors in order to create hospital-style settings for objects. The one success at the time was the furnishing of Aston Hall, Birmingham, at the instigation of Sir Trenchard Cox, the director of the City Museum and Art Gallery.

Thirty and forty years on the houses acquired in Robin Fedden's period tend to become a list of names, and it is only when they are looked up that the extraordinary variety of stories behind their acquisition come to mind once more; and the number of unappreciated risks that the Trust took – very few it could or would be prepared to take today.

10. The Boughton state bed in one of the innovative post-war Primary Galleries at the Victoria and Albert Museum that lasted until 1998.

What would have happened to the moated manor house with its soaring gatehouse at Oxburgh in Norfolk without the Trust – and later the HBC? In 1952 Sir Edmund Bedingfield, whose family had owned it since the first half of the 15th century, sold the whole place to a property company, which divided it into 70 lots, with all the trees to be felled and the house demolished for its materials. The night before the sale the Dowager Lady Bedingfield and two other members of the family managed to buy the house, selling their own houses in order to raise the money; and subsequently, with the support of several trusts, Lady Bedingfield was able to give it to the National Trust.

Also it is often overlooked how many places have come to the Trust because there were no direct heirs. Powis Castle, in Wales, came to the Trust because the 4th Earl of Powis's only surviving son had been killed in the war. His heir was a remote kinsman descended from the 4th son of the 2nd Earl who had died in 1848. Three days before the 4th Earl died at the age of 81 in 1952, he signed the transfer to the Trust. The 5th Earl also had no heir, and, on his death in 1974, he was succeeded by his brother, who was unmarried. So when the 6th Earl died in 1988, he was succeeded by a cousin who died in 1993; he was succeeded by his son, the present, 8th Earl. Without the Trust (and later introductions of conditional exemption) it is hard to see how the Powis trustees could have held the castle and estate together with five different holders of the title in 40 years. Moreover it would have been infinitely harder for the National Trust without the generous grants from the Welsh HBC. Nor could the contents have survived without several in lieu deals – and the successful outcome to the near disaster over Bellotto's *View of Verona* (Fig. 29) described on p. 167.

The two complicated arrangements made soon after the war over Ham and Osterley, which have already been mentioned, show how undeveloped was thinking and so legislation. In the case of Ham, Sir Leigh Ashton suggested that the Government should buy the property and put the Museum in charge, but its owner, Sir Lyonel Tollemache, did not like the idea of government ownership. So James Lees-Milne suggested the compromise of the house passing to the Trust. Thus Sir Lyonel gave the house to the National Trust, while the Government bought the contents for the Victoria and Albert Museum; and the Trust, lacking any endowment for the house, leased it to the Ministry of Works, which looked after the structure and the setting, and handed over the running of the house to the Museum.

A similar arrangement was made at Osterley, over which Lord Jersey had first approached the National Trust in 1938, before he opened it himself. However, talks ended when the house suffered bomb damage and were only resumed in 1944. In 1949 Lord Jersey gave the house to the Trust but without any endowment, and so it was leased to the Ministry of Works, and the Government acquired the furniture for the Victoria and Albert Museum, which continued to run it for the next 40 years as an out-station.

Ickworth, in Suffolk, came to the Trust because the 5th Marquess of Bristol had two daughters but no son, and neither he nor Lady Bristol trusted the heir. So they arranged for the house and contents to be offered in settlement of tax on Lord Bristol's death in 1956 while Lady Bristol gave the endowment to the National Trust. Sadly in two generations their suspicions have proved to be right, and in 1996 the 7th

Marquess sold the remaining contents of the family wing at auction. The Trust had already bought a Jacob More landscape, the only one of the Earl Bishop's commissions to survive, and also a Hugh Douglas Hamilton pastel of the Earl Bishop, both of which the 7th Marquess had sold, and at the auction, partly through the support of the Heritage Lottery Fund, the Trust bought pictures which it wanted to enrich the hanging, particularly in the Library (see p. 181).

Clandon Park, near Guildford, which belonged to the Earls of Onslow, was used by the Public Record Office for the storage of archives during the war. In 1945 the 5th Earl died; his son, like so many younger owners, was determined to return and did so before the PRO had completely moved out. However after five years he had to accept that it was an impossible situation and moved out again. Before that happened he offered the house to the Trust, but since there was no endowment, the Trust could not accept it; and then for several years the house stood empty. Finally in 1956 the house was saved by Lord Onslow's aunt, Lady Iveagh, who bought it together with seven acres from him and gave it to the Trust with an endowment. As part of the package the HBC agreed to contribute a then large grant of £20,000 towards the costs of repair. Lord Onslow still retained some of the contents, and in 1963 these were bought for the house out of the Land Fund. Even so Clandon remained a lame duck from the Trust's point of view, a splendid, cold and rather bare house that was also a constant financial drain.

In 1967 Mrs David Gubbay died, leaving her collection of furniture, porcelain and carpets to the National Trust with the request that it should be placed in a house within 30 miles of Hyde Park Corner together with an endowment of nearly £1 million. Unfortunately the Trust had known nothing of her intention and since she had made the bequest within 12 months of her death, the top rate of duty had to be paid on the endowment reducing it to £250,000. The Trust decided to place the collection at Clandon and in 1968–1970 it carried out what was for the time an unusually elaborate restoration and decoration programme at the house. However, there was a problem in that the objects were mostly too small in scale and delicate in character for such a monumental house and not well related to the Onslow possessions. The whole project of restoration and arrangement was very close to the heart of John Fowler who helped the Trust with it, as well as being a statement of attitudes to interiors at that time. It was also important for the influence it had on the thinking of the small band of people involved with the Trust's historic buildings, all the more important because it was being done at the same time as the Victoria and Albert Museum was working on Osterley. The situations in the two houses were quite different, but that only heightened the contrast in approaches.

The case was also important in that in the Finance Act 1972 all gifts and bequests to the National Trust were made free of Capital Gains Tax, death duty and aggregation.

Many houses and their contents came to the Trust gradually and by different routes. So it was at Uppark, in Sussex, where the most romantic part of the story that is so characteristic of the place now seems to be little known; it was told to me again by St John Gore, who was on the Trust's staff at the time. One Friday afternoon in the mid-1950s an unknown lady called at the Trust's office in Queen's Anne's Gate and asked to see whoever was in charge. On being taken to see the Secretary, Jack Rathbone, she said that she wished to give the Trust £70,000, a sum of money that seemed so large that he said that he could not possibly accept it just like that and would she not think the matter over and come back on Monday morning if she still felt the same way. She said that she had decided, but would come back. Jack Rathbone, not surprisingly, had a sleepless weekend at the thought of having possibly lost the money. But back she came on Monday and said that her favourite period of house dated from round about 1700. It happened that the Trust was then having fruitless negotiations over Uppark because of the lack of endowment, and so it was thanks to this anonymous benefactor that not only was Uppark endowed with £40,000 but Hanbury with £30,000. No one on the staff ever knew her name, and it has never been disclosed.

However, romance has been combined with years of negotiations over contents, with in lieu arrangements and purchases worked out side by side. In 1966–67 and 1969–70 there were in lieu deals over contents, and contents were bought in 1970–71, 1971–72 and 1976–77. However arrangements that look simple and tidy in official reports were, in fact, very complicated and negotiations were long drawn out. The first in lieu deal in 1966 and the second in 1969 were in respect of duty arising from the deaths in 1958 of Richard Meade-Fetherstonhaugh, the son of the donor of Uppark, and in 1964 of his father, the Admiral; the liability for tax was not high, so not much had to be handed over to the Treasury and lent to the Trust. The correspondence reveals the Treasury's concern about the weakness of the Trust's position over the contents in the show rooms, with it owning only about a third of them.

The houses acquired in the first 30 years of the Scheme were all pre-Victorian, except for Wightwick Manor, at Wolverhampton, given in 1937, but with the growing interest in 19th century architecture in the 1960s, following the establishment of the Victorian Society in 1958 and the rows over the demolition of Euston Arch in 1962 and the Coal Exchange the following year, it was largely a matter of time and opportunity before the National Trust looked forward. Then in the late 1960s Mark Girouard wrote a series of articles on Victorian country houses for *Country Life* with a book in mind that was eventually published in 1971. Although at the time some of the houses seemed impossibly ugly, they prompted the National Trust to ask him to compile a list of houses that in his view were sufficiently complete to be considered as candidates for preservation. In his paper discussed by the Trust in December 1971, Mark Girouard wrote that he knew of 500 Victorian houses, including notes on 256 in the catalogue in his book. However of those only 37 were still lived in by the families who had built them. He subdivided those into A and B categories, with six in A – Cragside, in Northumberland, Tyntesfield, in Somerset, Brodsworth, in Yorkshire, Thoresby, in Nottinghamshire, Mentmore, in Buckinghamshire, and Alnwick, in Northumberland. Today Alnwick and Tyntesfield are the only ones still to be occupied by their families: Cragside belongs to the National Trust and Brodsworth to English Heritage, while both Thoresby and Mentmore have been sold and their contents dispersed.

One of the houses on Girouard's B list was Standen, in Sussex, which was designed by Philip Webb in 1891. That was bequeathed to the Trust in 1972 by Miss Helen Beale, the youngest daughter of the builder, and, despite what was said at the time, the Trust quickly decided to accept it on merit: what took time was sorting out the finances.

The history of the National Trust's involvement with country houses is inextricably bound up with its acquisition of gardens and parks, as is explained on p. 272.

From the beginning of the Country Houses Scheme one of the fundamental problems was that of endowment, how to persuade donors to provide them and, just as important, how to calculate them so that they would support a place in the long term. Ongoing costs continue to be a problem with places accepted via the Land Fund and which the Government always refused to endow. Finally in 1976 all the problems led the Trust to ask Lord Chorley, who was a member of the Finance Commitee, to work out a formula for calculating what was needed to endow a place so that it would be safe for 50 years; and subject to minor amendments in 1983 and 1986 it has used it ever since.

According to the Trust's Accounting Policy Document, which explains how it works in detail, the basis of the formula is as follows.

Annual property expenditure		X
+20% (contingencies 12.5%, improvements 7.5%)		X
+20% (regional management fee)		X
Deduct annual property income		
Rents (less one-third)	X	
Other income	X	
Annual deficit	X	
+50% uplift	X	
Uplifted deficit	Y	
Capitalisation rate	Z%	
Endowment required		$\dfrac{Y \times 100}{Z}$

And according to its summary, the Chorley Formula converts a property's forecast annual deficit into a capital sum, the endowment required, by adding a factor for differential growth and capitalising at the current gross dividend yield.

That yield rate has averaged about 5% over the last 50 years. A 5% rate, taken with a 50% uplift, produces an endowment equivalent to 1.5×100, or 30 times the annual deficit.

The results of the calculation invariably cause shock, not only to Trust staff and committees, who find the totals hard to believe and difficult to ask for, but also to prospective donors or executors when they are presented with them, so that some of them withdraw and a few go off and make charitable trusts instead. They have also caused shock to the NHMF. However, in most cases the Trust discovers after a period of years that places are under-endowed. A number of private owners, who have a full understanding of the funding of their own properties, have come to see the Chorley Formula as being as good a way of calculating requirements as any and the results as being realistic.

In terms of date the formula may appear to belong in the later chapter on the National Trust, but it is so crucial to understanding many other aspects of the country house situation and events from 1976 that it is included here.

(f) *The Development of Architectural, Social and Economic History and the Perception of Country Houses*

One of the great advantages of English pragmatism is that official systems tend to evolve, albeit in a sometimes creaky way, in response to changing ideas, and anyone considering the history of country houses in Britain since 1945 has to relate private and public initiatives to ideas developed in books, articles and exhibitions. Indeed research and writing have underpinned developing attitudes and policies. In his book *The Rise of Architectural History* (1980) David Watkin provided an excellent framework in which post-war writing can be seen in a much longer historical perspective, but here some of the writing he discusses can be related to the development of preservation activity.

The restoration of peace in 1945 was soon followed with many useful books on historic architecture in Britain, starting with John Summerson's *Georgian London* in 1945. 1951 saw the publication of Rupert Gunnis's *Dictionary of British Sculptors*, and in the same year Nikolaus Pevsner began his *Buildings of England* series for Penguin which was to reveal for the first time the range of the greater and lesser riches of England (and is still revealing those of Scotland, Wales and Ireland) both to specialists and to the general public. H.M. Colvin produced the first edition of his *Biographical Dictionary of British Architects 1660–1840* in 1954. He gave a new degree of authority to all writing about English architecture, and particularly to that on country houses. The other key book was John Summerson's *Architecture in Britain 1530–1830*, which first appeared in 1953.

Most of the biographies of 18th century architects date from these years. Among them were books on Vanbrugh by Lawrence Whistler in 1954 and by Kerry Downes in 1977; on Hawksmoor by Downes in 1959 and 1969; on Kent by Margaret Jourdain in 1948 and by Michael Wilson in 1984; on Robert Adam by John Fleming in 1962; on Inigo Jones by John Summerson in 1966; on Chambers by John Harris in 1970; on Holland by Dorothy Stroud in 1966; on Dance by the same writer in 1971. The main additions to this group are John Summerson's new edition of his book on John Nash in 1980 (originally published in 1935) and books on James Paine by Peter Leach in 1988 and on James Gibbs by Terry Friedman in 1984.

In the mid-1950s Geoffrey Beard began to do research on craftsmen, particularly plasterers; over a period of nearly 40 years he has unearthed dynasties of plasterers and a huge company of craftsmen who were responsible for building country houses in the 17th, 18th and early 19th centuries, as can be seen in many articles and from his *Georgian Craftsmen and Their Work* (1966), his *Decorative Plasterwork in Great Britain* (1975) and his *Craftsmen and Interior Decoration in England 1660–1820* (1981).

Throughout the war *Country Life* had continued to publish its country house articles, with a remarkable number of them by Christopher Hussey, and that must be seen in part as propaganda at home and overseas, comparable with the exhibitions at the National Gallery and so on. Hussey had an extraordinary sweep and it is interesting to see him stepping forward into the 19th century in his writing in the 1950s when he was at work on his trilogy of volumes on English country houses, early, mid and late Georgian, which appeared in 1955, 1956 and 1958: those books seem to capture the enthusiasm for country houses at that time and provide the yardstick for the HBC, the National Trust and those seeking houses to take on.

What enormously enriched all post-war writing about country houses and allied subjects was the development of county record offices, which took in as gifts or loans a great range of local archives, in particular the papers of old county families, who might or might not remain in their houses; and in many cases they catalogued them. Thus huge caches of material were made available, with unknown drawings, inventories, accounts, bills and letters all coming to light, providing rich new fields for researchers to dig in. Much, of course, remained in muniment rooms of country houses or unrecognised in cupboards in store rooms, or even abandoned in outbuildings, but gradually, thanks to the co-operation of owners and archivists as well as the persistence of researchers, knowledge of houses has been and is being transformed.

In the 1950s there was increasing interest in the 19th century heralded by Peter Floud's exhibition of *Victorian and Edwardian Decorative Arts* at the Victoria and Albert Museum in 1952 and Henry Russell Hitchcock's *Early Victorian Architecture* (1954), followed by T.R.S. Boase's volume in the *Oxford History of English Art* series in 1959. This was confirmed in the foundation of the Victorian Society in 1958; and that was followed by other specialist societies, several of them, like the Society of Architectural Historians and the Furniture History Society, publishing excellent journals. However, despite the growing enthusiasm and the increasing number of people working in these allied fields, surprisingly few scholarly and readable survey volumes were produced for 19th century architecture except for Mark Girouards's *The Victorian Country House* (1971).

Yet another development towards the end of this period was in the growth of art history as a subject for study, both at university and in courses such as that run by the Study Centre in London, an idea later taken up by the auction houses. Before 1960 the only university course for undergraduates was at the Courtauld Institute in the University of London, but in 1961 a Part II course as part of the tripos was introduced at Cambridge and a number of other courses were started during that decade. The concentration in university courses was on the fine arts, with architecture generally as a secondary element, and the decorative arts almost entirely ignored. These courses coincided with the explosion of research for doctorates, and a growing number of people chose history of art subjects with some having a bearing on the field of country houses. Thus not only did more people want to work in the field, but they came to it with some formal training and sometimes considerable study.

The spread of art history in the 1960s was to have a more direct bearing on country houses, because sons and daughters, grandsons and granddaughters, nephews and nieces came to develop a new kind of network that linked together houses, museums and the sale rooms. These connections continue to be carefully nurtured by the sale rooms through their regional representatives as well as the London organisations, and their promotion of country house sales as quasi-social events.

The outstanding figure in the country house field trained in the auction world is Lady Victoria Leatham, who worked for Sotheby's as a regional appraiser for nine years before she was asked to take on the running of Burghley House, for which her father, Lord Exeter, had set up a charitable trust before he died. A collector by nature and devoted to Burghley and its collections, her years at Sotheby's not only opened her eyes to objects but made her at ease with them, so she was well prepared to take on the gigantic curatorial, conservation as well as management challenge of putting in order the diverse collections formed by her ancestors. That has involved research in the archives, which themselves had to be put into order, cataloguing, a great deal of lecturing, organising conservation, rehanging virtually the whole collection of pictures, putting on 13 annual special exhibitions between 1983 and 1995 devoted to hitherto unexplored aspects of the collection, and arranging exhibitions drawn from Burghley to tour overseas museums: 'Ancestors', as she explains, 'have to be prepared to travel.' If Burghley has presented Lady Victoria with opportunities for discovery that many museum curators dream of, few match her enthusiasm, energy and talent for fundraising.

The museum world has always been more cautious about welcoming people, but the Woodwork Department at the Victoria and Albert Museum in the late 1960s and early 1970s was unusually outward-looking: as well as clever young men from America and Holland there were several bright, glamorous girls who floated in and out between long, stimulating coffee breaks and organised departmental visits to houses they knew well. That was useful at the time, and 25 years later they are still seriously involved with houses and collections either as chatelaines or trustees.

3

◆

The Growth of Interest in Collections, Furniture and Historic Interiors 1945–1973

One of the most curious aspects of the history of the preservation of British country houses in the last 50 years is how attitudes to historic collections, contents and interiors trailed behind the appreciation of buildings and the development of architectural history. The step by step nature of English thinking may make that less surprising, but it is important to understand the effect it has had on the way places have been preserved, and how and why ideas began to develop in the mid-1960s.

What also has to be borne in mind is the influence of the art trade, which began to pick up about 1953–54, and the effect of almost continuously rising prices ever since on the nature of collecting, the work of art historians (but not those interested in architecture) and the attitudes of owners of inherited historic collections.

However, until about 1960 there was little understanding of the significance of historic collections in private ownership among people working in museums and galleries. That is to be seen in the way that they approached objects that were being considered as part of in lieu deals. I have already explained how the Finance Acts of 1953 and 1956 were amended to cover the acceptance of works of art, so pushing the Land Fund in a direction not visualised by Hugh Dalton.

The problem of approach can be seen particularly clearly in the negotiations over the pictures at Petworth. The great house had been given to the Trust in 1947 by the 3rd Lord Leconfield with an endowment but without any of the contents. That had been done at the instigation of his nephew and heir, John Wyndham, later Lord Egremont, who had considerable understanding of Whitehall, because he had been Harold Macmillan's right-hand man during the Second

World War (and later, in 1957, became his Private Secretary): in his own words he 'wanted to make sure that Petworth was preserved, and who could tell what the future might hold'. Lord Leconfield's death in 1952 created a death duty problem that not only ate into the family estates but threatened the integrity of the collection at Petworth built up over 300 years. The family and the Trust both wanted to preserve its character with great pictures and lesser ones, many acquired by the 3rd Earl of Egremont (1751–1837), the patron not only of Turner but of other contemporary artists who were out of fashion in the 1950s.

However the Government's adviser from the National Gallery only wanted to consider major pictures as individual objects in isolation, not in relation to their setting at Petworth; and in the end it took all the persuasion of Lord Crawford, the chairman of the Trust, who was knowledgeable about both works of art and the politics of museums, to get the Trust's view to prevail. As he wrote to the Treasury: '[The National Gallery] advises against accepting a number of pictures . . . The suggestion that they should not be included would absolutely wreck the house, leaving a series of spaces on the walls. The suggestion is quite lunatic, quite indefensible, quite exasperating . . . Owners won't face these obstacles and the years . . . of uncertainty and misery . . . If owners refuse to play – and if Wyndham sells – no one can blame them or the National Trust.'

Nearly 50 years later it is difficult to appreciate quite how difficult and how unfamiliar were the problems at Petworth for all concerned, but some idea can be gathered from a letter from Anthony Blunt to Robin Fedden dated 18 September 1956, written after he had been to see Lord Bridges, the Permanent Secretary to the Treasury from 1945 to 1956: 'Bridges first of all reminded me that the Gallery had thought that we had accepted some rather bad pictures, but the Treasury had taken the point that a country house needed to be well hung and is not like a picture gallery.' Blunt had explained to Lord Bridges that as a result of the rearrangement of the pictures that he had already carried out for the Trust he had reduced the number of pictures in the rooms open to the public by 50%; that John Wyndham wished to keep a number of pictures for his own rooms; and that in a few cases there were disagreements on valuations because the pictures themselves were controversial. After Lord Bridges had been called away his colleague asked Blunt: 'Would it in future be reasonable policy to say that the Treasury would in general accept paintings which would be regarded as important enough to gain exemption from death duties?' Blunt replied that he regarded that as perfectly reasonable 'because in my experience the galleries have been very generous in their recommendations for exemption,' but then he expressed concern about the possibility of the National Gallery rejecting the controversial pictures.

Even though Lord Crawford's view was accepted, the family still could not get the Government to accept its valuation, and in the end in 1956 had to agree to a figure of £553,148 in place of the £1 million it hoped for or lose any agreement and so the completeness of the collection. Anthony Blunt considered that grossly unfair on the family.

In recent years the present Lord Egremont has lent the Trust many more pictures for public display, particularly British pictures acquired by the 3rd Lord Egremont, thus reflecting Blunt's undated memorandum in which he wrote: 'Taste will change and it is likely that in fifty years the Trust will want to bring out and hang pictures that we have put away.'

The problem of selectivity affected the pictures at Dyrham Park, a house largely built in the years around 1700 and retaining a remarkably complete collection of pictures formed at that time. Most unusually, both the house and contents were bought in 1956 by the Government out of the Land Fund, because the tax liability that brought on the crisis was less than the value of the property. The house and contents were bought for £47,440 and £60,349 was spent on repairs. Unfortunately not all the pictures that were offered with the house were acquired, and the rooms have seemed on the thin side ever since.

A similar problem occurred at Hatchlands, where the house was given to the Trust by H.S. Goodhart Rendel, the architect, in 1945 but without any of the contents. He continued to live in the house until the late 1950s when he decided to move to France and sell the contents. At that point the Government agreed to help the Trust buy contents to the value of £2940 in order to furnish some of the rooms, but the Trust had to accept the loss of Salvator Rosa's *Apotheosis of the Italian Patriot Masaniello* (Fig. 11), because it would have absorbed too much of the allowance; and in the end it was bought by the Kunsthistorisches Museum in Vienna.

It seems that it was only in the late 1950s that scholars began to write about historic collections, the history of patronage and taste, and explore them in exhibitions. There were a few exhibitions drawing on pictures from houses in particular regions, such as *Fine Paintings from*

11. *The Apotheosis of the Italian Patriot Masaniello* by Salvator Rosa in the staircase hall at Hatchlands Park, Surrey, in 1953. It was lost to the house when the Government would not allow the National Trust sufficient funds to purchase the contents so that it could continue to be shown as a furnished house. The picture went abroad.

12. and 13. *Sir Robert Throckmorton* and *Elizabeth Throckmorton* by Largillière. Two of the unique set of five portraits formerly at Coughton Court, Warwickshire, which the Government refused to buy in 1964. In the end it bought the portrait of Sir Robert in its splendid frame to hang in the house, which belongs to the National Trust, but the portrait of Elizabeth went abroad to the National Gallery, Washington. The last portrait was recently acquired for the house.

ELIZABETH DAUGHTER OF S.ᴿ ROB.ᵀ THROCKMORTON BAR.ᵀ

East Anglia in 1964 and *Dutch Paintings from East Anglia* in 1966, both held at the Castle Museum, Norwich, but two early ones to have a theme were on the Grand Tour, *Eighteenth Century Italy and the Grand Tour* at Norwich in 1958 and *Italy and the Grand Tour in the 17th and 18th Centuries* held at Northampton in 1959. These were followed by the major *Italian Art and Britain* held at the Royal Academy in the winter of 1960. About

[77]

the same time Gerald Burdon wrote a pioneering article in *Italian Studies* on the Italian pictures acquired by Sir Thomas Isham in Italy in the late 1670s that remain at Lamport Hall, Northamptonshire. In 1962 James Lees-Milne published his *Earls of Creation*, a study of five 18th century English patrons.

In 1972 Frank Herrmann in *The English as Collectors* wrote about the relationship between the history of collecting and the current art market: 'We have today reached a stage in the history of collecting where one factor has become increasingly important. This is provenance. In the past the study of provenance has been confined to pictures and antiquities. As values go up it will be used increasingly for other categories of works of art. This alone makes the study of collecting particularly relevant today. Additionally the amalgam of taste, flair, fashion, patronage, connoisseurship, financial acumen, affluence and occasional flamboyance, makes it a fascinating subject that will gradually establish itself as an important aspect of our social history.'

Despite the weakness of appreciation of collections there were remarkably few occasions when the Government failed to step in to support a house that had been given to the Trust. The worst disaster occurred at Coughton Court in Warwickshire, an ancient Roman Catholic house where the Throckmortons have lived since 1409. With great difficulty, because of the existing family settlement, the family gave the house to the Trust in 1945 but retained all the contents. The most important pictures were the group of five portraits by Largillière (Figs 12 and 13) that Sir Robert Throckmorton commissioned in 1729 or thereabouts: this consisted of Sir Robert's own portrait, a glamorous picture in a fine original French frame, his second wife, and three members of his family who belonged to the Order of Blue Nuns at the Augustinian Convent in Paris. They were a unique group in England, not only because of the artist but because they were so revealing of Roman Catholic history in penal times. In 1964 the family decided to sell them and first offered them to the Government, which rejected them, So they went to Christie's, and after one of the nuns was sold for £65,000, the rest were withdrawn; subsequently Sir Robert's portrait was bought by the Government for £54,600, and it went back to the house. Sadly the portraits of two nuns went abroad, one to the National Gallery in Washington, and the other to a private collector in Australia (it is now in a public gallery). We will come back to the remaining portrait of a nun later.

The decoration of rooms was a suspect field and taken seriously by few people involved with preservation, except for the Duke of Wellington who took enormous trouble over the arrangement of Stratfield Saye, in Hampshire. But that was partly because after the war restrictions were so tight, with building licences only being removed in 1954, that it took almost 10 years before elaborate decoration became possible again. Also no one was working on its history. Among decorators working in historical styles Felix Harbord had a brilliant imaginative eye, but his talent was for creating theatrical versions of 18th-century interiors as at Kingston Russell, in Dorset, at Oving House in Buckinghamshire and at Luttrellstown near Dublin: he was not a restorer.

Here John Fowler was a more important and ultimately more influential figure with a remarkable country house practice. In the years after the Second World War, and particularly in the 1950s and 1960s, he created with his partner, Nancy Lancaster, a Virginian by birth, a country house style of their own time, combining ideas from the past with those from the present that grew out of the pre-war rediscovery of the 18th century. It became a beau ideal for her and her circle of friends, but at that time it was a private look, because few of John Fowler's largest jobs, like Grimsthorpe Castle, in Lincolnshire, for the Countess of Ancaster, Daylesford, in Gloucestershire, for Lord Rothermere, and Tyninghame, in Scotland, for the Countess of Haddington, were fully published at the time; and regrettably many were never adequately recorded. Ramsbury, in Wiltshire, when it belonged to Lord Rootes, and Mrs Lancaster's own Haseley Court, Oxfordshire, were illustrated in *Country Life*, but, of course, in black and white; and not a great deal of attention was devoted to the decoration.

John Fowler knew the value of exclusivity and wanted to protect his clients, so never encouraged publicity, and ironically his work only became more widely known through what he did in houses open to the public as at Wilton House, Wiltshire, where he painted Wyatt's cloisters to great effect in the 1960s, and for the National Trust in the late 1960s and early 1970s. What he did for the Trust has its own point, which is often missed today, but, because it was done in rooms to be looked at rather than lived in, it does not represent the real essence of his work, which was to make even the grandest rooms liveable in his own time, bringing out and enhancing their character but at the same time making them unformidable – 'degranding', he used to call it.

Of other post-war decoration not much of interest survives, except for the skilfully designed curtains made out of dyed American army blankets for Lady Onslow for the saloon at Clandon and the saloon at Basildon with hangings of baize put up by Lady Iliffe with the aid of her butler and sumptuous old silk damask curtains and pelmet cornices from Blenheim.

Here part of the problem was that after the death of Margaret Jourdain in 1951 virtually nothing was written about the history of interiors. They were omitted from writings about historic buildings and architecture, and also furniture studies had become stuck in the dictionary approach, of trying to sort out types into stylistic order. In fact the thinking behind Ralph Edwards' revised *Dictionary of English Furniture* published in 1954 was substantially the same as that found in the original three volumes planned before the First World War and first published in the mid-1920s. It was still strongly influenced by the collectors of English furniture who had been active in the early years of the century and dominated thinking until after the Second World War, but who have no real successors today. That partly explains why the *Dictionary* was not concerned with the context of furniture nor very greatly with the provenance of pieces. The only new element was that there was more on individual makers, a subject that Ralph Edwards and Margaret Jourdain had first tackled in a slim book in 1944.

Here research and writing did not pick up until about 1963 when Eileen Harris published her book on *Adam Furniture* and the newly founded Furniture History Society produced its first annual journal. Soon after that there began to appear a new kind of substantial article about furniture in country houses that was based on research in documents and supported by footnotes: these appeared in *Apollo, The Burlington Magazine* and *The Connoisseur*. The first seems to be Anthony Coleridge's article on furniture at Holkham in *Apollo* in 1964, and he followed that up with James Cullen at Hopetoun in *Apollo* in 1966, and furniture at Hatfield in *The Burlington Magazine* in 1967; in 1968 he published his book on Chippendale. The same years articles in the *Furniture History Society Journal* were devoted to Mersham and Nostell, and in 1969 Christopher Gilbert wrote about Chippendale at Dumfries House in *The Burlington Magazine*. The following year at the Ferens Art Gallery in Hull there was a remarkable exhibition devoted to William Constable of Burton Constable as a patron based on the researches of Ivan Hall. That exhibition and Ivan Hall's work were also to be of great importance to the Historic Buildings Council when it had to persuade ministers of the need for massive support for the repair programme at Burton Constable where the first grant was offered in 1972–73.

There were also signs of a renewed interest in textiles with Peter Thornton's *Baroque and Rococo Silks* in 1965 and Florence Montgomery's *Printed Textiles, English and American Cottons and Linens* (1970). About the same time there was a growing awareness of the need for the proper care of textiles and the development of facilities for their conservation as well as the training of people to work in the field.

Another new direction was opened up by Hugh Murray Baillie in an article with the formidable title of *Etiquette and the Planning of the State Apartments in Baroque Palaces* that he first gave as a talk to the Society of Antiquaries in 1966 and published in *Archaeologia* in 1967. As he explained, it grew out of his work as a Monuments, Fine Arts and Archives Officer in Germany after the war when he began to study the plans of state apartments in palaces and that led him to think about the William III buildings at Hampton Court Palace. This paper was to unlock many doors and ultimately to encourage a historical and so an interpretative and educational approach to the display of rooms not only in palaces but in country houses.

About the same time two other developments took place, one within the National Trust, starting about 1963 but building up from about 1968, and the other at the Victoria and Albert Museum starting about that year and revealed to the public in 1970. The Trust was faced with the need to open houses to the public and attract and satisfy an increasing number of visitors with rising expectations, and so with the need to carry out extensive programmes of redecoration. The first house where this situation arose was Claydon where in 1956–57 John Fowler helped the Trust by painting several of the splendid but dauntingly empty rooms. Their scale was such that it was impossible to furnish them, as had been done at Montacute, and so John Fowler introduced colour to play up the rich ornament and compensate for the lack of furniture, an approach that still seems to be the most sensible one, even if not strictly historical.

In 1963 the Trust faced a somewhat similar problem at Shugborough when the house was offered in lieu of tax. The whole house had been painted a creamy white between the wars, and by then looked flat and distinctly tired. So in 1965 John Fowler devised a series of schemes of decoration, using colour and pattern to give variety to the house and compensate for the sparseness of the furniture and lack of carpets in some of the bigger rooms, in order to create a more interesting experience for visitors. After that John Fowler helped the Trust on a number of occasions, combining elements of restoration and decoration to make houses more lively for visitors.

It was about that time that I became concerned that so little research was being done on interiors of National Trust houses being opened to the public and the Trust's lack of capacity to do it through existing pressures on the very small historic buildings staff. Then, in 1968, I met John Fowler, whose friends had been urging him for years to write down what he knew about decoration, and so gradually we developed the idea of writing a basic book together for the Trust's staff. That became our *English Decoration in the 18th Century*, which appeared in 1974 – and is now out of date.

Ralph Edwards, who had had an important influence on thinking about the selective acquisition of contents for houses after the Second World War, finally retired from the Keepership of the Furniture Department at the Victoria and Albert Museum in 1954. He was succeeded by Delves Molesworth, who moved across from Sculpture: he was a connoisseur with a great love of works of art and, although he had no particular interest in furniture, he started to rebuild the Department, recruiting young people including John Hardy and Desmond FitzGerald, Knight of Glin; he also brought in Peter Thornton, who had spent the years 1954 to 1962 in the Textile Department and so had a complementary approach and knowledge that was to be of crucial importance in the coming years.

In 1966 Peter Thornton became Keeper of the Department and started to give it a constructive new direction, looking at rooms and houses in the round in a way that was influenced by Scandinavian thinking. This was more significant, and difficult, than it sounds, because of the Museum's division by material that makes lateral thinking and action difficult. Also quite deliberately he made the Department more outward-looking so that it made sorties to houses belonging to the Trust or privately owned, writing reports, as was done for Hardwick and Hopetoun, and rearranging furniture. Not all their efforts were successful or admired but the warm reception in many houses, notably at Woburn, where the Duke and Duchess of Bedford were particularly welcoming, meant an important change in its position: the Department saw part of its job as being to help houses and to spread the idea that houses were complementary to museums, being able to show things in

14. The Dining Room at Osterley Park, Middlesex, in 1971. The rearrangement of the furniture according to the inventory of 1782 carried out in the late 1960s was to have a contested but gradually profound influence on attitudes to the preservation, arrangement, and showing of houses particularly by the National Trust.

context in a way that is impossible in a museum.

Up to that time the Department had regarded both Ham and Osterley as extensions of its galleries, doing a certain amount of swapping between the houses and the museum. Now the Department saw that both were well-documented entities, with Ham having a rare concentration of 17th century objects and Osterley representing the Adam period. So it set about showing both for what they were, without any additions.

Osterley was tackled first, and, when it was reopened in 1970 (Fig. 14), Maurice Tomlin, a member of the Department, described what had been done in *Country Life*: 'Hitherto furniture studies have concentrated on the development of styles and identification of makers, but recently more attention has been devoted to the arrangement and uses of furniture and attempts on paper have been made to reconstruct 18th century arrangements. It is this shift in interest that lies behind the changes at Osterley described in these articles . . .'

The Department rejected the concept of carrying on from where the former owners of Ham and Osterley had left off, a process which anyway had been disturbed by the Museum, but took the view that its duty was to display both houses as historical documents of particular periods, even if that involved carrying out restorations dependent on elements of subjective choice. It rejected the Rule of Taste as being essentially unsound, not being based on documentary and scientific research, and also being founded on a false set of values inspired by contemporary inaccurate enthusiasm for the 18th century; also it rejected the concept of pleasing the eye as a basis for decoration or arrangement. Thus as far as visitors are concerned, the appeal is essentially to their intellect, not to their spirits, and they have to be sufficiently well informed to make the leaps back in time or be helped to do so through interpretation.

All this might sound too specialised to matter, but in this lies the nub of the problem of preserving and presenting houses. The appeal of Ham and Hardwick, and, to a lesser extent, Osterley, had been to the spirit and the mind, and the duality has to be understood. That is central to much that has happened outside the private sector during the past 25 years.

However, the new attention that the Museum was giving to documented interiors was soon to have an important practical result, because in the Finance Act 1972 the original rules for exemption were revised: instead of objects having to be of a standard to be shown in a national institution, exemption was extended to what could be shown in a university or local authority museum. Thus when the Museum became involved in exemption cases it meant that almost everything in a historic house could be covered. This was also important in in lieu cases, as was seen at Cragside, as will be explained in a later section.

If the late 1940s, '50s and early '60s were years of country house demolitions, they were also years that saw the stripping of many country houses and sales on site or in London that were in many cases disastrous, because of inadequate research and cataloguing, as Sir Oliver Millar pointed out in his essay 'The Picture Collection' in *The*

Destruction of the Country House. Among the disasters he cites were the sales of the complete contents of Kimbolton Castle, Huntingdonshire, in 1949, a large part of the collection from Woburn Abbey, Bedfordshire, in 1951, and pictures from Panshanger, Hertfordshire, in 1953 including unrecognised family portraits, and the break-up of the Craven collection of portraits formerly associated with Hampstead Marshall, Berkshire, Combe Abbey, Warwickshire, and Ashdown House, Berkshire.

The list of houses stripped in these years is a melancholy long one. Among those that stand out in view of what has happened to the places later are Belsay Castle, in Northumberland, the most important neo-classical country house in the country which many years later was acquired by the Department of the Environment and is now shown by English Heritage; Highcliffe Castle, Hampshire, which through a series of disasters declined into ruin from which it is only now being rescued at huge public expense (Fig. 15); Croome Court, Worcestershire, where after many vicissitudes the landscape has been acquired by the National Trust; Brympton D'Evercy, Somerset, from which the contents were sold in 1947 when it became a school and to which the son of the vendor returned in 1974, had to sell in 1992.

There are many others: Ashburnham Place, Sussex; Hampton Court, Herefordshire; Aynhoe Park, Oxfordshire; Cobham Hall, Kent; Ince Blundell Hall, Lancashire; Northwick Park, Gloucestershire; Shardeloes, Buckinghamshire; Wardour Castle, Wiltshire. The stripping of 19th century country houses has included many now regrettable examples, among them Horsted Place, Sussex; Mamhead, Devon; Scarisbrick Hall, Lancashire.

Certain categories of objects tend to be sold before others. Silver and books are usually first choices for sale; in the years after the war sculpture found little enthusiasm with owners, but equally it was in little demand on the market. Many collections of marbles were dispersed, among them most of those from the historic collection at Wilton. Thus the remaining collections at Holkham, Petworth and Newby are even more precious. Italian Baroque pictures, many of which had been brought to England by Grand Tour collectors, were equally unpopular with owners and many were sold, as can be seen from the collection of Sir Denis Mahon. Thus not only were major works of art lost but the balance and character of numerous country house collections was upset.

[85]

15. The Hall at Highcliffe, Hampshire, as it was in 1942. Since then the place has had a desperate history with the loss of all its contents and much of its interior, but the Romantic shell is now being restored.

Today there are few signs of benefit in the contents of country houses. One of the few is Basildon Park, Berkshire, which was restored and furnished by Lord and Lady Iliffe in the 1950s and early '60s (Fig. 16). Here there are purchases made at the Ashburnham Place sale, and

16. The Octagon Drawing Room at Basildon Park, Berkshire. The saving, restoration and refurnishing of the house by the late Lord Iliffe and Renee, Lady Iliffe, who gave it to the National Trust, is one of the most revealing demonstrations of post-war taste and enthusiasms.

from Blenheim; Fawley Court, Oxfordshire; Ham House; Brockenhurst Park, Hampshire; and Eaton Hall, Cheshire. Without those opportunities it would have been impossible to recreate a complete interior at Basildon. As Lady Iliffe wrote later in the guidebook, furnishing the house 'was a continuous process, and even the Mentmore sale yielded one or two items, but due to present prices we came back with coal scuttles instead of marble-topped console tables.'

All this meant that in the late 1960s and early 1970s there was a real buzz in the air relating to houses, contents and decoration in the admittedly narrow circle of the people involved with the projects going on. But no one could have guessed how significant it was to be when *The*

Destruction of the Country House exhibition was being planned or what a thrust it was to give to the broader preservation campaign that developed in the face of the threats from Capital Transfer Tax and Wealth Tax.

PART II

4

◆

Country Houses and the Concept of the Heritage 1974–1998

(a) *The Country Houses of Britain, European Architectural Heritage Year and the Fight against Capital Transfer Tax and Wealth Tax 1974–78*

In the late 1960s and early 1970s country house enthusiasts and historic town enthusiasts tended to be found in different packs, and consequently there is a temptation to separate the two subjects and overlook the cross-influences at work. At that time the historic town enthusiasts were becoming more active and more influential, and the whole concept of European Architectural Heritage Year was primarily urban. My study and *The Destruction of the Country House* exhibition at the Victoria and Albert Museum were intended to counter that, and it was coincidence that one was published and the other opened within a few months of the first debate in the House of Lords on the new Labour Government's proposals for Capital Transfer Tax and Wealth Tax outlined in Green and White Papers.

The exhibition, in particular, created a double sense of shock, shock at what had been destroyed and shock at what was seen to be threatened; and what is so extraordinary is that it sparked off so many publications, particularly by Save, and a spate of county surveys of country houses extant and demolished such as *The Derbyshire Country House* by Maxwell Craven and Michael Stanley, first produced in 1984 and then republished in 1991, and *Lost Houses of Newcastle and Northumberland* by Thomas Faulkener and Phoebe Lowery, which appeared as recently as 1996. Without that sense of shock, which provided a focus, it would have been much more difficult, and arguably impossible, to have developed the campaign against the tax proposals. At the same time it got

EAHY off to a rousing start and, in Robert Hewison's view, marked the birth of 'the heritage industry'.

What no one, either in the Government or outside, anticipated was the explosive point that the tax proposals gave to the exhibition or the force of the campaign that was built on the basis of it and of my report. Nor could it have been foreseen how owners, acting on their own and through the Historic Houses Association (then a very small body with only 120 members), the national amenity societies – the Society for the Protection of Ancient Buildings, the Georgian Group, the Victorian Society and the Ancient Monuments Society (whose secretary was Mrs Jennifer Jenkins) – special groups like Heritage in Danger established in 1974, the National Trust and the National Trust for Scotland, and many museums together with many Members of Parliament, who were to form the All-Party Committee on the Heritage, could come together to make a strong case against the proposals. Not only were a wide range of people with specialist knowledge brought together for the first time, but they worked with people who understood or learned about the media; and threads of dedicated amateurism that were characteristic of the amenity movement became fused with tougher, political thinking. Country houses became part of the political scene once more, albeit in a new guise. For the first time, country houses and historic houses were seen as an essential part of a broader picture that also included the world of museums, galleries and libraries.

However, having been very close to what was going on at the time, it is difficult to stand back and see the campaign in a broader context, and here Robert Hewison's and Raphael Samuel's observations of the bigger picture are so useful. The latter comments on the change in style from the 1950s and '60s to the 1970s and '80s, with the spread of what he calls 'conservationism', the change from trying to make the old look new to 'instant oldness', the growing enthusiasm for the recovery of the past and 'the desperate desire to hang on to disappearing worlds', the discovery of family history, as opposed to old-style genealogy, and with it people looking down for their roots rather than up, so keen to find out about life below stairs, and the link between 'conservationism' and home ownership.

At the same time it should be recognised that some senior members of the Government also responded positively to the threat that they had created. In the autumn of 1974 Tony Crosland, the Secretary of State for the Environment, asked Lady Birk, a Minister in the House of

Lords, to look into the problem of historic houses; and, as a result of undertakings given at the Committee Stage of the Finance Bill the Chancellor, who had earlier said he would squeeze the rich until the pips squeaked, was also considering the position of historic houses in relation to Capital Transfer Tax, as he explained in a letter to Lord Montagu on 17 February 1975. Three months later the Chancellor was introduced to Commander Saunders Watson by local authority officials at a Labour Day rally in Corby: this gave the latter not only the opportunity to explain how the proposed legislation would effect Rockingham, but also the opening to send him a written paper. Commander Saunders Watson then wrote to George Howard on 12 May: 'I gained the clear impression that he was very sympathetic to the problem of maintaining historic houses and that if we could produce a workable scheme for a supporting fund which would not be open to abuse, then he would be very happy to look at it.'

It was essential to recognise and accept the weight given to public benefit and access in the papers relating to the legislation. It was out of that and the need for a phrase or term to cover the whole field that the concept of 'the national heritage' developed. Suddenly the word 'heritage' started to be used: European Architectural Heritage Year was announced for 1975; 'National Heritage' was used for a Museums Action Group in 1971, and then it was taken up in *Heritage in Danger* in 1974, *Save Britain's Heritage* in 1975, and the All-Party Committee for the Heritage started by Patrick Cormack in 1975 and his book *Heritage in Danger* in 1976. Indeed Robert Hewison has written: 'It is impossible not to conclude that the campaign against the wealth tax was a powerful stimulus to the spread of the word "heritage".'

All this enabled a massive campaign to be built up, culminating in a petition with over a million signatures being presented to Parliament.

Despite the degree of public support, the years from 1974 to 1980 were traumatic ones for country houses in Britain: it seemed that all the effort put into them since the Second World War would be wiped out within one generation as a result of the new taxation if it went through unamended; and that the only houses to survive would be those in various forms of public ownership or trusts. Indeed it was a harsh time for the country as a whole, with the end of the property boom, sharp inflation, energy shortages and, on top of that, a new Labour Government pledged to new capital taxation on a scale not seen since the time of Dr Hugh Dalton and intended to take advantage of the increases in wealth over the previous 20 years. Moreover the effects of Capital Gains Tax introduced in 1965 had already been greatly increased by inflation. It was a particularly grim period for owners, and at least one thought that there might be revolution and the tumbrels would be out. In a letter dated 15 October 1974, the Duchess of Devonshire wrote to me: 'Thank you very much indeed for sending me your brilliant and melancholy document. It is a food for thought, of a bitter kind. I am afraid the game is up, & that's all there is to it. Nothing can supplant the use for which the houses were built, however imaginative. We have been incredibly lucky to catch the tag end of it all, and struggle as we may there is no going back. Oh well. Sorry to be so depressing but we all know it's true.'

The Government's aim was to hit hard all those who appeared to have done well, and that included landowners, but Socialist thinking could make a distinction between people and places. Thus, while it disliked the idea of owners as much as it had done in the late 1940s, it soon realised the significance and vulnerability of the historic places that were caught up in their social and economic programme. So fairly soon it became an all-party matter to hammer out a solution to the complex problems of what had come to be called 'the national heritage'.

With the passing of time the tenseness of those years has faded from many memories or is unknown to a younger generation, so it is worth quoting from an article I wrote on 'Historic Houses and the Budget' in *Country Life* on 26 June 1980: 'As far as owners have been concerned, the last six years have been the tensest since the immediate post-war period, because all could see that nothing could survive the combination of existing kinds and levels of taxation, on income and capital, and inflation, and it was a matter of waiting to see whether public and political opinion caught up with reality before it was too late.' Or as William Proby wrote in *Apollo* in December 1989: 'CTT was, in effect, merely the culmination of a long period of inflation, high income tax and, most importantly, a political climate in which country house owners felt increasingly exposed and vulnerable.' He went on: 'It is difficult to overestimate the importance of those (heritage) reliefs – not that the fiscal measures themselves were all that radical, but they represented an acceptance by government (and a Labour government at that) that country houses had an important part to play in the cultural life of the nation, and that their survival should be actively encouraged. It therefore changed fundamentally the political climate towards country houses.' Ten years on that change does not seem quite as fundamental, because the cause of the Heritage has lost political ground and the Heritage Lottery Fund has serious problems.

In the end, after a great battle and intense lobbying of Parliament, improvements of lasting benefit were made to legislation. So it is worth considering how concepts of preserving individual buildings had been developing into a broader approach of considering buildings in groups, particularly in towns, with thinking about streets and squares expanding into consideration of areas, and preservation becoming conservation. Quite quickly the idea of the conservation area, which was developed for towns in the late 1960s, was extended to cover rural areas, particularly villages.

This had involved fundamental changes in approach and all the schemes of repair were based on a sense of partnership, between individual owners on the one hand and local and central government providing financial help on the other; and on many occasions that sense went beyond the actual money involved to a broader sense of commitment to a project and a place. Owners of country houses naturally do not like to see themselves as partners of anyone and rightly defend their independence, but, in fact, the survival of their houses, like other historic buildings and sites, depends on increasingly sophisticated systems of private and public partnerships.

Until then preservation of post-medieval buildings had been largely guided by aesthetic approaches and an admiration for Georgian architecture and the classical tradition down to the mid-19th century (the Royal Commission on Historical Monuments had rather timidly extended its brief from 1700 to 1715 in 1921, but it was only in 1962 that it advanced its terminal date to 1855). Now, however, thinking was beginning to move beyond the Rule of Taste into an enthusiasm for 19th century architecture, including industrial and commercial buildings, and to consider buildings in more historical and less aesthetic and visual ways. At the same time the rejection of the Rule of Taste made it more difficult to make judgements on merit, and the growing disenchantment with modern architecture led to a marked loss of confidence in what was new. As a result there was an increasing desire to hang on to what was familiar, even if it was recognised as not being of good quality and also expensive to retain. That was very largely a matter of townscape, but it was also to have a bearing on the way country houses were preserved, as can be seen in the rise of the 'leave it alone' school at Calke Abbey in the 1980s and Brodsworth and Chastleton in the 1990s.

The new approach was also related to the increasing awareness of social history that was to have a considerable influence on preservation thinking and enterprises. That too had a country house aspect, as can be seen in the Trust's restoration of Erddig, in North Wales, and its rethinking of the showing of Lanhydrock, in Cornwall, both carried out in the mid-1970s. And it had popular manifestations such as the television series *Upstairs Downstairs*. The world behind the green baize door had become so remote that the disagreeable aspects of it had been forgotten, and people were becoming curious to explore it.

(b) *The Expanding Role of the Historic Houses Association*

Private owners have survived because they are fiercely individualistic, and on the whole they are not sympathetic to what is now thought of as corporate thinking: they are naturally suspicious of bodies, whether they are local authorities, English Heritage or the National Trust, and they are not natural trade unionists. So although the idea of an association of owners went back to a scheme proposed by Sir Harold Wernher and Lord Montagu in 1952, it proved impossible to form one. However, a number of owners joined the British Tourist Association, as it then was, and then in 1966 the British Tourist Authority established its Historic Houses Committee, which concentrated on tourism and the opening of houses. Five years later Sir Alexander Glen, the chairman of the BTA, suggested that a Standing Committee for Historic Houses with subscribing members should be set up, in the hope that it would soon attract enough support to become an independent organisation.

That happened at the end of 1973 when the Standing Committee agreed to become the Historic Houses Association, but it still depended on the BTA for staff and office space. Lord Montagu of Beaulieu became its first chairman and the late George Howard, later Lord Howard of Henderskelfe, its vice-chairman. The combination was a formidable one of two very different characters, Lord Montagu being particularly interested in all aspects of opening and promotion and George Howard in wider political issues and taxation.

However, the nature of the threats of Capital Transfer Tax and Wealth Tax that emerged within four months of its establishment, in the spring of 1974, gave it a new significance and its work a new urgency.

How the Association organised itself and led the political campaign is a remarkable story that deserves to be set down in full before too long, revolving as it did round the Tax Committee of the HHA working closely with the Tax Group of the Joint Committee of the Amenity Societies, with Commander Michael Saunders Watson for the HHA and Jeremy Benson of the Tax Group as the leading figures. For both of them it was a completely new field. Michael Saunders Watson had come out of the navy in 1971 to take over Rockingham Castle, in Leicestershire, from his uncle, and he became involved with the HHA in the course of 1975, as was explained in the last chapter. Jeremy Benson is an architect specialising in the repair of historic buildings and at that time was deeply involved with the work of the SPAB and Georgian Group. However, since neither of them had any real knowledge of taxation or the ways of Parliament and all that was involved with lobbying, they had to teach themselves both the subject and the methods as well as find allies on both sides in Parliament to help them. At the same time the HHA organised a petition that attracted 1.25 million signatures that it presented to Parliament in 1975.

The HHA and the Joint Committee and many other bodies gave evidence to the Select Committee on Wealth Tax sitting in 1974 and to the Sub-Committee sitting in the summer of 1975, but the serious work on drafting amendments relating to the extension of exemption beyond single works of art to buildings and land and the protection of supporting funds and lobbying only really got under way when the Standing Committee on the Finance Bill for 1975 was considering the legislation. Both ideas had been around for many years, as has been shown, but this was the first time that they attracted serious political attention; not surprisingly it took a number of years and remarkable tenacity to persuade Members of Parliament of all parties, the Treasury and the Inland Revenue to refine the arrangements for exemption and maintenance funds – and that work is not finished. Here the All-Party Committee on the Heritage was particularly valuable with Robin Cooke, Patrick Cormack, Andrew Faulds and David Watkins among the allies.

Throughout the rest of the 1970s and until the replacement of

Capital Transfer Tax by Inheritance Tax in 1986, the HHA, and particularly its Tax Committee, which became increasingly professional through the support of outside experts, was principally concerned with these issues and lobbied hard and with considerable success.

Taxation continues to be a central matter for the Association, but after the Conservatives came to power in 1979 and the National Heritage Memorial Fund was set up in 1980, the heritage began to lose some of its mileage as a political cause. Moreover, as result of the general tax changes relating to income and capital, significant improvements made to the arrangements for maintenance funds in 1980 and 1982, which finally made them acceptable to the HHA, and because it became possible to make potentially exempt transfers in 1986, the Government felt that there were higher priorities for its attention and legislative time and it reverted to its traditional indifference to heritage matters.

Even in the mid-1970s taxation could not be the Association's sole concern, because the Government was keen to increase access to houses and gardens that lay at the centre of any new deal. However access and education went hand in hand, and it was fortunate that thinking about heritage education, as it soon came to be called, was just starting to develop. Lord Montagu had set up an education programme at Beaulieu in 1970 and appointed an education officer for the first time in 1972; and at Sudbury, in Derbyshire, which belongs to the National Trust, John Hodgson started another programme in 1972 and was trying to stir the Trust into taking a positive view of its responsibilities for education and appreciate its benefits. These and other initiatives led the HHA to press for 1977 to be designated Heritage Education Year, which led to various developments that will be discussed later.

By 1979 the HHA was able to stand on its own feet, moving out from under the BTA's wing, to its first office in Ebury Street, with Terry Empson becoming its first Director in 1981. Having been in the Foreign Office, he was interested in how the business of government worked in Whitehall and Westminster and he led the Association to develop in new ways. In particular it has concentrated on helping owners to become more professional, and there is an increasing group of them who look regularly to it for guidance and support, while many regard it as a valuable ally when they feel isolated. Also it tries to foster contacts with the next generation of owners who not only sometimes feel uncertain about what lies ahead, but find it difficult to talk to the older generation about their mutual concerns.

It now has 1500 owner members representing 280 houses and gardens open regularly to the public and 81 by appointment only, with another group providing access of different forms to about 150 houses. There are about 180 corporate members, who are involved professionally with houses, gardens and estates through their work as accountants, lawyers and land agents, and 67 who have houses in different forms of adaptive use. Probably only between 10 and 20 houses regularly open are not members, but there are many owners of houses not open who remain outside it. In addition the Association has 12,000 Friends, who pay a subscription and provide moral and political support. They have free entry to members' houses.

Making the case to Government involves watching not only legislation and directives from the British Government but also, increasingly, what is going on in and coming out of Brussels, although that is difficult without a professional (and unaffordable) monitor in Brussels. There are a bewildering range of directives apparently nothing to do with the heritage that have a bearing on the running of historic houses, such as regulations on part-time employment that could adversely affect the way opening arrangements are staffed, on catering and on VAT, but it is hard to know how to lobby against them because of the way the European Parliament and Civil Service are run.

The negotiations on VAT, on which a great deal of work has been done since 1986, have been particularly complicated because they have to be carried on in London and Brussels. Although it is clear that there is no hope of zero-rating, in 1991 the Council of Economic and Finance Ministers came to an informal agreement about standard and minimum rates of VAT, with the latter set at 5%. That was the first time that it was accepted that Brussels had any power to decide on VAT rates, but it said nothing about VAT rates in relation to historic buildings nor did it alter the arrangements in the United Kingdom. Since then the HHA has lobbied in Brussels for a lower rate of VAT for repairs; Customs and Excise has told Treasury Ministers that the British Government could reduce the rate if it wished to do so, and Chris Smith, the Secretary of State, has supported the idea. Even if the HHA has not met with success so far, the case is important because it shows how lobbying has to be done on two fronts.

Its work on repair grants since 1994 has been particularly successful, as will be shown later. From 1984 to 1992 English Heritage did not publish lists of the grants it had offered, and it was only when the figures for those years were issued in 1994 that it became apparent what a marked drop there had been in the offers to houses of all kinds including those in private ownership. Since then the HHA has worked hard and with success to make its case to English Heritage and also set out to improve relations between English Heritage and private owners in connection not only with grants but with listed building consent. It now looks as if there will be more money for grants for individual buildings over the next few years, but the situation will require careful monitoring.

That work has overlapped with making a case for support from the Heritage Lottery Fund. Partly as a result of its evidence to the Select Committee on the Lottery and also that given by English Heritage, it has won political support for private owners being made eligible to receive funds from the Heritage Lottery Fund. That is an important step forward. So has been the co-operation between the HLF and English Heritage, which should also help buildings in private ownership. But whether the change will produce substantial direct help for the individual country houses from the HLF seems unlikely, because of the increasing pressure on the HLF as a result of the major cut-back in its allocation and its priorities as perceived by public opinion. Also there is the view of some experienced in the repair of historic buildings who believe that it is English Heritage's job to fund and supervise long and complicated repair programmes and that the HLF, even supported as it is now by English Heritage staff, is not really the body to handle them.

Exemption of works of art has become another major field of concern with the abolition in the Finance Act 1998 of access by appointment, as is explained more fully on p. 138. For some time before that the HHA had been worried, because there had been difficulties over the accessibility of the list kept at the Victoria and Albert Museum, although the Inland Revenue now provides the information on disc and also on the Internet, where there are catalogues of items arranged topographically and by county.

As far as owner members are concerned the HHA helps in a variety of ways on aspects of opening, tourism and related subjects, the use of houses for functions and filming, which is a more important subject than might be imagined given the demand to use houses and their settings for feature films, television and advertising, and owners' needs for properly drawn contracts. Capital taxation naturally remains a major subject as can be seen from Terry Empson's *A Guide to the Operation of*

Maintenance Funds for Heritage Properties (1991). Also it tries to help over problems of hand-over from one generation to another and give advice to owners making plans for the future.

In 1992, thanks to a bequest and a number of gifts, the Association established a Heritage Conservation Trust to help owners with the costs of conservation of pictures and objects and provide advice on priorities for work. Its first grant went to the large Van Dyck of *John Count of Nassau* at Firle, in Sussex, and so far it has assisted with the conservation of 50 pictures in 12 houses.

In the sphere of gardens it has been keeping a watchful eye on development of the Register, arguing that it should remain firm to the original intention that it should not become a statutory equivalent of the system of listing buildings. Twice it has tried to establish schemes for the training of gardeners who want to work in private gardens, but it has been unable to find continuing sponsorship and so they have not continued.

One area where it has been particularly successful is in getting through to those whose own businesses are tied up with houses, gardens and estates, whether they be professional advisers (lawyers, surveyors, insurers and those concerned with property management), those concerned with the fabric of houses (architects, suppliers of specialist materials from lead and plaster to paint and horsehair) or those concerned with tourism and promotion (publishers of guide-books). That can be seen at the exhibition held as part of the Annual General Meeting. The 1997 gathering of over 70 stalls was evidence of the economic importance of houses to a wide range of business.

(c) *Conditional Exemption of Outstanding Buildings and Land from Capital Transfer Tax*

The idea of exemption for buildings and land can be traced back to thinking among Christopher Hussey and his friends in the late 1920s and early 1930s, and at least the principle was accepted in 1931 when gifts or bequests of buildings and land to the National Trust that were declared inalienable were exempted from death duties. The extension of that idea to historic houses in private ownership was recommended in the Gowers Report. However no Government would consider it until the Labour Government introduced it as a deferral of tax rather than absolute exemption as a palliative to Capital Transfer Tax on death in 1975. It covers land of outstanding historic, scenic or scientific interest, outstanding historic buildings and land to protect them, and historically associated objects as well as works of art, which had been exemptable since 1896. Thus it covers not only land in relation to outstanding buildings, but it can also include a Grade II house that is part of an outstanding landscape. In the Finance Act 1976 conditional exemptions were extended to lifetime transfers as well as those on death and maintenance funds were introduced. In return there have to be undertakings to maintain, repair and preserve the property and provide public access.

Owners were understandably suspicious of the conditions and some remain so, seeing the concept essentially in negative terms, because of the penalties incurred when the undertakings are broken and exemption is forefeited. In the first years disappointingly few applications for exemption were made. By March 1983, only 123 claims had been received by the Treasury and only 28 had been agreed. It is difficult to know how the system is working, because as part of the protection of the confidential nature of all individual tax details the Inland Revenue publishes no lists of places. However in answer to a Parliamentary question to the Chancellor of the Exchequer published in Hansard on February 23, 1998 there were 326 cases, 273 in England, 19 in Wales and 34 in Scotland. And in 1996–97 the estimated cost to the Exchequer was £5 million for land and buildings.

The replacement of Capital Transfer Tax by Inheritance Tax in 1986 and the possibility of making Potentially Exempt Transfers has meant that the number of applications for conditional exemption has dropped in recent years, but they do occur occasionally when an outstanding house and park have not been made over. Their rarity can be guessed by the small number of houses now opening for the first time.

If it was a new direction for owners and their advisers, it was a new field for the Government and its advisers, including the Historic Buildings Council and the Countryside Commission, who had to develop broad principles about what should be accepted, and what conditions of access should be attached, into workable practices. And it is probably fair to say that the HBC saw it largely in defensive terms, as being a way of protecting places, rather than in terms of the positive benefits that could follow from it.

One early problem to arise, for instance, was over outstanding villages in single ownership: could and should they be exemptable? This issue the HBC brought up in its report for 1978–79: 'There seems to us to be a strong case for exempting outstanding villages still substantially in single ownership since single management is far the most effective means of preventing minor but damaging alterations or unsuitable development, and also of providing a high standard of maintenance. Planning control and listed buildings legislation have not proved fully effective in either respect.' So it was a logical extension to the concept of the conservation area. A few years later it reported that estate villages could be expected to qualify for exemption.

Here it is important to realise that the concept posed a totally new kind of challenge to the Historic Buildings Council and the Countryside Commission – and here I write of the Historic Buildings Council for England, because that is the one of which I have personal memories in the years 1971 to 1985 – whose way of approaching buildings and areas had been expanding steadily since it was set up in 1953. With the expansion of conservation work in towns the Council had been strengthened in 1971–73 by the appointment of four people with experience of conservation in historic towns: Donald Insall, A.A. Wood, Elizabeth Chesterton and Edward Hollamby.

Thus when the HBC had to consider the first applications for exemption, it was able to combine its well-established knowledge of historic houses and architectural history with its new understanding of planning. Here the experience of Elizabeth Chesterton was particularly valuable, because she had worked not only on historic towns, producing the early report on King's Lynn in 1964, but on estates, for the National Trust, for Lord Montagu at Beaulieu, and for Dartington Hall in 1965. Those commissions had given her special understanding of how a well-run estate could be a positive agent for conservation, with its traditional aims and mechanisms anticipating what was coming to be called conservation thinking. The positive aspects were emphasised by the contrast with the essentially negative aspect of listed building control and the great difficulties local authorities had in managing historic towns and villages. Planning experience also showed how vital it was to give the spaces in which buildings stand adequate protection. Thus an idea that had been conceived mainly in historical and defensive terms was synthesised with planning concepts, so becoming both outward- as well as inward-looking. At the same time the HBC was feeling its way forward application by application and perhaps not knowing quite where it was going to end up in its recommendations. Unfortunately the HBC reports provide no detail on the early cases, not even listing them by name, but one day it will make an interesting study to compare what was applied for, what was recommended and what was finally agreed.

Looking at some of the applications which have gone through in the 20 years since 1976, and which are discussed here and in the last chapter, what is striking is how the concepts of exemption and maintenance funds have strengthened awareness of the value of entities in historical as well as planning terms and in particular the positive value of estates. The case for the economic relationship of the estate to the house had become familiar by 1974–75, if not necessarily accepted politically, but the broader significance has been greatly strengthened by the development of garden and landscape history since the late 1960s. Moreover the concept becomes politically easier when smaller estates of up to 4000 acres are seen as able to support themselves but no longer to provide a way of life for their owners in the way that used to be expected, perhaps over-optimistically, by their owners and, misguidedly, by non-owners.

Thus what owners have had to do for mainly tax reasons has many wider conservation benefits. Here it is interesting, and surprising, to see how exemption has worked out on two large estates, Sledmere, in Yorkshire, and Holkham, in Norfolk. It is just coincidence that two great estates crucial to the history of English agriculture in the late 18th

17. Sledmere, Yorkshire. A photograph taken in 1949 that shows how Sir Christopher Sykes's late 18th century house provides the key to his creation of the wide agricultural landscape in the Yorkshire wolds.

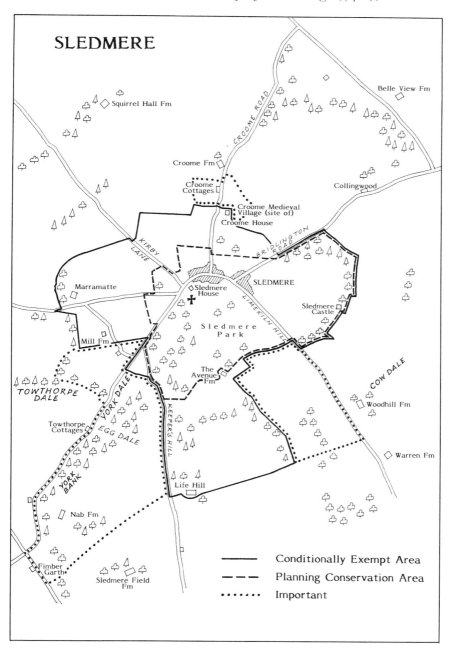

18. The area of the Sledmere estate conditionally exempt from CTT in 1983. This shows how the principal views to Sledmere Castle and Life Hill are protected, but how the broader agricultural history of the estate was not taken into account at that time. The map also shows the smaller Conservation Area.

and early 19th centuries came up for exemption at about the same time, and they show the way that thinking about historic landscape has been developing in the last 20 years. In the case of Sledmere Sir Richard Sykes died in 1978, while in that of Holkham the 5th Earl of Leicester died in 1976, but the exemptions were settled in the reverse order.

The house and park at Sledmere were exempted in 1983, the total area extending to about 1800 acres (Figs 17 and 18). The area covered the bowl in which the house sits, with the park and the two principal views from the house to Life Hill to the south-west and to the castle to the east, with some land to the north-west up to a farm called Maramatte. That is an area considerably broader than the conservation area of the village, park and house. However at that stage the definition of what was of historic interest was comparatively narrow, as can be seen from the first guidelines on Capital Taxation and the National Heritage issued by the Inland Revenue in 1977 and from the revised guidelines issued in 1986.

There the paragraph on Historic Land said: 'For a particular property to qualify as outstanding historic land it will need to have a very special historic significance in national or international terms. Land might be judged to be outstanding because of its association with a particularly important historic event. Earthworks and archaeological sites which have been scheduled as ancient monuments will clearly be eligible for consideration for exemption, but each case will need to be considered on its merits. In the case of an historic garden deemed to be outstanding in its own right the receipt or offer of a grant on the recommendation of the relevant Historic Buildings Council would be a prima facie indication that the standard for conditional exemption was met . . .' In addition the 'land adjoining an outstanding building and essential for the protection of the character and amenities of the buildings' could be included in a claim for exemption.

The three undertakings were simple: a. 'to maintain other land and preserve the character of such land having specific regard to its scenic and scientific interest'; b. 'for the maintenance, repair and preservation of the property qualifying under (the Act)'; and c. 'to secure reasonable access to the heritage property'.

Thus under that first definition of exemptable land it was not possible to get exemption on land that was part of a landscape of enclosure formed by Sir Christopher Sykes during his agricultural improvements. Nor was it even possible to make that case at the time, because little research work had been done on Sir Christopher: it will be only in 2001, the bicentenary of his death, that a full study of him by John Popham will appear. So according to the rules of exemption as then in force what was accepted was correct.

However, if the case had been completed after 1989, it would have been possible to advance arguments based on the significance of the broader landscape in terms of agricultural history and seek exemption on a bigger area, which would have been both more logical and economically viable.

This change came about at Holkham in 1989 (Figs 19 and 20), where it was argued by John Popham in his study of the development of the estate (eventually produced as Vol. 4 of the Holkham Management Plan) 'why the landscape outside the Park is of outstanding historic importance'. That argument, backed up by the evidence in R.A.C. Parker's *Coke of Norfolk: A Financial and Agricultural Study 1707–1842 (1975)*, was accepted, and as a result an enclosed landscape was accepted as eligible for exemption.

The present Lord Leicester inherited the property (but not the title, which went to his father who died in 1994) from his cousin, the 5th Earl, in 1976, and at that time about a third of the estate was made over to him. So it was fortunate that major parts of what had not been handed over were eligible for exemption under the new legislation. The park is the largest in Norfolk, and so 2927 acres were exempt as historic landscape. In addition 4496 acres of grazing, sand dunes and tidal saltings that extend for 14 miles along the coast were exempt for their natural history and scientific interest. Most of this land falls within the Norfolk Coast Area of Outstanding Natural Beauty and forms part of a National Nature Reserve managed in conjunction with English Nature. From a planning point of view the relationship of these two large areas in one ownership is of great value, because it is possible to balance the protection of the natural history element with the ability to cope with the increasing pressure of visitors to the Norfolk coast. About 500,000 people a year visit the beach, which is part of the Reserve.

About 90–100,000 people come into Holkham Park, where there is free access to the 500 acres of deer park and to all the roads, which include the spectacular drive from the south entrance, with its view southward to Kent's triumphal arch, and then to the obelisk and so down to the house, one of the finest approaches to any house in Britain. There are also two walks in the park, one to Samuel Wyatt's Great Barn

19. An aerial view of Holkham, Norfolk. This shows the relationship of the house
to the north-west part of the park, with the marshes, beach and sea beyond.

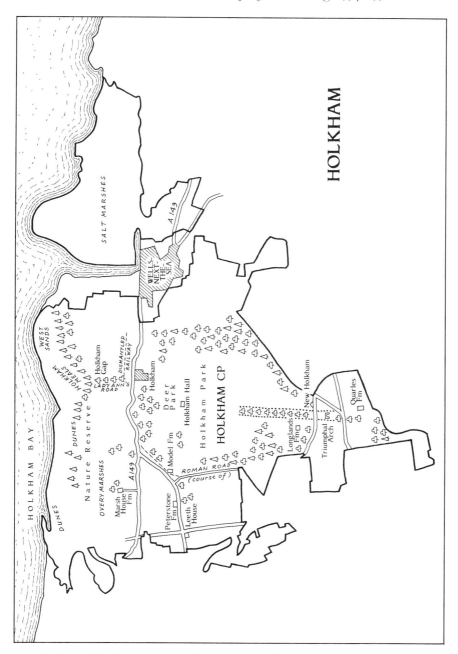

20. A plan of Holkham showing the total area of land conditionally exempt from CTT for historic and scientific reasons.

21. The Caravan Club's National Rally at Holkham in 1996 – a four day event that attracted 3,000 caravans.

built by Coke of Norfolk, and the other down to the lake, and inter-pretative material for these has been developed in co-operation with the County Council. Very large numbers of people come to special events in the park. Every other year, for instance, there is a Country Fair one summer weekend that attracts about 50,000 people; and in 1997 that raised £40,000 for local charities. In 1996 the Caravan Club held its four-day National Rally in the park with the house as a backdrop, and 3000 caravans and 10,000 people came (Fig. 21).

About 30,000 people visit the house, which is open for 90 days, rather than the 60 required as part of the exemption conditions. That earns about a third of its running costs.

When all this is considered, it shows how vital exemption has been in the past 20 years. If the 5th Earl had died even a year earlier, duty at 75% would have had to be paid on the full two-thirds of the estate, and that would have been a disaster both for the estate and for the collections. Indeed it is difficult to see how Holkham could have survived as an entity – and if the nation had had to step in as it did at Kedleston, the cost would have been more than £13.5 million.

As it is, part of the duty on the balance of the estate not exempt has been met from the sale of objects from the collection. These have included the Leonardo MS sold in 1980, and a Raphael cartoon which the British Museum undervalued and which was sold to the National Gallery in Washington. The group of 66 Old Master drawings collected by the 1st Earl were sold to clear debts resulting from improvements to the estate. In addition one in lieu *in situ* deal has been done over Guido Reni's *Joseph and Potiphar's Wife*, which hangs in the East Drawing Room (Fig. 22). That was a particularly important recognition of the relationship of the works of art at Holkham to their setting, and here it is worth bearing in mind a number of restorations carried out by Lord Leicester (see page 157).

One of the conditions of exemption is that there should be a management plan for the area; the Holkham Estate Management Plan is a massive document prepared by John Popham over four years between 1990 and 1994, and filling six volumes. The plan covers an area of almost 14,000 acres, because extra land has been included voluntarily by the estate. There are 53 listed buildings, of which four are Grade 1 and three Grade II*. The plan combines historical surveys of the park and estate that go back to the earliest estate map of 1590, 20 years before Chief Justice Coke acquired the place. That makes it possible to think out how to synthesise the different layers back to a plan of 1755.

One of the striking points about this document is its strong emphasis on historical research and use of archives as part of the basis for the future plan. That was not envisaged in the Countryside Commission's advice on the preparation of such plans issued in 1986, but it shows how thinking has been developing and is likely to be included in the next set of guidelines to be published next year.

The Holkham plan goes on to deal with assessments of work to be done in the years 1996–2000, with an outline for the next period from

22. The East Drawing Room at Holkham. On the east wall hangs Guido Reni's *Joseph and Potiphar's Wife* hung in the room in 1759 and the subject of an in-lieu in-situ deal in 1992–93 when it was accepted by the Fitzwilliam Museum, Cambridge for loan to Holkham.

2001 to 2005. Thus tax exemption is encouraging more positive management that takes greater note of historical and conservation considerations.

These management plans are increasingly detailed documents and on average cost £5000 to £10,000 to prepare because of the range and depth of the research required. But in many cases they will be eligible for grant aid from the Countryside Commission. On the other hand once the plans are done they help owners to save money in the long term, because by looking at everything they reveal the priorities for expenditure, in particular repairs to buildings and the importance of correct maintenance, thus saving on future costly repairs.

Naturally some owners hate the idea of having such a plan produced and then are fearful of what they see as interference in their affairs in its implementation in the years ahead. Against that others see exemption as having saved their estates and find that they can live with the system, making the best of it and developing a positive relationship with the bodies involved to get what benefits are possible.

However, as well as looking at the constructive aspects of conditional exemption and management plans for the place, the family and the community, it is only right to consider the potential downside for the family. Indeed some owners would prefer to sell rather than go down the exemption route. First the conditions are such that it may restrict development on the land covered, and no one knows what opportunities might occur in the future. Second, if an owner fails to carry out the undertakings and maintain the property, the Capital Taxes Office can say (but very rarely has said) that a place is no longer of outstanding importance, the exemption is withdrawn and the tax has to be paid. Then, if there has to be a sale, there will be CGT to pay as well as the relevant Estate Duty, Capital Transfer Tax or Inheritance Tax. The combined charge may be severe, particularly if there has been a considerable rise in value, because, first, CGT at 40% has to be paid on the difference between the original valuation and the current one, and the Inheritance Tax, again at 40%, has to be paid on the difference between the current value and the CGT paid. So the combined rate may approach 60%. On the other hand, if the sale takes place after a death, the base of the valuation goes up to the valuation on death and the calculation for CGT is based on the gain from that new value, so the total percentage paid may be lower. And always in the backs of owners' minds is the understandable fear of increasing control and interference from officials as well as demands for greater public access.

(d) *Maintenance Funds and Their Unexpected Conservation Value*

The phrase 'maintenance funds' appears to have been first used in legislation in connection with the National Trust in 1949 in relation to gifts of property and of land given as a source of upkeep, and it was borrowed for the Finance Act 1976 when they were introduced alongside conditional exemption of outstanding buildings and gardens to provide a form of financial protection and support for that property and protect it from the unavoidable effects of Capital Transfer Tax.

From the beginning the concept faced the problem of the rule against perpetuities which has been a feature of the English legal system since at least the 17th century and which limited trusts, as opposed to charities and companies, to the life of the settlor, the next life in being plus 21 years. Customarily the order of heirs was laid down in an entail, a legal shorthand for identifying whose unborn son or daughter should inherit. When the maintenance fund was first included in the Finance Act 1976, it was ruled that when a fund came to an end, the property had to pass to another heritage charity. Since the perpetuity rule limited the life of the maintenance fund, it was clearly a difficult concept to sell to almost all settlors.

So in the first two years none were set up. However in 1980 they were made revocable so that funds could be withdrawn, subject to the payment of tax, or could be resettled without payment of tax, thus allowing the perpetuity rule to be observed without the family losing control. Even so in the first seven years, up to March 1983, only 30 enquiries were received, and only five funds were actually set up. The HHA did not recommend them to its members until further changes had been made in 1982. By November 1986, 110 maintenance funds were set up, 82 in life. The number has also been limited by the access requirement: that has put off a number of people who open either not at all or only by appointment and would have to face 30 days and not be allowed to count groups on other days as part of their total number of days open. However from time to time new maintenance funds are set up in relation to conditional exemption schemes when there are assets that would otherwise be subject to an Inheritance Tax charge and the place is going to be open anyway.

Whereas a layman might presume that maintenance funds are a private equivalent of the endowment fund that the National Trust requires for its properties, they are much more limited in their application and heavily penalised in their tax treatment. The approved purposes are confined to maintenance and repair of the building and historically associated contents, but do not cover expenditure on works of art individually exempt; and they cannot be used to improve a property to make it more attractive to visitors, which in almost every case is an important element in maintaining success. So there are many expenses that a fund cannot cover. Income can (within limits) be accumulated and added to the capital.

Nor are they charitable funds. They are recoverable after six years, subject to penalties, and, while in being, pay income tax at the standard rate plus 10% and Capital Gains Tax. On the other hand payments into them avoided CTT and now avoid Inheritance Tax.

Part of the difficulty lies in their name if the old HBC and now English Heritage distinctions between 'maintenance' and 'repair' for purposes of grant aid are followed. Since 1953 that distinction has always been made, the theory being that an owner of an outstanding building must be able to carry out regular maintenance and running repairs unassisted, but may be helped with capital repairs to structure that occur once in a generation and sometimes once in a century.

The idea behind maintenance funds was that they should be able to cover both maintenance and repair costs, or at least an owner's proportion if grant aid was available. The difficulty of this concept is the great uncertainty about the scale of provision needed for capital repairs when they come, bearing in mind their unknown extent and constantly rising costs. While it is possible to estimate likely maintenance costs over the next five years, it is virtually impossible to plan and build up a comparable sinking fund for repairs. It is here that Capital Gains Tax treatment of the maintenance fund is so obviously discouraging.

What is needed is a fund that does not trigger off either Inheritance Tax or Capital Gains Tax on property that is transferred to it for sale to raise money for the approved purposes, but only incurs CGT penalties when withdrawals are made for other purposes or the place itself is sold. Clearly the tax treatment has to be such as to prevent abuses by those who might see it as a way of repairing a property with a view to resale after a few years and make a profit. But surely more note could be taken of their purposes, particularly in relation to repairs to listed buildings that have to be done and are unlikely to be supported by English Heritage? That body is unlikely to be able to cope with all the applications for help that it receives and go back to the 50–50 proportion of the 1950s and 1960s.

At present owners who look ahead and realise that major repairs are likely to become necessary later in their time or that of their successor probably take the view that the work will have to be met out of capital of some kind; and it is wiser to earmark that capital but not commit it to a fund for as long as possible.

When Inheritance Tax replaced CTT in 1987 and brought back the possibility of hand-over, that immediately reduced the relevance of the maintenance fund, and so only a trickle continue to be set up.

The original concept was that funds would usually be in the form of the supporting agricultural estate or investments and so produce a straightforward income that would be taxed like any other form of unearned income. The maintenance fund in land is the most interesting idea, because it can be added to the land conditionally exempt to create a large unit to protect both the house and estate. That, of course, reduces the family's own benefit but can make sense when the family has decided that the estate can only support itself and a house; and the family has to pay its own way.

With a squire's estate, where there is likely to be very little capital outside the property, it may be exceedingly difficult to create a maintenance fund except out of land. So it is interesting to learn of one case where development was permitted in a walled garden and the conversion of redundant farm buildings was agreed to because the sums realised from the sales of the site and the buildings were to go into a maintenance fund for an important house.

The HHA has worked with the Inland Revenue to encourage owners to set up token funds and, although the cost involved in setting one up is considerable, it seems worth doing in life or at least preparing for one so that a major endowment can be made on death under the terms of a will or by deed of variance of the will, provided it is done within two years of death. Not only can a settlor pay into a fund, but others can do so too. Thus not only is it known what land might be exemptable, but a fund can be built up gradually or be renewed. However an owner who does not open already is unlikely to want to do so, and, with the possibility of conditionally exempt transfers, an heir is unlikely to wish to do so either. On the other hand one attraction of a token fund is that investments 'pregnant' with chargeable gains passing to the maintenance fund under the owner's will can be sold free of CGT (except on the gains since the death).

The other point is that no one knows how long Inheritance Tax will exist in its present form, and it may prove useful to have a maintenance fund or at least a token fund in being.

Always a maintenance fund and conditional exemption have to be looked at together. The possibility of both means that an owner can hang on to property and can go on living in a house until death, knowing that it can be exempted and a maintenance fund can be created or increased at that time. Thus at one place it was possible to concentrate on handing over the outlying parts of an estate (and incurring the charges because the transfers were done under CTT) while the heart of the property, with the house, garden and park, was eligible for conditional exemption and a broad band round it could go into a maintenance fund.

The HHA has concentrated on the income tax and Capital Gains Tax treatment of revocable maintenance funds, but a few owners are interested in the idea of an irrevocable fund that is treated like a charity. Here there is the problem of perpetuities; at the end of the perpetuity period any capital left would have to go to the National Trust or another heritage charity. The HHA has suggested that in those cases the maintenance fund should enjoy additional tax privileges.

(e) *Mentmore and the Significance of the National Heritage Memorial Fund*

Even before *The Destruction of the Country House* exhibition opened at the Victoria and Albert Museum in 1974, the most important single country house crisis since that over Chatsworth in the early 1950s was starting to build up over Mentmore as a result of the death of the 6th Earl of Rosebery in May that year. At that time Mentmore and its collections were virtually unknown, because no account of it had appeared in any book or articles. Yet Professor Henry-Russell Hitchcock, the American architectural historian and author of the key *Early Victorian Architecture* (1954), regarded it as 'one of the finest of early Victorian houses and an exceptional example of the Jacobethan Revival at its best;' and it still contained the greater part of its very rich and varied collections of pictures, furniture and works of art that included many of a type not represented in other British public or private collections. The house and collection were the creation of Baron Mayer Amschal de Rothschild, the building being designed by Joseph Paxton and constructed in 1851–54.

Sometime in 1974 or 1975 Lord Rosebery began to have informal discussions with the Government about the future of Mentmore, and the imaginative idea developed of it becoming an out-station for the Victoria and Albert Museum, a mid-19th century successor to Ham, Osterley and Apsley House. In February 1976, Lord Rosebery made a formal offer of the house and collection for the bargain price of £2 million, which should easily have been found through the Land Fund. However the Government was quite understandably concerned about the running costs and hoped to find private money to underwrite the arrangement with the Victoria and Albert Museum. The Government's great error, however, was its failure to explore any other alternatives, so by early 1977, when it became clear that the private solution was not going to work, it was too late to seek any others, because time was running out for Lord Rosebery: he had to sell by May in order not to incur more duty on his father's estate. So on 19 January Sotheby's announced the sale of the contents.

At that point all hell broke loose. Spearheaded by Save's instantly produced pamphlet *Save Mentmore for the Nation* published in February, a public campaign was launched to acquire the house and collection, Save suggesting a two-year holding operation mounted by the Government to give it time to find a permanent solution. However, in March 1977 the Government finally rejected Lord Rosebery's offer.

In the end, while Lord Rosebery removed many important works of art to Dalmeny, the nation acquired a handful, two outstanding pieces of European furniture for £393,000, which together with a Gainsborough were bought before the sale, and seven less expensive lots withdrawn from the sale. However, the Treasury refused to accept in lieu of tax Drouais's outstanding portrait of Madame de Pompadour, and the National Gallery had to buy it out of its purchase grant. Sotheby's sale finally realised £6.25 million.

Mentmore and the Land Fund have become synonymous in many people's minds, and that is both unfair and unfortunate, because increasing use was made of the Land Fund in the 1970s and its functions were broadened. Among the country houses saved by the Land Fund in the 1970s were Cragside in Northumberland, Haddo House, Aberdeenshire, Brodie Castle in Nairn and, in the Fund's last year, Baddesley Clinton in Warwickshire. It also contributed to the acquisition of Tredegar House, Newport, Monmouthshire, by Newport Borough Council (Fig. 23), the repair of Chirk Castle as part of its transfer to the National Trust, and the acquisition of 18 Stafford Terrace, Kensington by Kensington and Chelsea Council. It also paid for the group of portraits at Arundel Castle, Sussex, that were accepted in lieu of tax and allotted to the National Portrait Gallery for permanent loan to Arundel.

23. Tredegar House, Newport, Monmouthshire. The Newport Borough Council acquired it with the aid of the Land Fund in 1974 and have developed it as a highly successful country house museum.

In the years 1946–71 the expenditure from the Land Fund amounted to £7,218,759. By 1980 that had increased to £19,347,210. Of course, there are regrets that more use was not made of the Fund and the increase in its last decade partly reflects rising prices; but surely now, when the National Heritage Memorial Fund, which succeeded it, is being run down by the Government, there is considerable point in remembering what the Land Fund achieved?

Within days of the Minister's rejection of Lord Rosebery's offer, on 9 March 1977, a debate was held on the heritage in the House of Lords, and that led to many questions being asked about the Treasury's handling of the Land Fund. The House of Commons' Environment Committee considered it in November–December 1977, and the acceptance of its report by the House in June 1978 led to Labour's White Paper on a National Heritage Fund to be instituted on 1 April 1980. However before that happened there was a change of Government, and as a result of the passing of the National Heritage Act, the National

Heritage Memorial Fund came into being on 1 April 1980.

In its first 18 years the National Heritage Memorial Fund achieved an amazing amount. Indeed it considerably widened concepts of what forms our heritage. But, as with so many constructive ideas in British life, it has been put under increasing pressure by Governments through the decline in the support it has been given since 1993 and the Government's reliance on the much bigger but much less embracing Heritage Lottery Fund.

The figures for the NHMF's funding are complicated, because of its initial grant-in-aid of £12.4 million in 1980–81, which was related to the balance in the old Land Fund, interest its funds have earned, and several extra allocations in 1984–85 (£25 million), 1986–87 (£10.5 million), and 1987–88 (£20 million). This reasonably generous support in the early years meant that it received £100 million in all by the end of 1989 and spent £103 million. But after 1987–88 that began to tail off. In 1987–88 its annual grant was set at £3 million. In 1990 that was raised again to £12 million for three years, but in 1993–94 it was cut to £7.8 million; in 1996–97 to £7.5 million; in 1997–98 to £5 million; and in 1998–99 to £2 million.

By the end of 1997 it had rescued 15 houses at a cost of £58.65 million. In addition the Heritage Lottery Fund had rescued Stoneleigh and Newhailes at a combined cost of £15.3 million. However, the combined figure of about £74 million excludes various supplementary grants, contributions from English Heritage and what has been raised privately. But given the reduction in its grant and cutbacks in the HLF it is difficult to see how future country house deals will be financed. Moreover, since the National Lottery was set up in 1995, Governments appear to have gone back on their promises not to regard the Heritage Lottery Fund as a substitute for their support for a wide variety of activities including the NHMF and have made severe cuts that put intense pressure on it.

So it is important to consider the contribution that the NHMF has made not only to houses, which is done here, but to gardens and parks and to works of art, which are considered in later sections. Also it is important to consider the effect the Fund has had on the National Trust. Until the NHMF was established, the Trust had great difficulty in taking the initiative over the acquisition of a major house, garden and park, because of the absence of endowments, and the impossibility of raising them by appeal. Places had come to the Trust either through the

24. Canons Ashby, Northamptonshire. The first house to pass to the National
Trust with the support of the National Heritage Memorial Fund in 1980–81.

initiative of donors or through in lieu or purchase systems depending
on the Land Fund. The creation of the NHMF immediately changed
that, because the Trust was able to go to it with a project and say 'Can
you help – quickly?' in a way that had not been possible before.

How that worked out can be seen with one of the Fund's first big
cases, Canons Ashby (Fig. 24), the Dryden family's ancient manor
house in Northamptonshire, which the Trust had been concerned
about since the late 1930s, but had been unable to secure, and whose
deteriorating condition and unsatisfactory tenancies had worried the
HBC for many years. At the same time the NHMF, with memories of
Mentmore vivid in its mind, was naturally particularly keen to show
what it could do to preserve country houses.

It was a happy coincidence that Gervase Jackson-Stops, the Trust's
Historic Buildings Adviser, had been keen on Canons Ashby ever since
he had discovered it when bicycling round the area during his school
holidays; and, since he continued to live nearby, he had kept an eye on
it. So when he read in the local press of the sale of the contents to be
held in July 1980, he asked Martin Drury, the National Trust's Historic

Buildings Secretary, whether the National Trust could find a way of buying them at the auction, if only as a holding operation, while the future of the house was investigated; and Simon Sainsbury, who had long been a staunch friend of the National Trust, agreed to make money available. Thus at the July sale the National Trust was able to acquire virtually everything it would want if it could get hold of the house.

By then John Dryden, one of the three brothers who owned the house, had arrived from Zimbabwe, and, when Gervase Jackson-Stops explained to him about the very recent establishment of the NHMF and how it was yet untried, he most generously agreed that the family would give the house to the National Trust if it could raise the money for endowment and repair. At the same time the Trust approached the NHMF, which very quickly responded by offering £1 million for endowment. Thus by January 1981 the Trust had constructed a package that involved the gift of the house from the Drydens, the £1 million endowment from the NHMF, the promise of repair grants from the HBC with an additional £500,000 for repairs from the NHMF, the contents given by Simon Sainsbury, contributions from the Landmark Trust to the repair of the tower and the conversion of a unit for its use as a holiday flat, and assistance from the Victoria and Albert Museum. At that point the Trust made a public appeal for the balance of £100,000 that was needed.

And by one of those strange coincidences, just after the sale of contents, the fine set of early 18th century needlework furniture that had been sold from the house in the 1920s or '30s reappeared on the art market; after a chase, the Trust was able to buy it back for the house. So it was back in position when the house was opened to the public at the conclusion of repairs in 1984.

Since then the Fund has played the central role in the saving of a series of houses. First, in 1981–82, came Charles Rennie Mackintosh's Hill House, Helensburgh, which the National Trust for Scotland was able to buy with the aid of a grant of £437,000 from the Fund. In the following year not only did the Fund contribute £2 million to the National Trust's acquisition of the grounds of Studley Royal, in Yorkshire, and begin to contribute to the restoration of the landscape at Painshill, in Surrey, but it was faced by threats to no fewer than five important houses. First came Fyvie Castle, in Aberdeenshire, which was put on the market in 1982; the National Trust for Scotland was able to acquire it and its contents thanks to the offer of £3.02 from the Fund. The other four, Weston Park, Shropshire, following the death of the 6th Earl of Bradford in 1981, Calke Abbey and Kedleston, both in Derbyshire and also following deaths, and Belton House, Lincolnshire, which was put on the market in 1983, could not be dealt with at once.

Early in the year 1983–84 the National Trust asked the Fund to help with the acquisition of Belton and Calke, but the Fund could not finance both straight away, and since Belton was the more urgent – and the more expensive – the Fund promised the Trust £8 million towards its acquisition, the largest single grant that it had offered at that point. The Chancellor of the Exchequer promised a supplementary grant to help over Calke, and in the year 1984–85 £4.5 million was found for that house and park.

In its report for that year the Fund said that it hoped to be able to announce solutions for Kedleston, Weston and also Nostell Priory the following year; and they were achieved in 1986–87 when the Government gave an extra £25 million to the Fund. It was able to offer £13.5 million for Kedleston, so that it could be accepted by the National Trust; £7,762,222 for a new charitable trust for Weston; and £6,102,360 for a new charitable trust for Nostell to hold the Chippendale furniture and look after the interior of the house, of which the National Trust only owned the structure.

In the case of Kedleston, a great house involving the conception by Brettingham and Paine and its revision and execution by Adam for Sir Nathaniel Curzon, 1st Lord Scarsdale, a patron of remarkable individuality, the idea that the Trust might one day be involved seems to have gone back to the time of Lord Curzon, who had succeeded his father, the 4th Lord Scarsdale, in 1916. Thus in the early 1970s there were discussions between the 2nd Viscount Scarsdale and the National Trust, and to that end the HBC supported repairs with three grants totalling over £28,500 in 1971–75. However since Lord Scarsdale was only tenant-for-life, he was not empowered to give or bequeath Kedleston to the Trust. In 1977 he was succeeded by his cousin, the present Lord Scarsdale, who was free of the entail and wished to assure the future of Kedleston.

First in 1980 Lord Scarsdale sold objects acquired by Lord Curzon, and the NHMF bought several in the hope that they might eventually go back to the house. Among them was an ivory-veneered sofa and two throne chairs with foot stools and a silver table garniture for £118,652.

Lord Scarsdale favoured the idea of Kedleston passing to the National Trust and, although English Heritage wanted to have the house and the NHMF tried to persuade him to establish a charitable trust, he was determined to carry out the idea that he had to some extent inherited and that was the basis of the deal.

The grants of £13.5 million, however, did not solve all the problems, because the Trust was expected to raise £2 million in addition to Lord Scarsdale's gift of the house. Also it has had to buy separately some contents from the family, including the Linnell sofas from the drawing room (see p. ooo), silver and pictures.

In 1986–87 the Fund gave the National Trust £254,200 towards its purchase of Sheringham in Norfolk, a fine Repton landscape with a good contemporary house. Although the house had not been altered since the library had been completed and furnished about 1840, that was the only room to preserve its contents, and while the Trust secured them, the economics of the deal and the lack of other contents argued for the leasing of the house to a tenant and the opening of the land-scape to visitors.

In 1989 the Fund provided £3.65 million so that English Heritage could acquire most of the contents of Brodsworth Hall, near Doncaster, which was given to it by Mrs Williams, who had inherited it in 1988. English Heritage undertook its repair at a cost of £4 million and did not seek an endowment – and so took on a considerable new liability just at the time when it was having to cut back on repair grants to individual buildings. The same year the Fund gave the National Trust £4.5 million which was an essential element in its ability to accept the grounds of Stowe, in Buckinghamshire (Fig. 35), which has proved to be one of the Trust's most ambitious projects as is explained in Chapter 6.

In 1991 Mrs Clutton Brock, the owner of Chastleton, in Oxfordshire, a house that had been of great concern to the HBC and English Heritage as well as the National Trust, decided that she must sell it rather than give it to the National Trust, as she had agreed. So because the Trust expects to receive houses as gifts and normally never buys them, the Fund, most exceptionally, bought the house, contents and park from her for £2 million and gave them together with a £2 million endowment to the Trust; and English Heritage offered £800,000 towards the cost of repairs.

In 1993–94 the Fund contributed to the National Trust's acquisition of more land at Gibside in Co. Durham (£309,000) and of the land-scape at Prior Park, Bath (£200,000).

Not only did the NHMF give the Trust a new kind of initiative, but also it encouraged its already rising standards of acceptability through making it consider merit and cost more closely than in the past. The expectations of visitors as well as the influence of new forms of history were already making the Trust more selective in what houses it took on, but inflation in all kinds of costs and values of property and objects has made any prospective acquisition a much more challenging proposition. Moreover the NHMF almost always requires a considerable element of gift from the family offering the property, and also expects the Trust to raise money. Thus when it came to the very difficult and long-drawn-out decision over Pitchford Hall, in Shropshire, the amount of public money for acquisition, endowment and repair seemed out of proportion to the merits of the place since the interior was not up to the quality of the romantic half-timbered house and the way it sits in its little valley with its tree house and church. (English Heritage wished to take it on, but could not get ministerial approval for their scheme.)

However, as well being encouraged by the NHMF both the National Trust and the National Trust for Scotland have been affected by the NHMF's wish to support individual trusts. Right from its inception the Fund wanted to find an alternative solution that involved smaller endowments, and it has now helped establish trusts for four houses. They are two places in Berwickshire, Thirlestane Castle (Fig. 56), to which it contributed £668,505 in 1984 and a further £250,000 in 1988–89, and Paxton House, to which it contributed £2,735,200 in 1988–89, Weston Park, Shropshire, to which it contributed £7,762,222, and Burton Constable in Yorkshire (Fig. 8), to which it contributed £5,417,284 in 1991–92. Also, having helped the Hopetoun House Trust with repairs, it acquired key contents in the state rooms from the family and endowed the Trust in 1995–96, offering a total of £4m.

The funding for the creation of a new charitable trust for Stoneleigh Abbey, in Warwickshire (Fig. 57), in 1995–96 and for Newhailes, near Edinburgh, to pass to the National Trust for Scotland in 1996–97 both came from the Heritage Lottery Fund, £7.3 million for the former and £8 million for the latter.

Here it is important to realise that neither of these last two operations could have been funded by the NHMF, because of the rundown in support it has been receiving from Government in recent years. And now with the reduction in the HLF, the huge pressures on it, the public perception of its role, and the likelihood of its swing away from country houses, it is vital that the strong feelings that led to the establishment of the NHMF are remembered and that the sense of commitment to them is honoured by all political parties. This is a kind of issue where the HHA has a role to play alongside the National Trusts, the museums and galleries, and the amenity movement – all the bodies who worked together so effectively in the 1970s.

(f) *The Gamble of Inheritance Tax*

When Inheritance Tax replaced Capital Transfer Tax in 1986, one owner said that it represented a new kind of gambling with the heritage. However, by bringing back the old rule whereby property made over seven years before a death was free of estate duty (but not Capital Gains Tax) and introducing a sliding scale of duty paid on transfers incomplete within that period, it gave many estates the vital chance to plan for the future that had been blocked by Capital Transfer Tax and so gave many owners a new confidence.

Making such transfers is a complicated business in itself and that is compounded by the need of the transferor to keep enough back to provide for himself and his wife and also by the personal problems that are discussed in Chapter 12. On the other hand it does give places a chance, particularly for those owners who do not like the idea of being tied into exemptions and maintenance funds, and want to give their heirs freedom of action. Also it encourages the older generation to hand over what has to be run as a business about the time they should be handing over anyway.

However, the situation for many families is already very complicated because they may be faced with property dealt with under three different sets of legislation on transfers and possibly with exemptions taken and maintenance funds set up because of CTT. And to be hit hard by Inheritance Tax may be the last straw. Moreover the effects of an unexpected death during the seven-year period of hand-over can be severe. It then becomes a failed PET, a Potentially Exempt Transfer, and under that it is possible to seek exemption on the property itself but not to set up a maintenance fund out of the other assets.

Furthermore any hand-over must not involve any reservation of benefit by the former owner or the gift will be disregarded on his death. The Revenue have recently challenged the use of procedures to avoid reservation of benefit, based on case law developed under estate duty, in a case called IRC v. Ingram. In the High Court the Revenue lost, but then won in the Court of Appeal; the case is now going to the House of Lords. The outcome could be important in a number of cases of transfers where a lease of a house is involved.

(g) *The Disappointment of the National Lottery*

When the Heritage Lottery Fund has contributed so much to British life and institutions in the past three years, infinitely more than was ever envisaged, it might seem perverse to see it as a disappointment to the preservation world – and also as a worrying distortion of the existing system. However both have happened, particularly as far as country houses in private ownership are concerned, and that looks like continuing. When the Lottery was still an idea, it was seen, not unnaturally, as an extension of the National Heritage Memorial Fund, and so the HHA discussed with the NHMF the possibility of the Lottery topping up maintenance funds to provide better endowment for houses. But, as soon as the HLF came into being, it was clear that that was not a realistic idea. Moreover the private sector was excluded from any help under the terms of the Act. It was partly as a result of the HHA's work that political sympathy for the private sector was aroused in the Select Committee on the Lottery and the House of Commons and so the National Heritage Act 1997 permitted the HLF to consider applications from private individuals. Thus it is an even greater disappointment that it looks as if the HLF will still not help houses in private ownership.

What has made this so galling is the scale of Lottery funding since 1995. In its first year it offered over £200 million to over 300 projects, and £450 million in 607 grants in the second, with a total of £892.7 million in 1558 grants by 28 February 1998.

However, at the same time this sudden influx of money has had a seriously distorting effect on the whole heritage scene through over-shadowing all the other official contributions to the financial pot covering the heritage and museums and galleries and, despite what was promised, giving the Government an excuse to cut back on them, even though they cover a wider spectrum than the HLF. Here the run-down in the support for the NHMF has been particularly disappointing after all the effort that went into getting it set up and all that it has achieved.

Moreover the HLF has been so big that it has been difficult for it to do things quietly, as happened with the National Heritage Memorial Fund; and ever since its first case, the contribution of £13.25 million to the acquisition of the Churchill Papers, which was expected to be a popular act, almost everything it has done has been subjected to intense questioning and on occasion hostile scrutiny in the media, which has made it nervous. There have been much greater problems to do with benefit than had occurred with the NHMF, perhaps partly because of the origin of the money in national gambling, and this concern appears to be leading the HLF to avoid the private sector, despite the go-ahead from Parliament.

Also the publicity has raised huge hopes, with the number of applications for grants having reached a total of 4630 by the end of February 1998: they total £3645 million, nearly four times the amount dispensed so far and 14 times the allocation in 1998, when it is being reduced from £450 million to about £250 million. That is going to mean support for fewer big schemes, with those in excess of £1 million becoming a rarity.

Thus major projects relating to the repair or endowment of privately owned houses are hardly likely to be seen as a first priority in the private sector by the HLF.

Endowments, in fact, have appeared a much more difficult field for the HLF than was originally envisaged. Among the few it has done are contributions of £1.43 million to Chetham's Library in Manchester, to the National Trust for Scotland for Newhailes and to the new charitable trust for Stoneleigh Abbey, in Warwickshire. So it seems unlikely that it will endow many new charitable trusts for country houses, particularly if a family is involved, and, anyway, projects like the NHMF's funding of Belton and Kedleston would be now almost beyond it. But would it be prepared to top up an endowment for a trust if part of the money could come from other sources?

If it is deeply disappointing to the HHA and many owners that the HLF is not going to do much for them, it has to be recognised that it is there to do what other bodies cannot do. So its contribution to repairs has to be looked at alongside the role and responsibilities of English Heritage for the whole range of historic buildings, secular and ecclesiastical as well as schemes of urban conservation. And given the great pressure on the English Heritage funds available for repair grants, which is examined in greater detail later, it was eminently sensible that the HLF in mid-1997 agreed to take over some of English Heritage's responsibilities that have no political implications, for churches and cathedrals and partnership schemes in urban areas: and it will enable English Heritage to do more for individually outstanding secular buildings, including houses. In 1995–96 the HLF made available £7 million to 90 places of worship and in 1996–97 over £18 million to 133 places as well as £4.5 million to cathedral projects. In addition in 1995–96 it made contributions to various English Heritage properties, including Charles Darwin's house at Downe in Kent, which had been newly taken on and received £1,783,000, and the cascade at Chiswick House.

As far as secular buildings are concerned, the HLF has so far only helped buildings belonging to public bodies, the two National Trusts and charitable trusts. Thus in 1995–96 it gave a grant of £276,993 to Towneley Hall, Burnley, a former country house that has long been a local authority museum. To the National Trust it gave grants for the acquisition of the park at Croome Court, in Worcestershire (nearly £5 million), for the Home Farm at Stowe (£792,300) and extra parkland at Osterley (£825,000) and to the National Trust for Scotland grants for the purchase of Mar Lodge estate, in the Grampians (over £10.25 million) and six houses on the south side of Charlotte Square in Edinburgh (£3.75 million). It gave the National Trust £55,600 for an improved access scheme at Cragside.

In 1996–97 among its cases involving buildings were Beckford's Tower at Bath, a survey of Samlesbury Hall, Lancashire, an education centre at Sulgrave Manor, Northamptonshire, and a small grant to Thirlestane Castle, a charitable trust founded by the NHMF. Its biggest country house project was to provide £8 million for Newhailes, near Edinburgh, so that the National Trust for Scotland could accept the gift, with the contents being acquired for £2.4 million and £6.4 million set aside for endowment.

Since then the HLF has given a grant of just over £3 million towards the restoration of Mogerhanger Park, in Bedfordshire, a house by Soane that suffered through many years of use as a hospital and might well have been lost if it had not been taken on by a religious community. After the hospital closed, the house and gardens were sold to a developer, who obtained permission to build 14 houses in the kitchen garden in order to fund the repair of the house which he intended to adapt for office use. After the scheme for conversion collapsed during the recession, the developer sold the house to the community but retained the site for the new buildings. Now thanks to the Heritage Lottery Fund a new partnership has been formed that will reassemble all the elements at Mogerhanger, and again the landscape elements has provided the key. The community has transferred the house to the Mogerhanger House Preservation Trust, while the local authority is using Land Fill Tax money to buy out the enabling development and the County Council is working on a plan for the restoration of the park, which it had divided into small holdings in 1919 when it acquired the place for use as a sanatorium.

The HLF's support for Stoneleigh, Newhailes and Mogerhanger has been crucial, but the reduction in its allocation means that there cannot be many more similar cases. It is worrying and disappointing that that still leaves unresolved the problems of certain buildings of the highest importance like the mausoleum at Castle Howard and the house at Stowe that English Heritage, and the HBC before it, have never been able to solve for a mixture of political and economic reasons, problems that have been around for 50 years and are getting more expensive every year. Stowe will not be an easy case for the HLF, which does not see itself as a fund for educational buildings, except in cases where the burden of repairs is exceptional, financial need is proved and there will be considerable public access; but the relationship of the house to the landscape and the National Trust's programme for the latter, which has been supported by the NHMF and English Heritage, have hopefully undone enough locks to encourage the HLF to make an exception for the house. However there will probably need to be a greater degree of public benefit than is provided by the present opening of the main rooms by the School.

The house at Stowe has received £430,176 in grant aid since 1988, most recently in 1993–94. However its problems remain daunting. After a good start on repairs, the introduction of new fire regulations for schools has meant that money the School intended to spend on repairs has had to go on new fire precautions. On the other hand the School has received a grant of $250,000 from the Getty Grant Programme for the repair of the colonnades on the north front. And it is on the basis of that and the repair of the Leoni arches that the School has applied to the HLF for a grant to tackle the whole of the north front that would turn it once more into a gleaming stone-white palace (see p. 137).

A somewhat similar case is the mausoleum at Castle Howard, which has the longest history of official foot shuffling. That started in 1955 when a grant was offered for works at Castle Howard, including the mausoleum, at the rate of 90%. At that time its main cornice was in good order and only needed minor repairs. These, however, were not carried out because of the greatly increased amount of repairs required on the house. Mr George Howard applied again for a grant for all the work at Castle Howard including the mausoleum in 1964, and by then the HBC's architects reported that £117,359 needed to be spent. After long negotiations a grant of £88,000 at 75% was offered for the mausoleum in August 1966, but again there were delays, and increased costs with a larger contribution expected from Mr Howard, and the project did not go ahead. After that, in 1988, at the Government's suggestion, there were negotiations with the National Trust so that it would hold the building and the Minister of Works would find the total costs of repair. But then the HBC tried to get Mr Howard to increase his contribution to the other works at Castle Howard because of his 'saving' in not contributing to the mausoleum: but, again, there were difficulties and delays, the Government changed, and nothing happened.

In July 1972, Mr Howard produced new proposals for the HBC, and by then the cost had arisen to £409,250 including fees. Talks continued between 1972 and 1978, and finally, in August 1978, a grant was offered. There were more negotiations in 1983 and although the grant offered was very large that left the estate with more to pay. However, the work of replacing the columns started in July 1980 and this first phase was completed by September 1983, at a cost of £1,200,000. Phase II was costed in October 1984 at £1,142,100, with the cornice and roof of the colonnade coming to £242,000 and work to the podium to £290,000. Since then there have been more talks with English Heritage and the NHMF, but no scheme has been produced; and no further work has been done. Clearly nothing will happen until the Government and English Heritage face up to it as they have had to do with the Albert Memorial.

Where the HHA hopes for help for country houses from the HLF is in the sphere of education. However, the problems are only partly to do with funding: they are as much those of the schools sending the groups, who have to incorporate visits with the curricula and pay for buses. Of course, education can contribute to the role of country houses in the community, but it is doubtful how many places would be able to boost their visitor figures without increasing their costs, and make a long-term contribution to their finances through developing an education programme.

During the course of 1998–99 it will become clear what the HLF can do for the private sector, and, if it appears that it can do little that gets to the heart of its problem, which seems likely, it will be necessary to stand back and think about the state of all historic buildings and how they are to be maintained and repaired. The problems of the private sector need to be related to those of the National Trust, and also to take on board recent Governments' failure to honour the idea of the National Heritage Memorial Fund, which seems to be unfamiliar even to some of those involved with it. Are we back in a situation comparable with that in the early 1970s which stimulated *The Destruction of the Country House?*

At present no body has a complete overview of country houses and historic houses and how all the different elements interrelate – houses and contents sold, houses saved through charitable and other trusts and houses becoming problems, how grant aid is going, not only for private owners, but the National Trust, local authorities and Buildings at Risk, what help the NHMF and the HLF are giving to buildings, how listed building consents are going and so on. Yet it is essential that such a record is made and kept going year by year: English Heritage's corporate plans and annual reports read like muddling puffs for a public company and say nothing about its concerns for buildings in other ownerships than its own. Would it be too much to hope that English Heritage would ask and help the HHA to produce it on an annual or biannual basis?

(h) *The Abolition of the One-Estate Election*

For the past 35 years the so-called One-Estate Election has been one of the most valuable tax arrangements for the protection of many country and historic houses, and consequently its withdrawl in the three years time outlined in the Finance Act 1998 is a blow of possibly unrealised severity against the Heritage. However it was never intended as a permanent arrangement, nor has it been a fair one as far as historic houses have been concerned.

In order to understand its significance it is necessary to go back to the Finance Act 1963 (as I explained in *The Country Houses of Britain Can They Survive?*) when Schedule A was abolished. According to Schedule A, every property was assessed for tax on its annual value, a figure close to its rateable value, but an occupier could set the costs of repairs on a five year average against that value and was only taxed on the balance.

In the case of small family houses, the costs of repairs were usually less than the annual value, and so the abolition of Schedule A meant the disappearance of a tax liability.

However with larger houses the change was for the worse, because their annual value was low and the costs of repairs were high, and so there was seldom any Schedule A to pay. Moreover the costs could be set against Schedule A demands on other property.

As a result of criticism of the measure, an option called the One-Estate Election was introduced. That meant that repair costs of the main house could be added to the repair costs of other tenanted buildings and then set against the whole income of the estate before tax. Almost all those who were able to opt for the Estate Election in 1963 did so and have hung on to it, but the option has not been open to any subsequent purchasers of properties where there was no Election in being or it had lapsed.

Only the Inland Revenue knows what places have such an Election and how important they are in architectural and historical terms, because they are not necessarily country or historic houses: some are unlisted farm houses. However it appears that many houses open to the public benefit from the One-Estate Election, and that, given the rarity of being able to pay for repairs out of the income from opening, it has been a vital element in the equation for those houses, because they have been treated alongside other tenanted buildings on an estate and set against estate income. However if all the costs of repairs and maintenance have to be set against the income from opening that may prejudice their Case-One assessment. Already there is a tendency to delay repairs because of costs and the decline in English Heritage support for historic buildings, and the removal of this way of setting off costs will be a further discouragement. The HHA alerted the Government to the possible consequences, and the Government has agreed to look at the possibility of an alternative relief but only for houses open to the public.

(i) *The Decline in Country House Literature*

An essential element in the success of the campaign against the tax proposals of 1974 was the bubbling up of enthusiasm for country houses and the development of fresh ideas about them in the late 1960s and early 1970s, and the number of books and articles being published on them and allied subjects.

A generation later there appear to be much less solid material appearing. The spread of colour illustration has opened the eyes of many people, particularly to interiors and gardens, but it has led to the dilution of written content. No architectural book has rivalled the success of Mark Girouard's *Life in the English Country House*, which appeared in 1978. Moreover costs of publishing illustrated books have led to a marked decline in the number of those of lasting value on English architectural subjects such as Giles Worsley's *Classical Architecture in Britain* (1996) published by the Yale University Press, now the leading publisher in the field. Those that do appear tend to be in fairly small editions and have a short shelf life, while articles become increasingly specialised.

It is particularly regrettable that no one has found a way of replacing the *Country Life* series of books on country houses that Christopher Hussey began to revise in the 1950s. His Georgian volumes have been reissued, but both text and plates are inevitably out of date now. However, the problem of replacing them is not just a commercial matter. The breadth of approach that would be expected today means that more would need to be said about interiors and contents as well as social history, so the volumes would explode under the weight of material. At the same time few authors have the confidence to take that broad approach. Thus while 18th century historical studies are very lively, country houses seem to have gone out of favour with writers, and the layman is now poorly served.

Monographs on single houses and architects of the classical period are now a rarity. The most recent studies of individual buildings are those on *The Building of Castle Howard* by Charles Saumarez Smith (1990), *Boughton House: The English Versailles* edited by Tessa Murdoch (1992) and *Spencer House: Chronicle of a great London mansion* by Joseph Friedman (1993) – and more recently has appeared *Royal Landscape* about Windsor Great Park. (Both *Spencer House* and *Royal Landscape* were heavily subsidised.) *Apollo* no longer devotes issues to single places, like Stowe in June 1973, Kingston Lacy in May 1986, Waddesdon in June 1987, and Woburn in June 1988, nor does anyone seem able to continue the studies of furniture makers on the lines of Christopher Gilbert's *Chippendale* or Helena Hayward and Pat Kirkham's *Linnell*.

Instead material tends to appear in exhibition catalogues and books relating to sponsored exhibitions such as *The Palladian Revival: Lord Burlington, his Villa and Garden at Chiswick* by John Harris (1994), which accompanied the exhibition held in Montreal, Pittsburgh and the Royal Academy, that on Houghton Hall held at Norwich and Kenwood in 1996, and that on Sir William Chambers at Somerset House, also in 1996. These remain useful works of reference to those who work in the field, but they are hardly convenient for 'the general reader'. Otherwise research appears in specialist journals such as *Architectural History*, *Furniture History*, *Garden History* and, increasingly, the more recently founded *Journal of the Georgian Group*. Lord Burlington has become a particularly difficult figure, with attention having concentrated on the vexed question of his Jacobite sympathies and masonic interests: so despite *Lord Burlington: Architecture, Art and Life* edited by Toby Barnard and Jane Clark (1995) there is still no life of him or a full study of his architecture.

Some 25 years ago the Royal Commission on Historical Monuments gave up publishing its inventory volumes such as the splendid sets on the county of Dorset and the City of York: they proved too costly to produce and the demand for them too limited. *The Country Houses of Northamptonshire* published in 1966 at a cost of £75 is likely to be one of the last of its type, although a companion volume on Northamptonshire churches is in the pipeline. Instead the Commission has been working on national survey volumes on building types such as mills, farmsteads and hospitals.

Nor has the National Trust found a way of making a proper contribution to the field of historical scholarship or to higher education through summer schools, courses, symposia or academic lectures: indeed, it almost seems to fight shy of it, relying on the unconvincing argument that it cannot afford to become involved. In place of its Year Books it supports an annual issue of *Apollo*, but its books on houses and gardens, with the exception of *Uppark Restored* by Christopher Rowell and John Martin Robinson (1996), *Textiles in Trust* edited by Ksynia Marko (1997) and *An Elizabethan Inheritance: The Hardwick Hall Textiles* by Santina M. Levey (1998), are disappointing. At the same time it has found it difficult to devise a format for guidebooks that is both more scholarly and popular, and the gap widens between the increasing amount of material that deserves to be made available and for which there is no outlet except in specialist national and local journals and the more pictorial approach that appeals to visitors. Thus its guidebooks have declined in quality, in terms of both text and illustration.

Moreover, as art history has become more popular in the 1980s and 1990s, it has tended to concentrate on the period after 1850 and has been influenced both by sociological approaches and by computerisation, both of which have tended to reduce interest in the study of buildings and objects. Thus many of those who have entered the field in recent years find their own barriers to the study of 17th and 18th-century country houses that were not there for those trained a generation earlier, and many find them hard to overcome.

One of the increasing dilemmas of the past 25 years is how to balance publication and security. A picture can be credited to a private collection and its recent provenance disguised, but a house cannot be hidden; and sometimes the risk of stirring up the wrong kind of attention seems too great. Thus many published accounts of country houses are now out of date; and that may matter when a building is trying to win support from the NHMF or the HLF.

The political achievements relating to houses, gardens and landscapes in the past 25 years have come about partly because specialist interests and popular enthusiasm have been in step. So it is disturbing to sense the academic curiosity in the period after 1660 becoming both more specialised and more limited. Interest has switched to the period after 1850, which is easier to work on, and, while that is producing some interesting thinking about country houses and revising opinions, particularly about Lutyens, it marks a turning away from the main period of country houses where there is still so much work to do. After all there has never been a book on the Marot period in England; no one has written a life of Lord Burlington, so it has been impossible to write a full study of William Kent; and one could go on like that through the 18th and early 19th centuries. If the field seems already worked on to those now embarking on research, it is more like a field that has not been ploughed for nearly a generation.

So while the problems of country houses are usually seen in terms of economics and politics, it could be that a new one is developing that is much harder to deal with: declining interest by those who fan the flames of enthusiasm. Since the popular enthusiasm of the 1970s was in part based on the specialist enthusiasms continuing from the previous decade, it was almost inevitable that there should be an intellectual change or reaction of some kind. So just as Evelyn Waugh's *Brideshead* was being made at Castle Howard for showing in 1981, Martin Wiener was at work on his *England and the Decline of the Industrial Spirit*, which argued persuasively against England's concern with its rural past and the damage that had caused. This was followed in 1990 by David Cannadine's *Decline and Fall of the British Aristocracy*. Thus there developed an anti-heritage, anti-country house view in the media and the press, particularly against the National Trust's houses, which in turn has created a defensive reaction within the Trust and the way it thinks about its role. That climate of opinion, coinciding with the populist view of the HLF, is naturally very worrying, and suggests that the intellectual interest in country houses needs to be rekindled.

On September 16, as the page proofs were being corrected, the Heritage Lottery Fund announced the offer of a grant of £4.9m towards the repair of the house at Stowe, which is not only a great encouragement to the new charitable trust set up to take over responsibility for the house and to those concerned for the future of Stowe as a house that provides the key to the gardens, but it is a most welcome demonstration that the HLF will continue to offer occasional large grants for preservation projects. In the case of Stowe £950,000 has also been offered to the National Trust for continuing work on the landscape, which means that one place is receiving close to £5m out of a total allocation of over £37m. What is also welcome is that access to the house and gardens is being increased, which means that there will be a greater opportunity for visitors to approach the gardens through the house and so appreciate the place as a whole, in particular getting the spectacular view that is obtained after walking through the house.

5

The Exemption of Works of Art and Attitudes to Historic Interiors, Collections and Contents 1974–1998

(a) *Threatening Changes to the System of Exemption of Works of Art in the Finance Act 1998*

'Attitudes to Historic Interiors, Collections and Contents 1974–1998' might sound academic and rarefied, but, as so often happens with country houses, new Beechers Brooks suddenly appear in the steeple-chase and transform the course through posing new threats that might at first sight seem specialised but in fact have much broader repercussions. So it has been with the exemption of works of art, where the existing system has been altered by the provisions of the Finance Act 1998.

They have been introduced by the Government in response to criticism of part of the system of exemption as it has developed in recent years but they effect the whole system. The concept of access in return for exemption was introduced in 1976, and at that time a Register was started of exempt objects for which an owner could not provide access either through opening a house on a regular basis or by loans to museums; and in 1982 the system was simplified so that it was easier for an owner to put objects on to the Register and provide access by appointment. The Register lists objects, but instead of giving the names of owners or their locations, because that would be a breach of confidentiality to which a tax payer is entitled, it provides mostly contact addresses. The Register now contains 18,000 objects in 800 different ownerships, but that only covers part of the total number, because it does not include objects in houses to which there is access on a regular basis. Nor does it cover objects exempted before 1976, when there was no access condition.

In the early years access to the Register, which was kept at the Victoria and Albert Museum and three other places in Northern Ireland, Scotland and Wales, was not satisfactory, but in recent years, as a result of criticism of the way the Register was run and the development of computer technology, it has been made much more widely available; and so it is now easy to see what has been exempt and how it can be viewed. It is the arrangements for access in certain cases, which can be complicated, that have caused problems, because there has been a certain amount of testing of the system to see how it is working; and a few published examples of the way requests have been handled by owners and their agents have been unfortunate. But at the same time there must be a strong presumption that these were tests of the system rather than genuine desires or needs to see objects; and no attention has been given to those where access presented no problems.

In addition to criticisms of difficulties of access through the Register there have been criticisms of standards for exemption, and it is clear that the present rules allow for the exemption of too many lesser objects that are neither of real national importance nor necessarily in the interests of owners who claim them because when they come to sell they may have to pay a high rate of tax on a greatly increased price.

Thus it is reasonable for the Government to consider how the system needed to be revised and tightened up.

However in tackling the Register and abolishing access by appointment as an acceptable condition and insisting that individual objects have to be pre-eminent or historically associated and on view to the public in order to qualify for exemption, it has gone much farther than the matter of the Register and gone into areas that do not appear to have aroused public discontent and criticism. Here is not the place to discuss the exemption of individual or small groups of objects not in country houses or historic houses but in smaller houses and flats, but it should be remembered that some of these are objects on loan from historic collections to other members of a family, particularly to those who have handed over, or to younger members who have inherited none of the core works of art, while others were formerly associated with a historic collection or a country house but for a variety of reasons have passed into other hands. Here the recent sales of objects by the

Trustees of the Olive Countess Fitzwilliam Chattels Settlement that were formerly at Wentworth Woodhouse in Yorkshire come to mind. Here because of the complexities of descent house and chattels have gone in different directions, but the system of exemption enabled the Trustees to retain Stubbs's *Whistlejacket* for a number of years, during which time it was lent to Kenwood, before selling it by private treaty to the National Gallery last year. In July 1998 the Trustees sold 93 lots at Christies, but shortly before the sale Van Dyck's portrait of *The Countess of Carlisle* was withdrawn at the request of the Tate Gallery, which was considering acquiring it by private treaty or through acceptance in lieu.

Moreover there are a number of problems relating to the exemption of objects in country and historic houses that are not open or hitherto open by appointment. The assumption is that it is easy to make everything available through opening or loans, but more thought needs to be given to the disruptive effect of access on the objects themselves, many of which are fragile, such as watercolours and textiles, or difficult to show, such as books. Long loans of major pictures may be possible, as can be seen in the National Gallery and the National Gallery of Scotland, but few institutions are geared to their short loan while furniture and works of applied or decorative art are very difficult to cope with as can be seen from the rarity of temporary exhibitions in those fields. At present all the Primary Galleries at the Victoria and Albert Museum are closed and when they re-open as the British Galleries in 2001, certain gaps could be filled by loans, but there will be no space to show a wide range of loans of furniture and there are no galleries for a study collection of furniture.

The Inland Revenue takes expert advice both on individual objects and historic association, over the latter usually from English Heritage which is reluctant to accept anything that has been in a house for less than 50 years. That denies the idea of a historic collection rolling forward and cuts out all signs of progress in the post war period that is much more important than is realised, as can be seen in a number of National Trust houses like Basildon, Croft and Dudmaston where the Trust has been influenced by the significance of recent acquisitions. That affects a number of houses in private ownership or in charitable trusts, like Burton Agnes, which was largely refurnished after the Second War by the late Marcus Wickham Boynton.

As far as access is concerned that is a matter between the Revenue and the owner. So it is hoped that the Revenue will be flexible on access.

It has already accepted that there can be no access to certain SSIs, and the same view should be taken of objects in certain situations, taking into account matters of security and conservation.

The worry of the new rules is that they will undermine owners' confidence in the system, particularly as the legislation is in effect retrospective and cancels admission by appointment on all cases since 1976 rather than starting in 1998, and discourage them from taking exemption in the future or sell objects now to buy out existing exemptions. The Government has expressed the hope that the legislation will not lead to sales, but it appears to have forgotten that the original and still basic idea of exemption was and is to keep objects off the market and so keep the pressure off museums, galleries and record offices that have never had sufficient purchase funds. Many of the objects exempt are of specialist significance and the system of exemption has provided that; moreover it has also enabled objects to be studied in their historic setting.

If one of the Government's hopes is that the change will provide more general access to great houses, probably they will be disappointed. The majority of these are already open, and it must be presumed that those not open do not have any post 1976 exemptions, have none at all or some objects on the Register. On the other hand there are a considerable number of smaller houses hitherto open by appointment, but it is unlikely that many of these will open regularly, because they realise that the costs and inconvenience of so doing will outweigh the likely income from it and may well consider how to buy their way out of exemption. However it is to be hoped that a compromise can be worked out with visits in pre-booked parties on certain advertised dates, as is already organised by the County Council in Northamptonshire.

With individually exempt objects each sale is treated on its own, but even so, because of the tax charges that each sale sets off, with duty payable at the rate at the time of exemption which might be as high as 80% on some estate duty cases plus CGT, it may cause great damage to a country house if an owner seeks to reduce the degree of exemption or clear it altogether; and with historically associated objects sales may threaten the entity, possibly leading to the loss of exemption of a house and its setting.

At the time of writing Inland Revenue guidelines relating to this aspect of the Finance Act were still awaited, but some unexpected problems may arise and there may be some sales that are disastrous for houses. So it is a great pity that the Government did not consider how the legislation might be revised in ways that was consistent with the development of thinking about historic entities and collections.

These changes give added point to the following sections explaining how thinking has developed in recent years and that were largely written before the recent changes were announced in the Finance Bill.

(b) *Research and Attitudes to Interiors*

In the late 1960s and early 1970s thinking about and research on interiors suddenly got going, largely as a result of the enthusiasm of the Furniture Department at the Victoria and Albert Museum, the challenges faced by the National Trust and the activities of the Furniture History Society. At that time historic interiors were really a new subject, without much literature and uncertain where it was going.

Here the work on Ham in the late 1970s, which followed on from that at Osterley, was significant, because it demonstrated how the thinking about Baroque planning explained by Hugh Murray Baillie in his paper of 1966 could be applied in a historic house. Moreover it encouraged research by a number of scholars, in particular Peter Thornton, whose *Seventeenth-century Interior Decoration in England, France and England* was published in 1977.

Furniture history was also developing very fast with much more use being made of bills and inventories, such as those for Ham House published in *Furniture History* in 1980, and furniture makers being looked at as closely as painters, sculptors or architects. Christopher Gilbert led the way in his two-volume study of Thomas Chippendale in 1978 and he was followed by Helena Hayward and Pat Kirkham in their companion study of Linnell published in 1980. Their publication of individual pieces together with designs and documents provided a rounded picture of a totally new kind, and that was to lead into detailed work on a host of subjects to do with interiors, decoration and furnishing.

Among those that have been and are being explored are historic paints and colours, most recently and fully by Ian Bristow in his two-volume study of historic colour and paint, *Architectural Colour in British Interiors 1615–1840* and *Interior House-Painting Colours and Technology*

1615–1840 (1996) (21 years after he began research at the Institute of Advanced Architectural Studies in York), wallpaper, upholstery, floors, carpets, picture hanging and, in recent years, picture frames. Some of the material has appeared in articles and books, but much of it has been related to restoration projects, as with picture-hanging schemes carried out at Stourhead, Wiltshire, by the National Trust, in the gallery at Temple Newsam House, Leeds, by the Victoria and Albert Museum at Apsley House and by Lord Leicester at Holkham (Plate VII). These are rarely fully published so that people can understand what has been done and why.

Thus there has been a new understanding of the significance of entities, not only designed interiors as at Osterley, but those that have grown up over the centuries, or more recently created interiors that are recognisable as period pieces, like those at Basildon (Fig. 16), entities with contents that are best covered by the elastic phrase 'historically associated'. That was recognised in legislation in 1976–77 extending exemption from objects of a quality to be shown in a local authority or university museum to those that are 'historically associated'. That had come about as a result of the concern over the effect that a Wealth Tax and CTT might have on the secondary contents of historic houses and was a natural result of the extension of conditional exemption to buildings and landscape and the introduction of the concept of maintenance funds.

Evidence of the new thinking about historic interiors can be seen in two restoration schemes carried out by the National Trust in the mid-1970s, at Erddig and Cragside. The negotiations over Erddig were particularly prolonged and difficult, because of the subsidence caused by mining below the house, but, when the house finally came to the Trust in an advanced state of decay as a gift from Philip Yorke in 1974, it was as near to complete as possible, with none of the usual sifting having gone on first, since Mr Yorke retained nothing of consequence for himself. Also it included unique material illustrating life below stairs and how the place had worked as a community. And it fell to Merlin Waterson, the young Historic Buildings Representative for the region, to plan its restoration and opening, co-ordinating and synthesising contributions and different approaches from John Fowler, Sheila Stainton's new team of conservators as well as Gervase Jackson-Stops, who worked with him on the unusually extensive archive. It was the first time that the Trust was able to make use of such material in a major programme of restoration, and that, combined with technical advances in conservation, and the social material, made Erddig into a turning point for the interpretation of country houses.

Before Erddig was complete, the Trust took on Cragside, in Northumberland, the house remodelled by Norman Shaw between 1869 and 1884, which was accepted in lieu of tax in 1977 and with a gift from the 3rd Lord Armstrong. It had been one of the six Category A houses in Mark Girouard's list of Victorian houses to be considered for preservation in 1971, but, when the possibility of its coming to the Trust was under discussion, it aroused strongly mixed feelings among members of committees, some of whom thought it was too hideous to take seriously. In the end it was the determination of Sheila Pettit, the Trust's remarkable Honorary Representative, who was able to charm, bully and shame all she came across within the Trust, the enthusiasm of the County Council for the project, the strength of local feeling for the Armstrong family's role in the 19th century industrial history of Northumberland and the popularity of its grounds and park that tipped the balance. It was typical of Sheila Pettit's free-range approach that, to bring home to the regional committee the serious state of the roof one winter, she made a tape recording of all the leaks and played it to them.

It was also an important case because it was the first since the broadening of exemption of contents to 'historically associated', and that enabled the Victoria and Albert Museum to recommend to the Government that virtually everything should be accepted as being part of the whole.

While the Victoria and Albert Museum at Osterley (Fig. 14) and Ham and the National Trust were spinning two threads, a third was being spun by English Heritage at Audley End (Plate II). When the house was acquired by the Ministry of Works in 1948, the 9th Lord Braybrooke left the contents on loan for 25 years with the condition that they should not be moved. At the end of that time his son, the Hon Robin Neville, wanted to sell some of them to the Government; and as a result of their purchase the Department of the Environment was able to reconsider the arrangement of the rooms. It had already restored the Adam rooms on the ground floor but had not been able to refurnish them. But now the strong archaeological tradition of the Ancient Monuments section of the Department was combined with the new thinking at the Victoria and Albert Museum. By then that included an interest in the Jacobean Revival contribution to the house made by the 3rd Lord Braybrooke,

I. The Library at Newby Hall, Yorkshire. Adam's dining room became a library in
the Regency period and its recent repainting is a synthesis of the two schemes.

II. The Saloon at Audley End, Essex. The property of English Heritage, the house was probably the first place where 19th-century antiquarian interiors were treated seriously.

III. The Drawing Room at Deene Park, Northamptonshire. It was redecorated in 1966 as part of a scheme of restoration begun in 1947.

IV. The Drawing Room at Raby Castle, Co Durham. A recent restoration of William Burn's rich interior of the 1840s carried out with some grant aid as part of a long programme of work on the castle.

V. The Dining Room at Elton Hall, Cambridgeshire. When the room was brought back into use in the late 1980s, it was decorated and arranged as a picture gallery cum dining room.

VI. The Tapestry Drawing Room at Hagley Hall, Worcestershire. In 1988 all the contents of the room were accepted as part of an in-lieu in-situ deal and left on loan in the house by Birmingham City Art Gallery. It was the first time a whole room had been dealt with in this way.

VII. *Perseus and Andromeda* by Chiari, one of the two original overmantels
recently replaced in the Saloon at Holkham, Norfolk.

VIII. The Gallery at Rockingham Castle, Leicestershire. In the early 1980s the conservation of the Victorian damask curtains was carried out with some grant aid to maintain the original character of the room.

IX. A Victorian watercolour of the gallery at Rockingham. This shows how little it has changed since it was decorated in the 1850s.

X. The Great Hall at Eastnor Castle, Herefordshire. Recently Mrs Hervey-Bathurst rearranged the hall and transformed its mood with the aid of Bernard Nevill.

XI. The Stone Hall at Houghton Hall, Norfolk. It is now arranged as an
architectural space and reduced to its original mahogany furniture.

who succeeded in 1825 and died in 1858, and his wife, who had redecorated the first-floor rooms over the Adam rooms. It was probably the first time that antiquarian interiors of the 1830s were treated seriously.

Thinking was gradually moving towards appearing to do less and less to interiors, to keep them as far as possible as they were at the time they came to the Trust, and that has been the dominant idea at Calke and Chastleton. It is a valid point of view, but it should probably be seen as that of one generation, a generation who sees houses as places to be studied rather than lived in and as appealing to the mind rather than the heart. Lord Crawford, always wise, foresaw that this was bound to happen. And probably it will be realised that just as it is impossible to maintain a lived-in look or to turn a clock back to an earlier time, it is just as impossible to stop a clock.

John Fowler often used the phrase 'pleasing decay', which came from John Betjeman, and that aspect of houses had a great appeal for him. However, there had to be an aesthetic balance between pleasing and decay, and if it was no longer pleasing, it was no longer acceptable. The problem of the 'leave it alone' school is that it is unwilling to make that distinction, and so quite often it is led into retaining decay that is definitely displeasing to many people, forgetting that an essential part of the point of a building is to appeal to the eye and the spirit.

What is often forgotten when looking at such rooms is all the specialised skills that go into achieving a unity, and one of the most remarkable threads running through the world of historic buildings including country houses in the past 25 years has been the development and flowering of skills among a new generation of craftsmen. When the interest in historic interiors was starting to gather pace in the late 1960s and early 1970s, it seemed that the traditional skills were in decline, but there has been a remarkable turn-round not only in the opportunities but in the response to them. Sadly it is the damage caused by the fires at Hampton Court Palace, Uppark and Windsor Castle that has provided the greatest opportunities. However, those jobs could not have been accomplished without all the earlier effort that had been going on to foster and encourage skills in restoration and conservation.

In the 1950s and '60s John Fowler seldom had the opportunity to have special damasks, especially silk damasks, woven, and no one was interested in doing simple traditional woollens, such as moreen; and he had great difficulty keeping Clarke's, his trimmings makers, going. Now, however, there are a number of specialist suppliers: Richard Humphries at Castle Hedingham who has a fine collection of cards for damasks usually produced for restoration jobs, and Anna Benson and Neil Warburton at Context Weavers at Rossendale in Lancashire are always eager to try to produce a new traditional simple woollen cloth, whether it be a moreen or camlet, or special muslins for sun curtains or holland for striped blinds. They started by making reproduction materials for use in car restorations, but have received a great deal of support from English Heritage and the National Trust. Similarly in John Fowler's day it was hard to get any hand block printing of wallpaper done, and it seemed a great extravagance. Now Tom Helme's Silvergate Papers and Allyson McDermott at Petworth have a growing collection of block-printed copies of 18th and 19th century documents. Fine hand-made trimmings continue to be made in England by Turner's, who have been in business since 1899, and now also by Wendy Cushing, but inevitably costs are high and, except in cases like the post-fire restorations of Hampton Court and Windsor Castle, it is rare for there to be sufficient funds for their use in restoration as opposed to decorative schemes. Special orders are complicated to put in, and they demand too much of the client for many private owners to embark on them without an inter-mediary, but it is encouraging that so many specialist suppliers find that it is worth their while to show at the exhibition at the HHA Annual General Meeting. Indeed one said that he found it better than showing at Decorex.

The non-interventionist school in reacting against earlier approaches is also usually reacting against the Rule of Taste and the enthusiasm of an earlier generation for the 18th century. Instead, as a result of the growing interest in the 19th century, there has been a fresh appreciation of past restorations, particularly during the antiquarian phase in the last century, and with it an increased appreciation of layers in a house. Also many people coming to work in the field now have a historical training, so they see houses primarily as documents whose value lies in the extent to which they have not been altered in recent years, particularly during the course of their preservation. It is worth remembering the advice written by Ian Lindsay in 1948 on *Notes for Guidance to Investigators* in Scotland: 'We may not like revival "baronial" but future generations may.'

Most recently this changing perception has applied to Chastleton. In 1990 it appeared to the National Trust as a remarkably untouched Jacobean house but now, after careful research and close study of the fabric, it is seen to have been very carefully handled by a succession of generations, almost all of whom have left their mark on it.

Commercial interests have also played a part that should not be forgotten. The auction houses place increasing emphasis on the importance of a good historical provenance for what they sell as the number of fine things coming on to the market declines and demand increases. Thus their cataloguing has become much more careful and that too has contributed to the information available. That can be seen with Christies' sale of the contents of Great Tew Park, Oxfordshire, in May 1987, which contained hitherto unknown furniture supplied by George Bullock and G.J. Morant; that of Mere Hall, Cheshire, held by Christie's in 1994, which included furniture by Gillow; and more recently Christie's sale of July 1997 which included the Weller-Poley suite attributed to Ince and Mayhew. All three were useful additions to furniture history.

Often the information gathered by the auction houses remains unpublished until a sale takes place, but the current inventories compiled by Christie's and Sotheby's for their clients with country houses have become increasingly detailed, with references to bills and old inventories included and extended as fresh discoveries are made. Thus they are essential confidential working tools and handy works of reference.

The new thinking about interiors that can be seen at Osterley, Ham and several houses of the National Trust, not surprisingly, had less immediate influence on houses in private ownership, partly because of the attitudes of owners and partly because of the preparation and costs of the work. However in the longer term the indirect influence has been considerable, and although many owners would deny its effect on them, it has come about through visiting houses, seeing photographs and employing architects and craftsmen who have worked for the Trust. Thus since about 1980 a number of houses have adopted an increasingly historical approach.

Among dramatic restorations have been that of the Elizabethan barrel-vaulted Long Gallery at Burton Agnes, in Yorkshire (Fig. 25). It had been divided up in the early 19th century following the collapse of part of the ceiling, and in 1951, after Marcus Wickham-Boynton had opened the house, he decided to recreate a third of the gallery with the

25. The Long Gallery at Burton Agnes, Yorkshire. Subdivided in the 19th century after part of its Jacobean ceiling collapsed, it was reformed and restored by the late Marcus Wickham Boynton in 1951 and 1975.

help of Francis Johnson, the architect who worked nearby in Bridlington, following the evidence of the surviving fragment of ceiling and using Georgian woodwork from Kilnwick Hall, near Driffield, which was demolished that year. Twenty-three years later, to mark European Architectural Heritage Year, Mr Wickham-Boynton decided to complete the Gallery, again with the help of Francis Johnson and Stead's of Bradford doing the plasterwork. It must be among the most ambitious private projects in recent years.

At Prideaux Place at Padstow a slightly later but more dramatic ceiling by the Abbotts of Barnstaple has been revealed (Fig. 26). It was always known that the ceiling was there – indeed it was possible for a photographer to crawl up through an opening in the later ceiling below to take details of it – and when the house was being repaired with the help of the HBC in the late 1970s it was decided to reveal the whole of the ceiling and recreate the Great Chamber, which had been divided up. That has provided the house with a useful large room which makes

26. The Great Chamber at Prideaux Place, Cornwall. The elaborate ceiling of about 1640 was revealed and the room restored as part of a programme of grant-aided repairs to the house in the late 1970s.

better historical sense of the house and can be shown to the public.

Among recent restorations of Georgian rooms one of the most dramatic campaigns has been carried out at Arniston, near Edinburgh. There William Adam's original concept of the 1720s was altered by his son John, who formed a large drawing room and dining room in the 1750s. These two rooms were dismantled when dry rot was discovered in 1957 during the course of repairs to the house, and then abandoned.

When Mrs Dundas-Bekker inherited the house in 1970, she began on a programme of repairs that went on for 25 years, with the unflinching support of the Historic Buildings Council for Scotland and Historic Scotland, but it was only in 1995 that she was able to tackle the dining room; since then she has been working on the drawing room. She points out that it took two generations to complete the house in the 18th century, and it will take that to complete its restoration in the 20th and 21st centuries.

In some cases owners have had professional help with decoration, but what has been more important is the way that they learned from the style of certain houses rearranged before and after the Second World War. Here the influence of Mrs Lancaster is probably crucial through what she did in the late 1920s and 1930s at Kelmarsh Hall, in Northamptonshire, and later at Ditchley Park, Oxfordshire, when she was married to Ronald Tree, two houses that were greatly admired at the time.

After the Second World War John Fowler in partnership with Nancy Lancaster developed his own style, which was considerably strengthened under her influence, and even those owners who never consulted him, picked up consciously or unconsciously ideas about colour, pattern and texture as well as visual and physical comfort; this enabled them to give their houses a new visual vitality that creates a synthesis out of the past and present.

John Fowler helped many owners of fine houses, but often without doing much visible decoration for them, and so to see him 'pulling out all the stops', as he used to say, in a country house it is necessary to go to Grimsthorpe Castle, in Lincolnshire, where he worked for many years for Lady Ancaster, the wife of the 3rd Earl. Lord Ancaster inherited in 1951 and did great a great deal to the structure of the house in that decade, and Lady Ancaster, who was a daughter of the 2nd Viscount Astor and so a cousin of Nancy Lancaster, loved working with John Fowler. He gave it a more relaxed and airy character, 'degranding' it by placing huge sofas covered in a giant check pattern in Vanbrugh's Great Hall, laying Hardwick matting in the King James Drawing Room and painting the 17th and early 18th century chapel in his inimitable succession of whites. Grimsthorpe was never open, and never photographed in Lady Ancaster's lifetime, but now it shows what the beau ideal of the country house interior on the largest scale was considered to be in the 1960s.

Here there is not the space nor can there be enough illustrations to show what has happened to country house interiors in recent years, but it is surely remarkable to be able to introduce a series of houses and rooms that tell such a positive story covering the past 40 years and show how thinking has developed and changed.

It would surely start with Stratfield Saye, in Hampshire, as restored and rearranged by the 7th Duke of Wellington. He had inherited unexpectedly from his nephew, who was killed in the war at Salerno in 1943: as a younger son of the 4th Duke, Lord Gerald Wellesley, as he had been hitherto, had had to make his own way in the world, which he did with considerable success as an architect in a stripped classical style fusing the Modern Movement with the Regency style, which was always his favourite period. In his case contemporary fashionable enthusiasms were related to his own particular fascination for the period of the Great Duke of Wellington, and he combined scholarly knowledge with an eye for interiors and decoration. Thus it was singularly fortunate that he should have inherited both Stratfield Saye and Apsley House, in London, which he gave to the nation as a munificent gift in 1947; and he devoted the rest of his life to the former, arranging it with rare sympathy both for its architectural decoration and for its collections mostly formed by the Great Duke.

The most ambitious revival of a great house after the Second World War is undoubtedly Chatsworth, with the state rooms tackled by the Duchess of Devonshire mostly in the late 1950s and early '60s. Not only did she rearrange the 1st Duke's state rooms on the second floor, giving them a sense of richness of texture and colour that complemented the elaborate carving and decorative painting, but she enlivened the 6th Duke's dining room and sculpture gallery; and also she worked on a number of other rooms such as the Mary Queen of Scots Rooms that have been opened to the public.

Another outstanding job spanning many years is Mr and Mrs Edmund Brudenell's restoration and reduction, rearrangement and redecoration of Deene Park (Plate III), which he began in 1947 and they completed in 1975. That house could easily have become one of the losses of the post-war period, a huge and underfurnished building of many periods, on which very little money had been spent since the death of the 7th Earl of Cardigan in 1868. In 1945 there was no gas or electricity – temporary power had been laid on for the six military units who had occupied it during the war – and no heating.

There was very little money – land had been let at 13s 6d an acre in the 1930s and only rose to 18s 6d by 1955 – but Edmund Brudenell's father allowed him to start to make improvements in 1947 when he was 18, a second bathroom, for instance, and electricity in 1948 and a little inexpensive painting before his coming of age in January 1950. However, the Great Hall remained lined with wrapping paper put up after his father sold the post-Civil War panelling. When Edmund Brudenell married in 1955, he and his wife moved into the house with his parents, because the estate could not afford a second establishment, and it was then that they decorated the Bow Room as their sitting room. However, they could not do much more until after the death of his father in 1962, and then they tackled first the drawing room and then the dining room. It was a case of one room at a time, but there was never a master plan and no idea that they would eventually restore and use the whole house as well as open it to the public, which they started to do in 1967. The work continued after that, with the east range being tackled in the early 1970s; and the whole house completed in 1975, except for the 7th Earl's vast ballroom, which was demolished in 1984 (see p. 312). In recent years they have shown an increasing amount of the house to the public and also made the house available to special parties during most of the year as well as using it for functions of many kinds.

Deene is one of the best shown houses in England, because visitors see it as it is lived in, and lived in as fully as any house in England, with all the main rooms regularly in use. Thus not only are the library and Ante Hall used on a daily basis, but at weekends life goes on in the Great Hall, drawing room and dining room, with spectacular flowers arranged both for visitors and for guests, with family and guests, current books and needlework tidied out of sight at 1.55 p.m. on summer Sundays. The whole is a remarkable performance that took the Brudenells many years to achieve; and the process still continues, as can be seen from the stained glass roundels recently made for the chapel that is regularly used by both family and village since the adjoining parish church became redundant.

The redecoration and rearrangement of Newby Hall (Plate I) in the late 1970s and early 1980s by Mrs Robin Compton is a particularly interesting response of a private owner to the challenge of showing a house to the public as part of a fully commercial operation and making it looked lived in when only a few of the rooms are used occasionally and some never. When her husband inherited Newby in 1977, that had to happen because of the scale of the garden rather than of the house. The rethinking involved not only repainting the famous Adam rooms but adding a series of bedrooms and other rooms to extend the tour and to give the house a more lived-in and human feeling.

The repainting of the Adam rooms was done at a time when academic thinking about historic colour and paint was trying to solve the problem such rooms presented but usually producing results that were neither convincing nor agreeable. Mrs Compton, while aware of what was going on, took a more moderate, common-sense view and thought more about the visitors to the house. Here she was helped by the painters Charles Hesp and Denis Jones, who had previously worked for Bellerby's of York, a firm whom John Fowler had come to rely on for most of his northern work, both private and for the National Trust. And Hesp and Jones have worked for the Trust at Erddig, Lyme, Dunham Massey and Attingham. In the hall at Newby, for instance, which Mrs Compton had always found unwelcoming and cold, she slightly altered the disposition and tones of the colours to give visitors, who frequently come on grey days, a warmer greeting. In the Tapestry Room the ground colours of the Boucher-Neilson tapestries are now so faded that it would have been absurd to repeat Adam's original drawing (even if it had been carried out), and again she modified the existing scheme to suit the altered balance of the room. In the library, which Adam had designed as the dining room but whose purpose had been changed in the Regency period, she used some of the colours that were part of the Regency scheme. The National Trust would now feel unable to be so free; and also, since Newby was painted, considerable progress has been made in the painting of Adam rooms, as can be seen at Kedleston and Osterley. But a private owner still has that freedom and I find the approach at Newby refreshing; as with any paint scheme it will not last for ever and in the future can always be replaced or revised.

At Burghley since 1981 Lady Victoria Leatham has been faced with a challenge on the Chatsworth scale of great Baroque rooms with darkened painted ceilings, acres of brown woodwork enriched with lavish naturalistic carving and hundreds of Old Master pictures hiding under discoloured varnish. Burghley before her day was a daunting place for visitors, unless they were specialists and knew what they were looking at. However, she has transformed the whole house, restoring all 18 state rooms, renewing wall hangings, repairing furniture, conserving tapestries and beds, and cleaning pictures and frames as well as arranging a series of special exhibitions exploring aspects of the collection and drawing on recent research. Again the task is unending. The painted ceilings and walls are still not done, and although it took four years to clean and restore the staircase with Verrio's ceiling of *Hell* and Stothard's *Horrors of War* on the walls, English Heritage refused to grant aid the work. Now the Heaven Room has to be faced and that will be another four-year project.

One of the most remarkable and most interesting of these recent transformations has been at Eastnor Castle, Herefordshire, a huge and austere castle-style house designed by Smirke for the 1st Earl Somers (Fig. 2), embellished by Pugin for the 2nd Earl and enriched in an Italianate style in the 1860s for the 3rd Earl. Both the scale and the styles are daunting to anyone brought up on the Rule of Taste before and after the Second World War; and no one could have blamed the late Mrs Hervey-Bathurst if, facing it as a bride in 1947, she had said 'No.' Happily she had a great affection for the place she had inherited and was prepared to work very hard in practical ways, as was explained on p. 32. That dedication she has passed on to her son, James, the present owner, who was born in 1949, nine years before the establishment of the Victorian Society. In 1968 Alistair Rowan, a devotee of castle-style houses, wrote the first full modern account of it in *Country Life*.

Where Eastnor has been remarkably lucky is that James Hervey-Bathurst's wife read 19th century novels while studying English literature at university and so was able to approach Eastnor through the characters who had created it. Thus while Mrs Hervey-Bathurst has been challenged by the house, she has also been exhilarated by it, and, initially with the aid of Bernard Nevill, she has responded to it very positively (Fig. 27 and Plate X); it is probably no accident that she has been working on it in the period that Alexandra Wedgwood produced her two catalogues of Pugin drawings (in 1977 and 1985), Clive Wainwright published *The Romantic Interior* (1989) and the big Pugin exhibition was held at the Victoria and Albert Museum in 1994. She has rearranged and partly redecorated the principal rooms for occasional family use and at the same time made the house much more sympathetic and exciting for visitors as well as working for the corporate life that is essential to the financial equation, with the two aspects of Eastnor's public life providing the justification for all that has been done. That in turn has

27. The Great Hall at Eastnor Castle, Herefordshire, as it was in 1968. Its present appearance is seen in Plate X.

encouraged them to bring back into use all the bedrooms in the main building that had been abandoned in 1939, an act that is best described by the no doubt politically incorrect idea of recolonisation. Thus a group of people can have the experience of staying in a castle that is redolent of Disraeli or Trollope novels. Surely no one could have done what the Hervey-Bathursts have done before the 1980s? Now they have worked on 53 rooms in five years and have seen the numbers of their visitors doubling to 18,000 by 1993 and reaching 50,000 in 1997. The new income combined with on-going grant aid from English Heritage is funding the extensive and long overdue roof-repair programme.

The drawing room at Raby Castle, in Co. Durham (Plate IV), is different from the other rooms mentioned here in that it shows a private owner approaching a major interior on lines parallel to those that would be adopted by the National Trust or English Heritage, and it is also unusual in that its restoration involved a grant from English Heritage. That was offered in 1993, following on from grant-aided restoration of John Carr's aisled hall, one of the most dramatic 18th century interiors in England. The octagonal room lies at the end of it, and was originally designed by Carr as a circular gothick climax to it. However in 1843 William Burn began to recast it for the short-lived 2nd Duke of Cleveland, who succeeded in 1842 and died in 1848. It is a striking essay in elaborate ornament and strong colour, with yellow damask for the walls and red and yellow damask for the curtains and upholstery combined with a great deal of gilding and picking out in red, with additional shots of strong green in a pair of malachite tables bought for the room in the early 1860s. In the course of this century the room has gone sadly downhill, with most of the yellow damask wall hangings rotting beyond repair and only sections of the draped valances surviving, and most of the original furniture removed from sight because of its condition.

Very soon after Lord Barnard began to carry out his major programme of repairs to the castle in 1976, he started to think about how to restore this room, making a first enquiry about a grant in 1978, when it seemed that machine-made silk and cotton damask was the best that could be aimed for. Happily nothing was done at that stage, because of other priorities, and only in the late 1980s did Lord Barnard begin to consider a more comprehensive project and one carried out to a much higher standard. By then it was only reasonable to conserve the five narrow wall panels flanking the windows and reuse the surviving outer tails of the draped valances for the three windows. Their conservation has been assisted by English Heritage, which has also supported the limited repair of the architectural gilding in the room. However English Heritage did not contribute to the reweaving of the yellow or red and yellow damasks, and, since Lord Barnard wanted to use the room occasionally, he decided not to seek grant aid for the restoration of the furniture by Morant, which had become so decayed that it had been removed and stored, so that there would be no conditions over its future display or use. The result is a splendid example of the richest taste of the 1840s and done to a standard that would have been unthinkable 15 to 20 years earlier.

The way the work was divided into what was grant-aidable and what was not arose out of discussions between Lord Barnard and English Heritage. It is easy for English Heritage to say that it cannot afford to do much grant-aided work of this kind when it has more pressing cases of repairs to structures on their last legs, but interiors are an essential part of buildings and their appearance is a crucial element in the appeal of houses to visitors and so their ability to earn some of their keep. Thus a room like the Burn Drawing Room needs to be seen not as an isolated project but as part of the long-term programme of work at Raby.

An even more recent rearrangement of a house has been at Houghton, in Norfolk. For the last 80 years it has seemed one of the most splendid in England, and in that period the late Marchioness of Cholmondeley gathered there works of art inherited from her parents and from her brother, Sir Philip Sassoon, one of the principal collectors in Britain between the wars, and brought from her London house in the 1980s. Since her death in 1989 her grandson, the present Lord Cholmondeley, has had to do a great deal of work on the services of the house and carry out a lot of conservation work. He has also been interested in the more historic approach to houses and has thought about Sir Robert Walpole's intentions: combining evidence in the 18th century inventories with photographs taken about 1920, which show the house much emptier than it became by the end of his grandmother's lifetime, he has taken a much more architectural line, particularly in the Stone Hall and in the White Drawing Room. The Stone Hall (Plate XI) always looked wonderful and staggeringly rich with all the carved and gilt green velvet furniture from the drawing room in it, but that did not belong in there and threw out the balance of the series of rooms: the room looks much more striking as an architectural space and reduced to just its original mahogany furniture. It was a brave decision to take.

One new element that has been a significant influence on country house interiors in the past 25 years has been the growth of interest in picture hanging and arrangement, which has developed out of the visual interest in historic decoration on the one hand and the history of collecting on the other. There have been a series of interesting campaigns in private houses and those belonging to the National Trust, local authorities and charitable trusts. Among them have been Burghley, Elton, Harewood, Holkham, Ickworth, Kingston Lacy, Osterley, Paxton, where the Gallery has been restored and the original idea recreated with the help of the National Gallery of Scotland, Petworth, Stourhead and Temple Newsam.

Of all these schemes arguably the most rewarding of the private exercises has been at Holkham, where Lord Leicester has put back the original overmantels of *Tarquin and Lucretia* by Procaccini and *Perseus and Andromeda* by Chiari (Plate VII) in the saloon and of *Jupiter and Juno* by Gavin Hamilton in the State Bedroom, and recreated the Landscape Room. The last started in 1990 when he decided that the hangings were beyond recall and that it would be better to go back to crimson damask, as specified in the 18th century inventories, so as to recreate the original sequence of materials: caffoy in the saloon, cut velvet in the drawing room and then damask in the Landscape Room. The damask was successfully woven by Richard Humphries in a pattern of the Kent period. At that stage Lord Leicester put back four more of the original pictures bringing the total to 17 out of the 22 listed in the inventories of 1760 and 1765, but since then he as put back all the pictures that remain in the collection (one pair of Locatelli were sold in the late 19th century) with marvellous results.

At Elton the approach in the dining room (Plate V) has been freer. When the house was illustrated in *Country Life* in 1957, that room was not photographed as a whole, presumably because it was not fully furnished, and Arthur Oswald only showed the chimneypiece and overmantel, presumably because they came out of the 18th century library. Now it is the most dramatic room in the house with its 1860 Italianate detail set off by varnished broken red walls, inspired by the Gallery at Attingham, and close hung with a strong pattern of pictures combining Italian Renaissance religious pictures, family portraits, flower pictures and so on, worked out by Alec Cobbe. The decorative effect is splendid, a reinterpretation rather than a reconstruction of a classic hang that gives a rarely used dining room the feeling of a picture gallery and makes a climax in visitors' tours of the house.

Here as in so many of the schemes carried out in recent years in private houses the impetus has been a combination of family feeling and a desire to show off the house and its contents to visitors as effectively as possible. Without opening, all the effort and expense might have seemed hard to justify, and the satisfaction lies in the combination of private and public pleasure.

Research on interiors has led to a much greater understanding of houses, but it has also raised standards of what is thought significant and worthy of preservation. As yet that has not been fully digested, but it has become much harder to argue the case for preservation of a country house that depends on a degree of public funding when the interior is not as strong as it was 25 or 30 years ago or at least seemed to be at that time.

That was the nub of the problem at Brympton d'Evercy in 1992.

Whereas until the sale of its contents in 1947, it was one of the most admired houses of its type in England, as can be seen from Christopher Hussey's poetic description of it in *Country Life* in 1927, once it had lost its contents, it seemed to have lost its soul; and while it remains a singularly beautiful building, the preservation lobby outside the HHA was not prepared to make a case for it to the NHMF.

A rather different but comparable situation happened over Pitchford, as is explained on p. 270: there finally the National Trust declined to become involved in an exceedingly complex and expensive operation that would have depended entirely on public money, because the costs and the interest of the interior were so far out of balance. Yet if the house had been considered a generation earlier not only would the sums have been far less but the interior would not have raised so many questions about merit.

In the case of Appleby the loss of virtually all the contents other than the portraits, which had been acquired by Abbott Hall, at Kendal, influenced the National Trust's decision not to become involved: it was too late. These three cases show how crucial contents are to the point of houses when it comes to trying to devise preservation schemes.

(c) *The Development of Conservation Thinking*

One of the important new threads in the late 1960s and early 1970s as far as country houses were concerned was the increasing awareness of the need for proper care of interiors. On the one hand that meant higher standards of day-to-day maintenance, traditional housekeeping brought up to date in a world from which the traditional housekeepers and their trained staffs had vanished. On the other it meant the need for improved facilities and trained people who could prolong the life not only of great works of art but of the huge range of textiles and all the other materials that are to be found in houses as well as museums. If it was a movement that started in museums, it soon spread to houses, and it has had a number of surprising results.

First, and very important, it has helped to make the routine work of looking after the inside of a house, particularly one open to the public, seem worthwhile; tasks which had been regarded as a menial and unworthy part of domestic life in the late 1940s and '50s have acquired a new point and satisfaction.

Second, it has meant a recognition of the damage caused by light and atmosphere, and so blinds and sun curtains have been ordered for windows, shutters have come back into use and also some houses are now put to bed in the winter. As a result of those precautions and better standards of care, things have lasted longer and rooms stayed fresher. I have been particularly struck by this at Clandon, Sudbury and Beningbrough.

Third, it has changed attitudes to preservation and restoration, making it possible to repair elements of schemes of decoration and so keep entities together. That has already been seen in the Octagon Drawing Room at Raby but it can also be seen in the Gallery at Rockingham Castle, Northamptonshire (Plates VIII and IX), a room formed by Salvin in 1850 and not only containing fine pictures and French furniture but still retaining its original graining and wallpaper of that time, supplied by Cowtan, and also its original crimson damask curtains. By the late 1970s the curtains were in a very sad way, and even 10 years earlier would have been discarded and replaced: by then, however, the development of conservation facilities at Osterley meant that they could be repaired – at a price – and rehung, so that the complete mid-19th century scheme of decoration in the room has been retained. Commander Saunders Watson applied to the HBC in 1981 for a grant towards their conservation and was told that, although in principle the work was grant-aidable, one could not be recommended at that time because it was held that structural repairs had a first call on the funds available, but that if he applied again at the end of the financial year, when the work had been done, it might be possible to offer a grant. In the end he was offered £1600 towards a total bill of £4826 for what was done in 1980–1981 and in 1984 a further £500, the whole project costing £15,000 as well as a great deal of voluntary labour. Thus the grant contribution was modest, but at least the idea was accepted.

Fourth, first through the National Trust's early textile workshops at Knole and Blickling and then through the National Association of Decorative and Fine Arts Societies, it was discovered that volunteers giving their time on a regular basis could do a range of tasks in country houses, particularly to do with the conservation of textiles and the care of books in a library, tasks that could never have been done if they had to be paid for at even modest rates. Not only have NADFAS volunteers achieved a great deal all over the country, but those giving their time have had satisfaction and interest as well as welcome company through working together.

The final aspect of the concern for conservation is that it is now recognised that places can be literally worn out by the pressure of people through opening. Therefore a price has to be paid in terms of some reduction in present pleasure, so that they do have a future; and the more important and delicate the interior and the more it is shown to visitors, the more rigorous have to be the controls over light and atmosphere. Consequently important but delicate rooms cannot be left as casually lived in, particularly in houses owned by the National Trust and charitable bodies. Hours of opening have to be limited – the Trust now aims for 1000 hours of controlled daylight a year, 600 for visitors, which gives four hours a day, five days a week and a 30 week season, and 400 hours for maintenance and cleaning, an hour a day. However, as Julia Marsden has explained over Felbrigg, 'there is great pressure on the houses either to increase light levels during the opening season, often in response to complaints from visitors; or to extend open hours in order to host a range of activities and generate income.' In certain places numbers have to be restricted as at Canons Ashby and Chastleton.

Country house interiors, and that usually means state rooms or rooms of parade, rather than rooms for daily living, have come down to us from the past partly because they were little used and so seldom exposed to light and partly because they were well cared for by servants who covered up tapestries and put case covers on seat furniture and gilt furniture following strict rules. Great houses far from London were often visited for comparatively brief periods; and a few, because of the accidents of family history, were seldom used for decades and even centuries. That is why houses like Boughton and Houghton are such marvellous places today. Thus there are great risks if such houses are opened a great deal more than they are already.

One of the downsides of the house-opening movement in the years after the war is that it coincided with the departure of trained housekeepers and servants who knew how to look after things. Here the National Trust was in a worse state than some private houses, because it was often starting again from scratch. To a generation influenced by the Modern Movement to enjoy light rooms, it was not obvious what damage all kinds of light did to hangings, curtains and upholstered furniture; and they faded if they did not actually fall to pieces in most houses open to the public.

As far as the Trust was concerned, Robin Fedden took the view that the Trust did not need to do more than an enlightened private owner, and the lack of success in the early 1960s over repairs to the Venetian Ambassador's Bed at Knole, which proved to be disastrous, was also a deterrent. However in the mid to late 1960s the Trust began to be aware that it had to face up to the challenge of decaying textiles in its houses and the need to install blinds and sun curtains to filter the light during opening hours. That grew out of reports on the textiles at Hardwick and Knole by Karen Finch and recommendations from George Wingfield Digby and later Donald King, successive Keepers of the Textile Department at the Victoria and Albert Museum, which owned the Hardwick tapestries.

At the same time museums were becoming more aware of the needs for conservation, and that thinking was conveyed to the Trust by Lord Rosse, who was chairman not only of the Trust's Historic Buildings Committee but of the Standing Committee on Museums and Galleries.

All this meant a great deal to St John Gore, who succeeded Robin Fedden in 1973, and it was he who encouraged the new standards of housekeeping and also the development of new conservation facilities. Thus in 1977 Sheila Stainton, who had first begun to work on Trust textiles in 1961, became the Trust's first housekeeper. Soon after that she and Hermione Sandwith began work on turning what had been a shoe box of cards of do's and don'ts into what became *The National Trust Manual of Housekeeping*, which was first published in 1984 and, against all the publisher's prognostications, proved to be a bestseller.

The key marker here was the Victoria and Albert Museum's saving of the Erddig bed, which Philip Yorke allowed the Museum to take out of the house in 1968 at a time when it was at serious risk from water pouring through the leaking roof and the future of the whole house was very uncertain. Initially the Museum was reluctant to be involved with this outside job, and Sheila Landi, who carried out the amazing conservation work, has subsequently written that, when she went to see the bed *in situ*, she 'was privately instructed to find that it would be an impossible enterprise'. Characteristically she didn't; and her decision to take it on was significant in two ways. Not only was it 'probably the first object of its kind to receive the serious attention of a conservator rather than that of the desperate housekeeper', but it was also the first time the Museum had tackled a major object that was to go back to its historic setting when that could be made sound.

From then until the late 1980s, first at South Kensington and from 1976 in its own conservation studios at Osterley, Mrs Landi carried out work on the Museum's possessions and on those belonging to other bodies, particularly the National Trust, and private owners. Thus she worked on the Vardy bed from Hardwick and the state bed from Audley End for English Heritage. Now, however, the Museum had constructed a new department at South Kensington, but has become inward-looking again.

The National Trust, however, has become more or less self-sufficient and, having had textile conservation workrooms at Erdigg, Knole, Hughenden and Blickling, it has now concentrated all its textile conservation resources at Blickling. The key to these workshops lay in Karen Finch's report on Knole where she estimated that the King's Bed would cost £50,000 to repair, an unfaceable figure at that time. It was she who suggested that it could be done by volunteers working under professional supervision. So the workshop was set up, the HBC paid for the supervisor, and after 13 years the work was brought to a triumphant conclusion.

Inspired by what the Trust has done, NADFAS has helped a number of houses with textile repairs and conservation work of other kinds, as is explained on p. 253, and several owners have organised their own teams concentrating on textile repairs, as at Bowhill, Chatsworth and Hatfield, where a team has been at work since 1976. In that year Lady Salisbury, who had been originally inspired by Lady Meade-Fetherstonhaugh at Uppark and been introduced by her to the use of *Saponaria officinalis* in the late 1960s, invited Mrs Joan Kendall to come to Hatfield and organise a group to work on lines approved by the Victoria and Albert Museum. That consists of 40 people who come one day a week and specialise in particular objects or special problems. In the early years they concentrated on objects in the state rooms, starting with four Sheldon tapestries and then conserving and tackling the state bed.

At Burghley Lady Victoria Leatham began work on tapestries in 1982 and by 1988 the set of Mortlake *Bacchanals* in the Blue State Bedroom, the Gobelins set in the Queen Elizabeth Room, and two sets of Vanderbank tapestries, the *Elements* and *Grotesques*, had been done. Also the late 17th century bed in Queen Elizabeth's Room was restored with conservation of the old materials done by Sheila Landi. Sponsorship has made a crucial contribution to this programme, Rémy Martin, for instance, who were sponsors of the Burghley horse trials, paying for the work on that bed, related chairs, stools and window curtains. The boldly embroidered 17th century hangings on the bed in the Black and Yellow Room have also been conserved by Sheila Landi.

The challenges of conservation at Burghley have led to the conversion of the stables, which were no longer required for horses, into conservation studios rented to freelance specialists, who do work for the house and other clients. There is Michael Cowell for picture restoration; Blair Jeary for book conservation and bindings; Sheila Landi for textile conservation; Mervyn Thorpe as a blacksmith; Gwyn Watkins, a stonemason; Barry Witmond, a silversmith. Thus not only have some 350 pictures been put in order, but huge tasks like the Grand Staircase with Verrio's ceiling of *Hell* and its walls painted by Thomas Stothard with the *Horrors of War* have been tackled; a huge dent has even been taken out of one of the two silver cisterns.

However one of the ironies of the situation is that as enthusiasm for textile conservation has grown, facilities have been set up and people trained to do the work, there has been no growth in grant aid to help private owners. The work is highly labour intensive, and therefore expensive, and the costs often have little relationship to the value of an object on the open market. However at the same time the grant funds of the HBC and since 1985 English Heritage have been under increasing pressure and they have done very little in this field. Thus the major jobs tend to have been confined to those belonging to museums, which in effect means the Victoria and Albert Museum, and the National Trust.

As a result there appears to have been a certain withering of enthusiasm in the private sector, and fresh thought needs to be given to how to deal with old materials in country houses. If they are allowed to disappear, a large part of the patina of interiors will go too, and yet it is too big and too expensive a task to bring them up to museum display standard. It has been suggested that effort should be concentrated on first aid and making objects safe and stabilised so that more work can be done in the future when funds may be available. As it is, owners are discouraged by the estimates they receive and the knowledge that they are not going to get any support.

There is a particular good example of this at Doddington Hall, Lincoln, where two bedrooms (Fig. 28) shown to the public are lined

28. The Holly Bedroom at Doddington Hall, Lincolnshire. One of two tapestry-hung bedrooms fitted up in the early 1760s to create an antiquarian effect and now in need of extensive conservation work.

with 17th century tapestry that was much cut about, probably in the early 1760s when the rooms were refitted and the old tapestry was tacked up to give an air of antiquity in keeping with the carefully restored Elizabethan exterior. From a museum point of view the tapestries are not of great significance, nor are they of great value in commercial terms, but they are of great rarity in terms of the history of taste and for that reason are suitable candidates for grant-aided conservation. However, since they were a salvage job in the 18th century, they are particularly difficult to deal with now, because they are held up by their 18th century nails and when they are taken down they will probably collapse: so it will be a laborious job to take them down, clean them, attach them to a new backing and rehang them. Ten years ago the estimate was the unfaceable figure of £75,000 for each room.

(d) *The Changing Role and Views of Museums*

Most of the great museums in Britain are 19th century foundations and conceived metaphorically, if not literally, as temples of art, to inspire and improve as well dominate their visitors. In the late 20th century they house greater collections, but they have less authority than they did, partly because they are challenged by many other kinds of institution and a broad range of sites and sights including country houses. Nor do they now always seem to be the most relevant repositories for particular works of art and historical objects, as can be seen from the support

29. Bellotto's *View of Verona* in the Drawing Room at Powis Castle, Powys. In 1981 it was saved for the house in Wales rather than sold to the National Gallery in London as a result of the National Trust's campaign and the support of the National Heritage Memorial Fund and other bodies.

given to the National Trust by the NHMF in 1981 so that Bellotto's *View of Verona* would stay at Powis Castle rather than be acquired by the National Gallery and removed from central Wales to London (Fig. 29). That is implicit in much of the legislation relating to works of art in the past half-century, and it has been expressed in a number of decisions and actions taken by museums themselves in the past 30 years. Also it has been recognised by the National Art Collections Fund, which now occasionally helps the National Trust with acquisitions. The first time this happened was in 1979 when the NACF contributed £1000 towards the Trust's purchase of Thomas Phillips's portrait of the 3rd Earl of Hardwicke for Wimpole Hall. In 1988 the Fund contributed £250,000 towards the Trust's purchase of Linnell's spectacular merman sofas for the drawing room at Kedleston. By 1997 it had contributed no less than £540,000 to Trust purchases for its houses.

That change in museums is one of the encouraging developments of the past 25–30 years, and it involves both national and regional institutions. Here it is conceivable that the thinking has come to London rather than from it, and certainly in the early 1970s the National Gallery of Scotland under Colin Thompson was much more aware of the importance of historic collections in Scotland and the need to protect them than was the National Gallery in London concerned for comparable collections in England. As he wrote of the portraits by Gainsborough and Reynolds in the dining room at Bowhill: 'In this environment where they are still family portraits looking down from the walls on their descendants, the value of each portrait bears no relation to its price on the market for each one is an organic part of the whole situation, and is seen to be so by the public who go to visit the house. By comparison, the pictures screwed on to the bare, antiseptic walls of our galleries are like corpses laid out in a morgue.'

Also it is important to remember the loans from country house collections to national institutions. The outstanding one, of course, is the loan from the Duke of Sutherland of his pictures to the National Gallery of Scotland. But at the present time a visit to the National Gallery in London will reveal a number of important pictures on loan from historic private collections in country houses, although they are seldom named. Similarly a visit to the new Silver Gallery at the Victoria and Albert Museum will reveal some important loans from unidentified country house collections.

Relations between country houses and the curatorial staff of regional museums can be very important to the latter, particularly for loans to temporary exhibitions. Here the Castle Museum at Norwich and Temple Newsam at Leeds can produce lists of exhibitions stretching back over many years that have drawn on country houses in their areas.

However in certain fields, notably the decorative arts, interior design and furniture, country houses can do much more in Britain than museums. That can be seen in the way major cities, mainly in the Midlands and the North of England, took on country houses that had been swallowed up by their expansion and adapted them as museums: these include Aston Hall, Birmingham; Temple Newsam, Leeds; Astley Hall, Chorley; and Heaton and Platt Halls, Manchester. Other examples include Christchurch Mansion at Ipswich, Lydiard Park, Swindon, and most recently and successfully, Tredegar, in South Wales. But not all have been able to build up collections worthy of their settings.

Here the role of the Victoria and Albert Museum is particularly significant, because since the late 1960s it has become increasingly interested in keeping things where they belong and helping to achieve that. This can be seen in the way that in 1986–87 it acquired, with the aid of

30. The pair of bookcases by John Channon at Powderham Castle, Devon. These key signed pieces were acquired by the Victoria and Albert Museum in 1985–86 so that they would remain on loan in the house for which they had been made.

the National Heritage Memorial Fund, the Powderham bookcases (Fig. 30) in order to lend them back to the house, and in the way that it conserved the Erddig bed. Earlier it was involved in the acquisition of the seat furniture from the Painted Room at Spencer House, lending it first to Kenwood and then back to Spencer House, and with Temple Newsam lending back the Vardy tables for the dining room; similar thinking led to its acquisition of the Stoneleigh communion table in the hope that it would go back to the house. Through operation of the Museums and Galleries Commission Acquisition Fund it has since 1976 helped the National Trust make a number of acquisitions for its houses, the first being for chattels for Uppark in 1976. There is a limit of £80,000 a year and a purchase price of £300,000 for an object, but subject to those conditions the Trust can ask for £2 for every £1 it raises. By 1997 that scheme had produced £627,000 for the Trust.

The Museum is now considering how to return to their correct settings the room from Sizergh Castle, in Westmorland, and the state bed from Boughton House in Northamptonshire, which it conserved in 1976 but no longer has sufficient space to display.

That thinking has slotted in with the Museum's long-cherished plan to rethink its Primary Galleries: since the Second World War these 14 large galleries have shown the development of the decorative arts in England from 1450 to 1900. The Museum's collection is undoubtedly the most important of its kind in the country, and so in the world; but it also has to be recognised that, since it has never been built up with the Primary Galleries in mind, it lacks balance and has many surprising weaknesses. Nor has it sufficient space to display all the major objects it owns or might acquire in the future, because, unlike other departments, it does not have galleries for a study collection.

When the galleries were set up, the period rooms played a central role and they have always been popular, but in recent years curators at the Victoria and Albert Museum and most other museums have been less than enthusiastic about them, and the new display in the Victoria and Albert Museum will include fewer rooms than in the past. One of the arguments in support of this is that since the late 1940s a range of much finer rooms with their original furniture have become available to visitors through the opening of country houses in Britain.

The V and A rooms have become, like old friends, battered by time and, while they will be missed, it has to be accepted that of the late 17th and 18th century rooms only the Music Room from Norfolk House, in

London, is of the highest quality. Also surprisingly the Museum has no sets of furniture other than the Glemham Hall set bought for the Norfolk House room in 1970. It does not own a complete set of drawing room or dining room furniture, for instance, and it cannot arrange a dining table of any date with chairs and silver or silver gilt.

Probably the nearest to a complete room in a decorative arts museum in a historic house is the Gallery at Temple Newsam, which has many of its pictures and most of its furniture. And now, since its recent restoration with a copy of its original green flock wallpaper, it is once again one of the outstanding interiors of the early 1740s in England. However, although Temple Newsam has built up the finest collection of furniture outside London, it has not yet another complete room.

That situation and way of collecting as well as matters of funding mean that no museum in Britain can step in and try to buy all the furniture designed for a room when it is put up for sale. That can be seen with the saloon at Brocket Hall, Hertfordshire, from which part of the Chippendale furniture was sold in 1994; or with the chairs sold in 1990 from the set in the Music Room at Powderham from which the Victoria and Albert Museum acquired the fine grate by Thomire. Nor was it possible to hold together that part of the furniture from the Great Room at Arlington Street, London, sold from Aske Hall, Yorkshire, in 1997, even though it was the only set of chairs designed by Adam and made by Chippendale and the Victoria and Albert Museum already had one side chair; or the furniture including the framed portraits from the dining room at St Giles's House, in Dorset (Fig. 31), even though that house is crucial to mid-18th century furniture studies.

Looking at the limited role that museums can play, we can see why the documented collections in country houses are so important, and why the National Heritage Memorial Fund was so right to step in in the way it did at Kedleston, Nostell, Paxton and Burton Constable, where the documented furniture plays such a central role in the entity.

The Leeds City Museums, and in particular Temple Newsam, have long had an open approach to country houses in other ownerships. Thus when the first in lieu *in situ* case came up, the Doddington Reynolds, Leeds was prepared to accept it. A little later Temple Newsam stepped in with the NHMF to save the Burton Constable wine coolers (Fig. 32) and then the specimen tables from the gallery there when they would otherwise have gone abroad. So when the NHMF was trying to establish a charitable trust for Burton Constable it naturally

31. The Dining Room at St Giles's House, Dorset. The pictures and furniture that were an integral part of this room have been dispersed in recent years.

looked to Leeds for help, and the contents of the house were given to it; and the staff at Temple Newsam have been very active in the running of the Burton Constable Foundation.

The National Portrait Gallery has not the space to show all its pic-

32. The Dining Room at Burton Constable, Yorkshire. Beneath the side table can be seen one of the cisterns made for the house and whose sale by auction and acquisition by Temple Newsam at Leeds indirectly led to the establishment of the charitable trust for the house and its contents.

tures in its galleries in St Martin's Place, and so in 1972 it embarked on a scheme with the National Trust to display early portraits that were more or less contemporary with Montacute, where the Trust had always been short of pictures. After that it embarked on a second scheme for hanging late 17th and early 18th century portraits at Beningbrough, a house built in the first quarter of the 18th century and where again the Trust was short of pictures. Since then it has embarked on a third partnership scheme, for Victorian portraits, and also involving the Victoria and Albert Museum and the Royal Academy, at Bodelwyddan Castle, in North Wales, a house that had been used as a school and was bought by Clwyd County Council in the early 1980s. That opened to the public in 1988. Since 1994 the castle has been run by the independent Bodelwyddan Castle Trust, with Denbighshire County Council, the successor to Clwyd in 1996, the principal funding body.

In Scotland there have been a number of loans from the National Galleries of Scotland to foundations in houses and houses in public and also private ownership. The most ambitious schemes have involved the National Gallery at Paxton House, Berwickshire, and Duff House, Banff. At Paxton, which was established as a charitable trust by the NHMF, it was desirable to restore the early 19th century picture gallery from which the pictures had been sold in 1892: with the support of the National Gallery of Scotland that has now been hung with pictures from the Gallery's reserves.

The more ambitious Duff House project shows in an interesting way how thinking about houses and museums have come together in recent years. Most unusually William Adam's great house was taken into guardianship in 1956 and then repaired between the late 1960s and early 1980s; but no satisfactory use could be found for such an ambitious building with no contents in a remote place. However by the late 1980s thinking had changed so much about the relationship of houses and museums that Historic Scotland began to think about establishing a gallery there. Finally in 1989 Historic Scotland, the National Galleries and the local authorities agreed to explore the possibility of creating a country house gallery in the house, and that was opened to the public in 1995.

One of the most imaginative cases has been the purchase by Abbott Hall, an independent historic house museum at Kendal, of the Hothfield portraits formerly at Appleby Castle in Westmorland. It was felt essential that the large collection should be kept together and in a place as close as possible to their historic home; and, while many of the pictures are of archival rather than artistic significance, among them is one of the most remarkable icons of the 17th century, the Great Picture commissioned by Lady Anne Clifford, which Abbott Hall has lent back to Appleby Castle.

The coming together of museums and country houses is not often commented on, but anyone who has even one toe in the two spheres must realise how they now shade into each other, performing complementary roles at many levels rather than being embattled opponents as they seemed 30 years ago.

(e) *The Working of In Lieu and the Significance of In Lieu In Situ*

The system of accepting works of art, objects and archives in lieu of tax is particularly difficult to write about in the summer of 1998, because in recent years a number of problems have built up and it is not clear how the changes in the Finance Act 1998 will effect the working of the system. The most welcome and indeed long requested proposal is that no longer will the acceptance of works of art in lieu of tax be regarded as public expenditure with the Revenue to be compensated for revenue forgone and for calls on the Public Expenditure Reserve to be approved by the Treasury. If that goes through, it should make the operation of the system much simpler and swifter, and hopefully it will also unblock the log-jam of cases in the pipeline that, according to Hansard, now represents a value of £52 million.

In the past private treaty sales could be arranged for any exempt or exemptable object, but from now on they will be possible for any object that is already exempt or could be exemptable as being pre-eminent. Thus if objects cease to be exempt, they will be harder to sell by private treaty under the new rules. Also it has to be settled who advises on the pre-eminence of objects. Here it may be relevant that the Commission on Museums and Galleries advises on the pre-eminence of objects in in-lieu deals. For bodies such as the National Trust historical association will continue to be appropriate.

However, in order to understand what might happen from now on, it is necessary to understand how the system of accepting works of art, objects and archives in lieu of tax established in the Finance Acts of 1953 and 1956 worked remarkably well both for public institutions and the National Trust until the early 1990s. Moreover the extension of the acceptance of works of art for houses belonging to the National Trust to houses in private ownership open to the public was starting to solve a number of problems. However, since 1993–94 the value of the acceptances in lieu has never reached the allowance indicated by the Treasury in the mid-1980s, when it extended its allocation of £2 million, introduced when the NHMF was set up, to permit drawing on the Public Expenditure Reserve up to £10 million–£12 million a year.

In 1993–94 there were 17 cases totalling £3 million that were accepted; in 1994–95 27 cases totalling £6.6 million; in 1995–96 20 cases totalling £9.5 million; in 1996–97 18 cases totalling £1.4 million. The most recent figure, given in the Report of the Museums and Galleries Commission for 1996–97, strikes a warning bell, suggesting various possibilities: the system may be running out of steam, there may be a temporary log-jam, or it may relate to the general cutting back of the new Government on the arts and heritage fields. In fact the cut-back or log-jam goes back to the last Government.

In recent years a considerable proportion of the cases have involved post-1850 works of art and objects; these have tended to come from new collections rather than from historic collections in country houses, as was so in the 1960s and 1970s. However a number have come from the latter, and, since several owners of notable historic collections have died in recent years, it might be presumed that at least some objects would have been offered in lieu. But what has happened to them? Are they stuck in a secret Government log-jam?

What is so curious about this is that the system does not involve any real money being expended by the Treasury, but rather the expenditure arises from its traditional approach to bookkeeping when anything forgone is seen as expenditure.

The presumed backlog probably includes a few cases whose lack of resolution will be causing real inconvenience to owners, who cannot make any move until they know where they stand. So that also brings the system into disrepute and encourages owners to go straight to auction, gamble on getting a better nett price, with the near certainty that most of the objects of international appeal will go abroad because no British institution can acquire them against the figure on the export licence.

However, from the point of view of country houses what is also very serious is the decline in in lieu *in situ* cases. There were none in 1993–94, 1994–95 and 1996–97, and only one in 1995–96. That involved three pieces of French furniture at Longleat, which were allocated to the Victoria and Albert Museum for long-term loan to the house, the first time furniture had been dealt with in this way.

The in lieu *in situ* system is such an excellent way of keeping objects in their historic setting and fits in so well with the thinking that has lain behind Getting Things Back Where They Belong (explored on p. 183), as well as solving tax and other major problems that occur in country houses, that it is worth considering some of the cases that have been accepted since the mid-1970s.

It was the success of the in lieu arrangements with the National Trust that led in the early 1970s to the idea that the practice might be extended to the private sector. A good test case was needed, and conveniently one came to light at Doddington Hall, Lincolnshire. The only way to settle it was for a sale of contents that would have been very damaging to the house and contradicted the efforts to preserve it through the repair programme being funded by the Historic Buildings Council. So a large Reynolds portrait of the Earl and Countess of Mexborough was offered in lieu in 1974, and eventually, after nine years of negotiation, it was accepted by the Treasury and allotted to Leeds City Art Galleries for permanent loan to the house.

A significant early case involving a charitable trust was over a group of important historical portraits at Arundel Castle, Sussex, which were accepted in lieu of tax in 1975 on the death of the 16th Duke of Norfolk and allotted to the National Portrait Gallery for display at Arundel.

The other cases have been Van Dyck's *Betrayal of Christ* in the Gallery at Corsham Court, Wiltshire (1984) (Fig. 33), Lawrence's portrait of Sir Mark Masterman Sykes and his wife and brother Tatton at Sledmere (1986), a pair of Roubiliac busts in the library at Mellerstain (1988–89), the Beechey full-length of Sir Bellingham Graham in the Great Hall at Norton Conyers (1982); six portraits by Cotes in the drawing room at Cawdor Castle (1985); Lucas de Here's *Tudor Succession* at Sudeley Castle (1989); Beechey's portrait *The Children of the 1st Lord Porchester* at Hichclere (1990); and Guido Reni's *Joseph and Potiphar's Wife* at Holkham (1992–93) (Fig. 22).

The first complete room to be preserved in this way was the Tapestry Drawing Room at Hagley Hall, Worcestershire (Plate VI), one of the most remarkable rooms of the 1750s, which was formed round a set of slightly earlier Joshua Morris tapestries and included the related furniture.

For the system to work well there needs to be an appropriate museum in the area, not only to hold the objects but to be satisfied with standards of security and atmospheric control. Here the 1985 extension of government indemnity to cover objects belonging to non-national institutions has helped, but costs of conservation and security remain a serious problem for any accepting institution, because of potential liabilities. Also there are only limited benefits for the ratepayers who contribute to the running of local authority museums. So it is reasonable for receiving institutions to expect at least a conservation budget.

33. The Gallery at Corsham Court, Wiltshire. The big picture on the right is Van Dyck's *Betrayal of Christ*, which was the subject of an in-lieu in-situ deal in 1984 and is lent to the house by Bristol City Art Gallery.

It is disturbing that the Department of Culture, Media and Sport has brought out new guidelines for acceptance of in lieu *in situ* cases that include a normal access provision of 100 days a year. That would restrict future deals to houses that are show places, like Longleat and Arundel, and take no account of the role of major objects in smaller houses, like Doddington and Norton Conyers, which may be open between 30 and 60 days, or of the conservation needs of objects, particularly those involving textiles, where attention needs to be paid to the National Trust's advice on the exposure of contents to light.

There could be very serious consequences if some of those offers now in the pipeline that were begun under the rules existing at the time have to be dealt with under the new ones. They could lead to very damaging sales as well as upsetting the delicate financial situation of at least one house.

What is needed is more of these deals, not fewer.

(f) *The Pressure to Sell and the National Defences*

The most worrying aspect of the country house scene in Britain is the constant draining of works of art and contents. The process has been going on for over 100 years now, and still it continues. In fact there must be very few, if any, historic collections in country houses from which nothing of importance has been sold in the past 25 years, as can be seen from *Private Treaty Sales: Christie's Sales to the Nation 1956–1982*, and its *Sales to the Nation 1957–1990*, from the list in Michael Sayer's *Disintegration of The Heritage* and from the annual reports of the Reviewing Committee on the Export of Works of Art (but it is not always clear where objects come from).

Owners hang on to inherited works of art for as long as possible, and they get depressed when they have to make sales. However at the end of the day these are the non-productive, indeed income-consuming, assets that sometimes have to be sold. So the changes relating to exemption of works of art in the Finance Act 1988 threaten to upset the present delicate balance in many places.

Sales usually take place for a combination of reasons – to settle capital taxes on death or possibly arising through a transfer, to raise money to fund repairs or endow a charitable trust, or to pay for estate improvements. Sometimes they occur to provide for members of a family under the terms of a will or to settle liabilities that have occurred through ventures going wrong. In some cases the objects are an integral part of a historic collection, but not always, since they may have been inherited in recent years, possibly from another collection. Many of them are subject to existing exemption claims, and so their disposal means a hefty charge for that as well as CGT, so the difference between the gross price achieved, particularly at auction, and what the vendor finally receives may be very great. On the other hand most owners would prefer to solve their problems if they can through the disposal of one major item rather eat away round the edges of a collection.

The sales are a matter of both quantity and quality, because collections continue to be creamed off and lose their stars. Quite apart from major groups of Old Master drawings from Chatsworth and Holkham, there have been a wide range of pictures and sculpture including several Van Dycks from Althorp; the Florentine cabinet from Badminton; the *Bromley Davenport Altarpiece* by Taddeo Gaddi from Capesthorne Hall,

Cheshire; the Bernini bust, a recent discovery, as well as Gentileschi's *Finding of Moses* and Guercino's *Erminia finding the Wounded Tancred* from the Gallery at Castle Howard, where they were the key pictures; Hals's *Young Man with a Skull* from Elton; Terbruggen's *The Concert* from Eastnor Castle; Fra Bartolommeo's *Holy Family with the Infant St John* from Firle Place, in Sussex; Holbein's *Lady with a Squirrel* and de Troy's *La Lecture de Molière* from Houghton; Van Dyck's *1st Duke of Hamilton* from Lennoxlove; Bermejo's *St Michael Triumphant* from Luton Hoo; *The Fortress of Konigstein* by Bellotto from Madresfield Court, Worcestershire; Ingres's drawing of Lord Grantham from Newby; *Daniel and Cyrus before the Idol Bal* by Rembrandt from Port Eliot, Cornwall; Titian's *Venus and Adonis* from Somerley Park, Hampshire; Constable's *The Lock* from Sudeley Castle, Gloucestershire; *The Courtyard of a House in Delft* by de Hooch from Wrotham Park, Middlesex.

However it is not satisfactory just to compile a token list of losses from houses, or try to compile a list of houses from which groups of things have been sold, which would include Althorp, Houghton, Luton Hoo and Mount Stuart. As with taxes, which need to be looked at collectively as well as individually, sales of works of art have to be related not only to the in lieu system, which has already been discussed, but to the working of private treaty sales, the export system and the purchasing powers of public institutions. Each element depends on there being enough money in it to make the whole have a chance of working relatively effectively. Here it is impossible to go into each part in any detail, but at least it can be suggested how they fit together.

In the first reports the Trustees of the National Heritage Memorial Fund were concerned about the situation. In 1980–81 they said: 'We are deeply worried . . . by the continuing pressures on owners of important heritage items to dispose of them to meet tax demands or, quite simply, to cope with recession and provide for the future . . . The nation finds itself in the contradictory situation of encouraging, even demanding, conservation on the one hand and of discouraging it, or making it financially impossible, on the other.'

The following year it returned to the theme: 'The future of the great house and its historically associated contents still poses the greatest problem so far as the man-made heritage is concerned. Our objective is to retain the characteristics of a house as a setting for the outstanding works of art it contains, often collected over many centuries and now a legacy not to be casually dispersed. Wherever possible, we seek to preserve an outstanding house and its contents intact.' Eighteen years on, the drain continues, and it is difficult to see how it can be checked, but any study of historic houses must draw attention to its effect.

The fullest list of sales up to 1992 is to be found in Michael Sayer's *The Disintegration of a Heritage* and, while there are a number of successes with contents saved for houses or for museums, a considerable number of important objects have left the country. In whatever way the list is looked at, it is a formidable one, and the first problem is the way that the Government's purchase grants for the national institutions have been frozen since 1985. Thus if an outstanding picture or work of art appears on the market and a public institution has not been able to secure it at that stage, the only way to retain it in the country is for an institution to object to its export if a licence is applied for. That means that the object has to meet the standards laid down by the Waverley Committee and the institution also has to be able to raise the sum on the export application.

As the Reviewing Committee reported in 1990–91: 'We do not know how we could have put more strongly the case for adequate grants for our museums and galleries. The Waverley system, formulated in a period of post-war austerity, assumed that public collections would have sufficient funds to make pre-emptive acquisitions of important works of art and that, in the last resort, Treasury grants would be available to acquire objects in cases where the Reviewing Committee had recommended that a decision on the licence should be deferred but public collections have been unable to raise the necessary funds . . . grants are still frozen at their 1985 levels . . .'

The Reviewing Committee's reports make dismal reading, because year after year the pattern is repeated, with objections being raised to the granting of licences to export, but then no institution being able to put in a bid, particularly if the price of the object is very high. In 1992–93, for instance, when 15 cases worth a total of over £22.5 million were deferred so that British institutions could try to make bids, only five were successful; and they were for the more modest items whose total value only came to £747,880.

The situation has been helped to some degree by the introduction of the Heritage Lottery Fund, which produced £18 million in 1995–96 and about £18.5 million in 1996–97 towards the costs of purchasing pictures, furniture, works of art and manuscripts, but that will go down again in 1998. Also the system of partnership funding caused problems for institutions. For instance, with the Firle Fra Bartolommeo in 1995–96 the National Gallery of Scotland would have had to raise £3.5 million as its 25%, and yet its purchase grant for the year only came to £1.3 million. Similarly, when the Walker Art Gallery in Liverpool needed £650,000 as its 25% for the former Ince Blundell *The Journey of The Three Kings*, that was only slightly less than the total purchase grants for all the National Museums on Merseyside.

On the other hand occasionally some cases do have a happy outcome. Two successes in country house terms were the Burton Constable wine cisterns (Fig. 32), which were acquired by Temple Newsam in 1988, and the gallery tables from the same house, also acquired by Temple Newsam after they were sold by auction in 1989. Both the cisterns and tables are now back in the house, but without the export system they would have gone abroad – and possibly the house might never have become a charitable trust, because it was their sale that provided the warning signals that something needed to be done about its future.

In 1996 the 7th Marquess of Bristol sold the contents of the family wing at Ickworth, and included in the sale were a number of pictures removed from the main house in 1956 when it passed to the National Trust. The Trust was anxious to secure many of these in order to restore as far as possible the arrangement of pictures that had survived largely untouched from 1830 to 1956 and also the character that they had given the house. Thanks to the support of the HLF, the first of its kind in that sphere, the Trust was able to secure 16 lots of pictures at auction for £214,000. That has enabled it to recreate the original hang in the library, the largest of the rooms after the entrance hall, by combining purchases with pictures already in its ownership. Only an Andrea del Sarto is now missing, but that left the house some years ago, and so it has been replaced by a copy of a Guido Reni bought at the sale. The result is a double gain, because not only is the library greatly enriched, but that has released two of the major pictures in the house, the conversation pictures by Hogarth and Gravelot, to be hung in the smoking room, the third major picture room in the house, where they are seen to greater advantage, with visitors being closer to them, and the room itself is greatly strengthened by their presence.

How is the private treaty sale mechanism working? Sometimes it does not, because there is not a sufficient tax liability arising from a past exemption to make it worthwhile for the vendor to take that route.

Sometimes it does not work because valuations cannot be agreed between the vendor and the purchaser; and in a sufficient number of cases the vendor is proved to be right even making allowance for the tax to be paid and the douceur to be waived. Owners feel that galleries want to negotiate down for what is the generally accepted price taking the douceur into account, so that lowers the price and the amount of the douceur.

Among the successfully concluded private treaty sales of works of art from country houses in recent years are the Hals from Elton, the Holbein from Houghton, the Terbruggen from Eastnor and the Bermejo from Luton Hoo, all mentioned at the start of this section; the portrait of Lord John and Lord Bernard Stuart by Van Dyck, formerly at Broadlands and sold in 1988 to the National Gallery; portraits of Mr and Mrs Fleetwood Hesketh by Wright of Derby, formerly at Meols Hall, Lancashire, and sold to the Walker Art Gallery, Liverpool, in 1991; a terracotta bust of Sir Andrew Fountaine by Roubiliac, formerly at Narford Hall, Norfolk, and sold in 1992 to the Castle Museum, Norwich; *The Iron Forge* by Wright of Derby, formerly at Broadlands, and sold in 1992 to the Tate Gallery; and in 1996 Durer's *St Jerome* from the Bacon Collection sold to the National Gallery, and Hogarth's portrait *The Jones Family* formerly at Fonmon Castle, in Wales, sold to the National Museum of Wales. In 1998 the Victoria and Albert Museum acquired by a hybrid arrangement of private treaty sale and acceptance in lieu the only recorded surviving set of silver wine fountain, cooler and cistern that had been recently discovered at Shirborne Castle, Oxfordshire.

In recent years there has also been a much more active market in family archives, and a number of the collections have only been secured through the support of the National Heritage Memorial Fund (marked here with an asterisk). Among those from country houses or relating to old English families there have been negotiated sales of papers from Melbourne, Derbyshire;* Ugbrooke, Devon,* including the Secret of Dover; the Duke of Abercorn's Scottish archive; the Marquess of Lothian's Scottish papers;* the Duke of Marlborough's papers; the Brownlow of Belton papers;* the Chichester Constable papers; the Sir William Petty papers and Lansdowne papers from Bowood.*

(g) *Getting Things Back Where They Belong*

If the continued draining of contents from country houses and the creaming off of their historic collections are the most serious and insoluble problems, they have become much more obvious as a result of recent research and a consequent desire to get things back to where they belong. While it is like trying to dam a torrent with pebbles, the thinking and initiatives connected with these repatriations have become important; and the successes, which are generally unrecognised, are worth listing. Moreover it is worth thinking about the increasing influence of research on contents and collections that got under way during the 1960s and the arrangement of houses by the Victoria and Albert Museum, the National Trust and English Heritage at Osterley, Ham, Erddig, Cragside and Audley End. This has brought about a much stronger awareness of the point of complete rooms and complete houses. First it influenced the broadening of the rules of exemption of works of art and then the introduction of the concept of in lieu *in situ* for houses in private ownership. It has also influenced the thinking of the NHMF and the HLF, certain decisions at the Victoria and Albert Museum, and the National Art Collection Fund's help to the National Trust.

So far little, too little, has been done for houses in private ownership, except for those few in lieu *in situ* cases listed on p. 176, but it is surprising how many owners try to acquire pictures of family interest that sometimes come from other houses being sold up or appear unexpectedly on the art market. Among examples that come to mind are Jonathan Richardson's portrait of the 1st Lord Leicester painted just after his return from Italy which was sold from Shotesham and bought by the present Lord Leicester, Fleming of Rydal portraits and one of Sir George Fletcher's second wife from local houses that have been added to the gallery at Hutton-in-the-Forest, Reynolds's hitherto unknown portrait of Mary Duchess of Montagu that was bought for Deene, and the big Wootton conversation picture of Sir Robert Walpole and his family bought for Houghton.

Immense effort has to be put into each success in this field, and their number is limited by the amount of money available. But surely the increasing number of examples also underlines the illogicality of the present situation where there is no relationship between the official help given to structures and to their contents?

Although the movement seems to have started in 1965 at Dyrham, in Gloucestershire, with the state bed being lent back to the National Trust by the Lady Lever Art Gallery at Port Sunlight, it only really got under way after 1975, and it has gathered pace as can be seen from the selection of cases that follows. Others could be cited at Burton Constable, Dunham Massey, Farnborough, Kenwood, Powis, Uppark, Stoneleigh, The Vyne and Wimpole.

Temple Newsam at Leeds has been one of the most active places. It started to acquire furniture original to the Gallery as early as 1939, and has made subsequent purchases in 1947, 1976 and 1983. In 1989, after the library table by William Hallett was rediscovered in New York, that was bought back with the aid of the NACF and other funds. In 1992–93 a pair of mid-18th century Brussels tapestries probably given to Lady Hertford by the Prince Regent were identified at a country house sale in Ireland and bought with the help of the NHMF and NACF. Then in 1996–97 the state bed made in Paris in 1770 was bought with the help of the NHMF and other bodies after an export licence was withheld.

The National Trust has been making increasing efforts to buy back the contents of houses, in part through the generous support of the NHMF and the NACF. In the case of Kedleston that process started even before it acquired the house, because in 1980–81 the NHMF made several purchases of objects sent for sale by Lord Scarsdale in the hope that they could eventually return to the house. Then in 1986–87 it helped the Trust acquire the so-called Rembrandt *Head of an Old Man*, which had been sold to pay death duties in 1930, so that it could go back on its original hook in the music room. The same year the NHMF bought the Kedleston silver epergne from the dinner service as a holding operation and in 1988 the Trust acquired it and also part of the dinner service, the latter with the help of the Victoria and Albert Museum and the Museums and Galleries Commission.

Among other Trust examples there has been the acquisition of the early 16th century Flemish triptych from the altar of the Roman Catholic chapel at Oxburgh Hall, Norfolk, a building not in the ownership of the Trust. To that the NHMF contributed £100,000. Then in 1990–91 the NHMF contributed £75,000 so that the National Trust could acquire for Coughton Court, Warwickshire, a group of medieval illuminated devotional manuscripts which had been in the house since the late 17th century. This was followed by the acquisition from the family of the portrait of Ann Throckmorton as a nun, the last remaining of the portraits by Largillière. That was achieved with the aid of a grant of £225,000 from the NHMF (see also p. 78).

Among examples in houses belonging to charitable trusts, in 1992–3 the NHMF contributed £123,000 so that the newly formed Paxton Trust could buy back for the newly restored Picture Gallery three of the original tables supplied by Trotter in 1814.

So far there has been only one case of a museum acquiring a major object to keep it in a private house. That was the Victoria and Albert Museum's purchase in 1985–86 of the unique pair of bookcases by John Channon at Powderham Castle, Devon (Fig. 30), for loan back to the house. Towards that the NHMF contributed £465,000.

In the case of the sale of the house and contents of Littlecote, Wiltshire, in 1985–86, the NHMF gave the Royal Armouries £94,000 towards securing the Civil War armoury that had belonged to Colonel Alexander Popham, a Parliamentarian owner of the house, and also contributed £185,000 towards a remarkable early 18th century bird's-eye picture of the house. The intention was that the armoury and picture should remain in the house as long as it was open to the public, but after the closure of the house and its sale again, the loans were withdrawn. The loans will be renewed by the Royal Armouries when they are satisfied with the security, environmental and access conditions.

Even this sample list is surely longer and more varied than might be expected and it confirms how much more seriously those who work professionally in the field regard the importance of completeness of rooms and houses, and how much more detailed thinking about country houses has become during the past 25 years.

6

◆

The Increasing Importance of Gardens, Parks and Landscapes 1945–1998

One of the principal elements in the history of country houses since the Second World War has been the build-up, indeed in recent years almost explosion, of interest in gardens, parks and landscapes, with many of the more elaborate preservation initiatives being garden and landscape-led. That enthusiasm has involved a bewildering number of threads that sometimes intertwine with those of houses and sometimes pursue an independent course. They include the revival and development of private gardening from the 1950s onwards, in which ladies played an important part; changing methods of work and styles of planting introduced to overcome rising costs and make use of improvements in machinery; new ways of growing plants; and the introduction of new species. In addition there have been the special challenges of gardening in places open to the public that involve trying to lengthen the season of interest to satisfy visitors. Also the increasing influence of garden history since the mid-1960s, as it has become an academic subject in its own right, has been important, and with it the development of schemes for the preservation and restoration of historic and also 20th century gardens. That combined with having to think out the implications of conditional exemption of the settings of buildings from first CTT, and now Inheritance Tax, has encouraged the expansion of preservation thinking from gardens to parks and parks to landscapes.

Moreover it is important to stress that the growth of specialist understanding has been matched by popular enthusiasm. The British have always been a nation of gardeners and the greater opportunities for garden visiting that have occurred through house and garden opening since the end of the Second World War meant that it has become an enormously popular pastime that gives pleasure and stimulus to people of every degree of knowledge. That can be seen from the great success of the National Gardens Scheme through which 3218 gardens were open in 1997, 372 of them for the first time.

On top of that comes the broader role of gardens, parks and landscapes as places of recreation and leisure, with those in private ownership attracting an estimated 45 million people a year, three times the number who visit the houses. Thus if it was possible to express the post-war interest in houses and gardens as two lines on a graph, they would not follow the same course.

In order to clarify the picture of what has happened, the period is divided into two stages, from 1945 to 1973, and from 1974 to 1998.

(a) *The Revival of Gardening after 1945 and the Growth of Garden History 1965–1973*

It is arguable that private gardening got going before work on houses and interiors after the war, because it was less hampered by rationing and restrictions. Certainly that is the impression given in *The English Woman's Garden* edited by Alvilde Lees Milne and Rosemary Verey in 1980, a book that explains a great deal about attitudes in the post-war period. Of the gardens described by their owners, Lady Heathcoat-Amory began to plan in earnest at Knightshayes, in Devon, in 1946; Lady Haddington began when she went to live at Tyninghame, in Scotland, in 1952; Lady Salisbury went to live at Cranborne, in Dorset, in 1954, and began to garden at Hatfield in the early 1970s. However the chief figure, who influenced them all, is missing, because she had died in 1962: Vita Sackville-West. So were two others who had been influential after the war, Margery Fish of East Lambrook Manor, in Somerset, who died in 1969, and Mrs Reiss, who with her husband, Captain F.E. Reiss, bought Tintinhull House, also in Somerset, in 1933 and gave it to the National Trust in 1954, seven years before her death.

Alongside these ladies were the professional garden designers and writers. Among them were Russell Page (1906–1985), the author of *The Education of a Gardener*, who after the Second World War worked more abroad; Sir Geoffrey Jellicoe (d. 1996), who was a designer of landscapes rather than gardens; and Lanning Roper (d. 1983), an American who settled in England after the war and turned to gardening, first as a writer and then as a designer. Jane Brown's book *Lanning Roper and his Gardens* (1987) is not only an excellent portrait of him but also provides a picture of the world in which he wrote about gardens and gardening in the years after 1950 and worked as a garden designer from the late 1950s until the early 1980s. It is especially interesting to see how he increasingly became a conservator of historic gardens from the mid-1960s, looking after a number of gardens belonging to the National Trust. Scotney was particularly important to him, because he had been a friend of Christopher and Betty Hussey since about 1952; and it was through Christopher Hussey's influence that he began to write for *Country Life*, which published articles by him over a period of 30 years.

Most of these post-war gardens were initially entirely private, only being open occasionally through the National Gardens Scheme and for local charities, but with older and established gardens related to country houses house opening and garden opening started to interlock, with the one stimulating the other. Sometimes it was the garden that was opened first, and the costs of the garden rather than of the house that were the determining factor.

Certainly that was so at Newby, in Yorkshire (Fig. 34), where the late Major Edward Compton had created a garden extending to 40 acres between the wars, employing about 12 gardeners up to 1939. To put that into perspective a leader in *Country Life* on 28 December 1935 reckoned that in a large garden one man could look after two acres and the cost of a garden of 10 acres was £550 a year. However a staff of 12 was unthinkable in 1945; and even with seven gardeners it was essential to open, a concept that Major Compton accepted with reluctance in 1948–49. However he was not prepared to accept change in the way the garden was run (or costed); and understandably did not want to hand over control to his son, Robin.

So it was only after Major Compton died in 1977, after a reign of 56 years at Newby, that Robin Compton, who had trained himself to be a professional plantsman, and his wife were able to take over and restore the garden as well as reform the way it was run; and it is the balance between restoration and reform that is the key. Mr Compton has retained all the vistas and perspectives created by his father, who was a friend of Lawrence Johnston of Hidcote and much influenced by his sense of architecture in gardening, but he has introduced changes to

34. An aerial view of Newby Hall, Yorkshire, showing the long herbaceous borders
leading from the house to the river.

make that possible. Hedges provide the framework for the design, but by the end of Major Compton's time they took four men four weeks to clip by hand; also some of them had grown too thick and were difficult to reach. Thus with the great herbaceous borders that form the spine of the garden, running down from the house to the river and framed by yew hedges, Mr Compton has narrowed the hedges to plant grass paths between them and the backs of the borders. This gives space for a small tractor and trailer with a two-tier platform from which men can operate long power-driven hedge clippers. By such rethinking all the hedges are now done by two men in two weeks. The borders also involved a great deal of staking and tying up, but now the plants grow up through fine netting. Mr Compton has also introduced a watering system covering the whole garden, which has replaced a laborious system of water carts. Mowing too has become more significant, and sophisticated variations in the way it is done make an important contribution to the look of the garden: there are now five main types of grass cutting at Newby, all done by machines.

Garden opening also now involves additional problems of security and public liability. So, sadly, occasionally fine and visually important trees have to be felled or areas closed to the public. Also access for the disabled has become more important and that involves not only simple ramps down steps, as into the Rose Garden at Newby, but altering the 19th century stonework framing the Statue Walk to provide a ramp up to Sylvia's Garden. Moreover, as with the interiors of houses, there are many problems to do with wear and tear, with grass paths, for instance, not standing up to the weight of visitors' feet, particularly in wet weather. But what should be done? And how should alternatives be paid for, if changes have to be made?

Newby illustrates the challenges and rewards of a great garden on the grand scale, and the improvement in its quality and interest in the past 20 years, combined with the creation of the Adventure Gardens for children in part of the old walled garden, is reflected in the growth of the number of visitors from 34,000 in 1978 to 55,000 in 1980, when the first phase of improvements was complete, and to 106,000 in 1990, with 70% now coming to the garden and 30% to the house.

From the early days of the National Trust's Country Houses Scheme it considered both houses and gardens, and one of the first major places to be offered was Stourhead, Wiltshire, in 1938. However it was not finally given to the Trust until 1946.

After the war, prompted by Lord Aberconway, the owner of Bodnant, in North Wales, and the President of the Royal Horticultural Society, the Trust began to think about what it might do for major gardens that were not attached to historic houses and particularly great 20th century gardens. Here it is right to recognise the contribution of people like the Earl of Rosse, who had been brought on to Trust committees when he came out of the army. He had great experience of gardens through his own notable garden at Birr in Ireland and the increasing problems of his parents-in-law's garden at Nymans in Sussex. It was out of this that grew the National Trust's parallel Gardens Scheme. Negotiations over Nymans began in 1948, although it did not finally come to the Trust until 1954, and the first 20th century garden to be accepted was, in fact, Hidcote, in Gloucestershire, also in 1948. That was followed by Bodnant in 1949.

By then the Historic Buildings Council was getting down to work, and one of the categories of building that it discovered to be in urgent need of help was garden buildings. In its report for 1954 it stated: 'Soon after we were appointed we discovered that there was one type of building which was in even greater danger when the Act became law than the historic house on which public attention has been concentrated. We refer to the garden buildings which have played so prominent a part in the history of English architecture. Many of the finest examples were in an advanced stage of decay by 1953, for owners who had made great sacrifices to try to keep the roof over their heads had naturally not been able to do so much to preserve temples, gazebos, obelisks and ornamental bridges in their gardens. Although many of these buildings have no use, or only occasional uses, we feel that the case for their preservation is strong . . . In 1954 we have, therefore, recommended grants for the complete restoration of Vanbrugh's Temple of the Four Winds at Castle Howard, for a programme of repairs to some of the most important buildings at Stowe, and for the group of buildings at Hagley . . .'

The emphasis on the 18th century was to be expected given the enthusiasms of the time, but what is surprising two generations later is how new a subject the landscape garden appears to have been and how few had been photographed. Again Christopher Hussey's role was important, but, although he had written *The Picturesque* as early as 1927, his first article on a landscape was that on Stourhead in 1938. It was only after the Second World War that he described more, starting with Rousham, in Oxfordshire, in 1946 and Stowe in 1947.

The Rousham articles also related to Margaret Jourdain's pioneering book *The Work of William Kent*, which was published in 1948 and to which Hussey contributed the Introduction. By then Dorothy Stroud, who had been Hussey's secretary at *Country Life* before the second war, had gone to Sir John Soane's Museum and resumed her pre-war idea of a study of Capability Brown, which appeared in 1950. Vanbrugh was receiving a new degree of attention first in David Green's *Blenheim Palace* of 1951 and then in Laurence Whistler's *The Imagination of Vanbrugh and his Fellow Artists* (1954). In 1958 David Green produced his study of Henry Wise, *Gardener to Queen Anne*. By then Christopher Hussey was planning what became his *English Gardens and Landscapes 1700–1750* (1967). In his preface he explained: 'Historians of garden architecture in England are few, but linked in friendship by shared pleasure in their subject . . . I began to concern myself over twenty years ago with the project of *Country Life*'s building up photographic material for a book on 18th century gardens and landscapes . . . Thenceforward I arranged the photographing . . . of at least one garden during each of a number of years, with the idea that the eventual book should supplement the 18th century volumes of *English Country Houses* already under consideration.'

The HBC's concern for garden architecture was encouraged by this new direction of research and writing, and how it bore practical fruit can be seen not only in individual grants but in the way grants led to schemes of preservation.

At Shugborough, in Staffordshire, the park had been seriously damaged by an American camp during the war, leaving its rococo and early neo-classical park buildings in decay, and so Viscount Anson, the Earl of Lichfield's heir, asked his old army friend, Lord Euston, now Duke of Grafton, about what could be done. That led to an application for and offer of a repair grant in 1955; and presumably it was the preliminary discussions about it that had stimulated Christopher Hussey to write three articles on the house and two on the landscape in *Country Life* in 1954. He ended them by saying that despite the military camp 'Shugborough is still a landscape of unique historic interest and, potentially, a regional amenity of first class importance.' Then, as a result of the heavy duties incurred on, first, Lord Anson's death in 1958 and then

Lord Lichfield's in 1960, the trustees, greatly encouraged by Lord Lichfield's widow, offered the house and its contents together with the park and its monuments in lieu of tax. In 1960 it was transferred to the National Trust with a lease to the Staffordshire County Council since there was no endowment.

Five years later the HBC offered a grant for the restoration of the garden buildings at Westbury Court in Gloucestershire, which is arguably the first post-war scheme of its kind and the start of the current movement for garden restoration. After the place was sold in 1960, the undistinguished house on the site was demolished by a speculator who hoped to build 10 houses flanking the canal. In 1963 planning permission ran out, and to its credit not only did Gloucestershire County Council refuse to renew it but with Gloucester District decided to buy the whole place so that they could give the garden layout to the National Trust for restoration. However it was only in 1967, thanks to the support of a benefactor, a public appeal and a grant from the HBC for the buildings, that it was able to do so. Restoration began the following year.

At Stowe (Fig. 35) there were no more HBC grants for the repair of buildings between 1954 and 1968, presumably because of the School's inability to produce matching funds, but nevertheless the School worked on 10 structures between 1950 and 1968. However, as a result of the intervention of Sir Ralph Verney, one of the governors of the School, who was deeply concerned at the deteriorating state of the buildings and the School's lack of a policy, the HBC was invited to visit Stowe. As a result a report was produced showing that £70,000 needed to be spent and the work could be tackled at the rate of £7000 a year. The following year the Stowe Landscape Committee was established to oversee the place, and in 1967, because the HBC was concerned that there was no way in which the settings of the buildings could be protected, it asked the School to give covenants over the heart of the property to the National Trust. A programme of grant-aided work then began, with offers of £13,500 and £14,960 in 1968 and 1969. But after that the pace slackened, and throughout the 1970s only six small grants, all less than £10,000, were offered; and the figure only rose to £27,500 in 1982–83.

In the late 1960s garden history began to give itself a capital G and H, to attract a larger and younger following who were attracted to the new Garden History Society, much more concerned with documentary research and so drawn to vanished and vanishing gardens and landscapes. In this it was a slightly younger sister of furniture history, but the proponents of both subjects were determined to prove that theirs were catching up with their older sisters, architectural and art history, and provided as much meat for PhDs.

How garden history was developing can be seen from the titles of some of the books. Edward Malins's *English Landscape and Literature 1660–1840* came out in 1966, and Christopher Hussey's *English Gardens and Landscapes* the following year.

The 1970s were a more productive decade. In 1970 came the first monograph on a landscape, *Landscape and Antiquity: Aspects of English Culture at Stourhead 1718–1838* by Kenneth Woodbridge. In 1971 Eileen Harris published in *Country Life* a series of three articles on the then virtually unknown Thomas Wright, who was, among other things, one of the key figures for rococo gardens and landscapes. In 1975 John Dixon Hunt and Peter Willis brought out *The Genius of the Place: The English Landscape Garden 1620–1820*. That was followed in 1976 by *Lost Demesnes: Irish Landscape Gardening 1660–1845* by Edward Malins and *The Knight of Glin* and *The Figure in the Landscape: Poetry, Painting and Gardening during the 18th Century* by John Dixon Hunt. *Charles Bridgeman and the English Landscape Garden* by Peter Willis, the first study of a gardener treated on the same scale as a major architect or painter, appeared in 1977. In 1978 John Harris published *Gardens of Delight, the Rococo Landscape of Thomas Roberts the Elder*.

By then writers were looking both backwards from the period 1700–1850 and forwards. Thus in 1979 Roy Strong published his *The Renaissance Garden in England*, while there was a growing interest in Lutyens and Jekyll from the late 1970s that stimulated the Lutyens exhibition of 1982 and also Jane Brown's *Gardens of a Golden Afternoon – The Story of a Partnership, Edwin Lutyens and Gertrude Jekyll*, which was published the same year.

The growing interest in parks and landscapes was also fanned by the threats from road builders, and there were a series of *causes célèbres* starting with Saltram in 1968, which the Trust fought and lost. Its case was not a strong one because it knew a road scheme was in the pipeline when it accepted the place in 1957 and declared it inalienable. It had, however, to fight the case because of its declaration over the land, its justification being that the road was considerably wider than that proposed a few years earlier. The Trust's rightness can also be seen from an aerial photograph that shows what a precious lung Saltram is for Plymouth and how its position has been weakened in recent years.

The year after Saltram came the campaign against the proposed Kendal link from Exit 36 on the M6 that was planned to cut across the avenue in the park at Levens Hall, in Westmorland. That had been planted by Guillaume de Beaumont in 1694 as an approach to a view over the narrow gorge of the River Kent. The garden at Levens had always been recognised as of great historic interest, but the significance of the park on the other side of the road was less widely appreciated. So the researches in the muniments by Annette Bagot FSA, the wife of Robin Bagot, the owner, which revealed unsuspected evidence about Beaumont's work in Levens' park, was crucial to the case against the line of the road. As a result of the public enquiry the route was altered so that the road avoided the avenue and the park and was carried on a bridge a little way up the gorge. It was probably the first time that garden history in its modern form played such a crucial role in a preservation battle.

Several other cases come to mind, among them the bypass at Petworth, in Sussex, the road through the valley at Farnborough, in Warwickshire, and the new M54 linking Telford to the M6 that cut through the park at Chillington in Staffordshire in the mid-1970s. Chillington, which was designed by Brown, lay in an area of then still remote and unspoilt country with the park and estate at Weston, Boscabel House, where the future Charles II hid after the battle of Worcester, and Tong with its beautiful church. Yet it is within eight miles of Wolverhampton. Both the Shropshire and Staffordshire County Councils were against the line of the road as was the Government's own inspector. Even so, and despite Staffordshire having declared the park a conservation area, the road was built only 35 yards from the back of the Greek Temple, listed Grade 1, and cut the White House off from the great lake as well as destroying the peace of the place and so much of the pleasure of the walk round the lake.

(b) *The Expansion of Restoration and Conservation in Gardens, Parks and Landscapes 1974–1998*

The years 1973–1974 conveniently make a break in the history of gardens and parks since the Second World War. Here again *The*

Destruction of the Country House exhibition in 1974 was a landmark, because it considered not only the house and its contents but its gardens and park and showed some of the current threats – the bypass at Petworth, the route of the M40 at Farnborough, in Warwickshire, the proposed sewage works in the park at Audley End, dereliction at Gibside, in Co. Durham, the decaying state of the garden at Biddulph Grange, in Staffordshire and of Chatelherault in Scotland. For the first time it brought to gardens and parks the same informed militancy of approach that had been developing in architectural circles in the late 1960s and was to be such a valuable stimulus to efforts in the years ahead. Moreover one important development was already in the pipeline when the exhibition was being planned, the Town and Country Amenities Act of 1974. That empowered the Historic Buildings Council to recommend for the first time grant aid for aspects of historic gardens other than buildings, and so was to open up a new direction for conservation in Britain that has proved and continues to be of unsuspected significance.

It was a logical step bearing in mind the development of thinking about areas through the concept of the conservation area and the general expansion of thinking about the built heritage and the environment. Thus in its report for 1975–76 the HBC wrote: 'As a result of the Town and Country Amenities Act, we have been asked to advise on historic gardens of outstanding importance which are not associated with buildings outstanding in themselves. Six such applications were under consideration at the end of the year covered by this report.' The following year it reported on its recommendations of grants for the pool that formed part of the layout created at Melbourne Hall, Derbyshire, about 1700, and the early 19th century Swiss Garden at Old Warden, Bedfordshire. Since then English Heritage has helped a number of garden schemes and now recommends grants to the value of about £200,000 a year.

The HBC had always been able to make up its own mind about what buildings it regarded as 'outstanding', but whereas it could usually check its thinking against the listing description of a building, there was no such background information on gardens and landscapes; and no one had any idea of the scale of the problem. The Garden History Society was already working on its first survey, which was produced as its *Preliminary List of Gardens, Parks, Grounds and Designed Landscapes of Historic Interest in England and Wales* in 1976. The following year Jennifer

Jenkins, then chairman of the HBC – despite the opposition of the D.o.E., reluctant to expand its vision because of shortage of funds – set up an informal gardens committee of the HBC to prepare its own preliminary list on a county by county basis that was to be complete by 1981.

It was this project that helped change attitudes within the D.o.E. and led the National Heritage Act 1983 to empower English Heritage to compile an official Register on lines similar to listing but without statutory powers: the idea was partly to 'highlight their importance to developers and statutory bodies and act as a warning against unsuitable development'. The following year it started on this Register of Parks and Gardens of Special Historic Interest; Scotland followed on in 1987. Since then the concept of the Register has evolved and become considerably more elaborate, reflecting the increasing sophistication of thinking and knowledge about the subject. The original version, compiled between 1984 and 1988, consisted only of written descriptions, with no plans or illustrations. By April 1988 it contained 1085 sites in 44 counties. That led to the development of the revised Register with descriptions and maps; also owners had to be notified that their property was on the Register. With the kind of places considered here notification did not create serious problems, but with historic layouts now in multiple ownerships it was a complicated process to discover who owned what and inform them.

At present English Heritage is carrying out a third revision to be completed in 2000 that involves visiting every site, checking and rewriting the descriptions where necessary, producing accurate maps and meeting owners. Then in 2001 a gazeteer listing all the sites will be published.

From the beginning the Government has stressed that the Register will not become statutory, like the lists of historic buildings, but naturally owners, and the HHA on their behalf, have been concerned that official attitudes might change. The best explanation of the principles put to me was that there has to be a distinction made between the framework of a garden and the details of planting, which are like decoration and constantly changing. Whereas colours and materials in rooms fade at different paces and in different ways, plants grow, often very quickly, and then peak before needing to be replaced. Thus any garden, whether it is recognised as 'historic' or not, is always in a greater state of transition than a house or any other building.

It seems that English Heritage is satisfied to rely on local authorities to use the Register in making plans and in protecting sites from development; and it accepts that inclusion on the Register does nothing to influence the way the land is managed or, if it is farmed, the way that is done. By June 1998 there were about 1200 sites on the Register, 10% Grade 1 and 28% Grade 2*.

What has also influenced the D.o.E. and from 1984 English Heritage has been their own involvement with the practical aspects of gardens and landscapes through running their own properties, particularly Belsay in Northumberland. Throughout the late 1960s and early 1970s efforts were made to find a solution to the problematic future of Belsay, with the finest complete neo-classical country house in Britain (but already, alas, without its contents), its ruined old castle with its pele tower and Jacobean mansion, and its remarkable picturesque garden linking the two. Finally it was acquired by the D.o.E. in 1982, but not much had been done by the time English Heritage took over; and it was the finding of a suitably qualified gardener and the management of the garden that ultimately led to English Heritage establishing its Landscape Division with its own specialist inspectorate about 1986. This new staff immediately began to think about management plans for historic landscapes that combined historical research and practical work, a concept that had been developed in the early 1980s in connection with the landscape at Chevening in Kent.

The combination of the Register, the production of grant-aided management plans and its experience running its own gardens also had an effect on English Heritage itself, broadening its approach to both its own properties and those in other ownerships.

The other important element has been the Countryside Commission, set up in its present form as the successor to the National Parks Commission under the Countryside Act 1968. It was conceived as a rural equivalent of the urban conservation idea, being charged with conserving and enhancing the natural beauty of the countryside, providing access and becoming a grant-giving agency. It first began to consider the role of landed estates when it promoted the idea of country parks, of which several were set up in the early 1970s by owners of country houses, among them the Duke of Wellington at Stratfield Saye and the Earl of March at Goodwood. However it was not until 1982, after the Commission became an independent body supported by a grant from the D.o.E., that it began to turn its attention to historic gardens and parks, combining its concern for enjoyment and leisure with conservation and historical thinking, a fusion that owed a good deal to Paul Walshe, who had been one of the original members of Jennifer Jenkins's unofficial gardens committee.

Its first case was at Blenheim where the landscape had suffered severely from the loss of all the elm avenues as a result of disease and of the beeches as a result of the drought of 1976. In 1982–83 the Commission funded a management plan for the whole landscape and since then it has grant-aided planting schemes at Blenheim every year.

At the same time as all these developments, conditional exemption of the settings of outstanding buildings from CTT presented a new challenge to those who had to advise on how to make the concept work on the ground, because it meant bringing together historical thinking, visual sense and a planning approach; and it is probably no accident that exemption for gardens and parks and settings should have followed so soon on the heels of the introduction of grant aid for gardens, that both should have come about as a result of the new kind of enthusiasm for garden and landscape history, and that they should have encouraged a much broader approach to landscape.

Just when English Heritage was trying to strengthen the Register and stimulate more management plans, the great storm of 16 October 1987 swept across the south-east of England and into East Anglia, wreaking havoc in gardens and parks as well as to planting in urban areas. At the time it was looked on as one of the great natural disasters of the century, but 10 years later many of those involved with landscape conservation see it as a turning point that helped to develop attitudes to the conservation of parks and landscape in England and promote a renewal of much over-mature planting that few people had had the courage to fell. Then before everyone had recovered there came the second great storm, on 26 January 1990, which caused damage from the Scilly Islands right across Southern England to North Norfolk. Together the two storms turned what had been rather tentative and underfunded projects by the Countryside Commission and English Heritage into a great opportunity to promote more positive schemes that marked the start of a more broadly based approach to parks and landscapes backed by special government funding.

Here it is important to stress that none of this could or would have happened without the preparatory work and all the research that had taken place over the 20 years that had culminated in English Heritage's

Register. That enabled English Heritage and the Countryside Commission to respond to the storm damage on many known sites and to press the Government for additional funding to help with the preparation of schemes for the clearance of fallen trees and replanting on outstanding sites where at least a degree of public access could be provided.

Rethinking after the storm produced the need for a new type of management plan that not only covers the area and deals with its history but sets down how it is to be looked after in the future and what needs to be done. Thus in the last 10 years parks and landscapes have been starting to attract a degree of considered attention that many have not received for well over 100 years.

As David Jacques wrote in English Heritage's *Conservation Bulletin*, June 1991: 'The whole exercise is proving rewarding in more than just the obvious sense that damaged landscapes are being repaired. First, the realisation that an historic landscape needs specialist attention, just like a historic house, is taking root among owners. Families who have owned their properties for generations may not have employed a designer since the 1850s, when the formal gardens next to the house were installed . . . Now with the encouragement of grants, restoration and management plans are being written which will serve the owners well in the long-term care of their parks and gardens . . . It is fair to say that there is much more expertise in dealing with historic landscapes available today than two years ago.'

Of the some 240 sites known to be damaged in 1987, about a third were judged to be outstanding. Then followed the second storm in 1990 with damage on 200 known sites, and of these 80 were found to be outstanding. Among the places helped were Helmingham, in Suffolk, Combe Bank and Knole, in Kent, and Gunton, in Norfolk.

The legislation of the mid-1970s not only encouraged the idea of charitable trusts for houses, but it led to the establishment of trusts for gardens. Indeed the first use of an educational trust for preservation was for the garden at Knightshayes, in Devon, which was set up by the late Sir John Heathcoat-Amory in 1955.

Among preservation trusts for gardens that for Painshill, in Surrey, has achieved the most publicity and attention. It owes its survival to Elmbridge Borough Council, which bought 64 hectares of the site between 1974 and 1980, but major work only began a few years later when Land Use Consultants produced a master plan for the site funded by the NHMF. Since then it has received generous grant aid.

A more modest trust, but one that was to bear the most unexpected fruit, was the Stowe Garden Buildings Trust, which was set up in 1986 by a group of friends, mostly old boys of the School, who loved the place but were not interested in the School. Their idea was to build up an endowment fund whose income could be used to help the owners of Stowe sustain a steady programme of repair. The Garden Buildings Trust's aims were explained in an article in *Country Life* on 24 August 1986, and that prompted a reader to make a generous and imaginative offer of £1.8 million to the National Trust if the governors of Stowe School would give it the grounds. The National Trust, of course, had held covenants over part of the site since 1968, and, also, in 1985 it had bought the Oxford Avenue, the last piece of Stowe property to remain in the hands of the family and the first that the Trust had ever bought to add to covenanted land; and in recognition of that the School had extended the area covenanted.

The School's generous response was to offer to the National Trust 275 acres of the grounds with 37 buildings. It took until 1989 for the Trust to accept that, because the complete financial package depended on receiving £4.5 million from the NHMF. Immediately work began to go ahead both on the buildings and their setting, and so far £4,344,000 has been spent on the restoration of buildings, among them the temples of Concord, Venus, Friendship and Ancient Virtue (Fig. 35).

The Trust has also acquired part of Stowe Castle Farm, Home Farm and the deer park and so now holds just over 1000 of the original 6000 acres. The transformation of the buildings and landscape has been one of the most remarkable achievements of the National Trust and now there is an air of optimism about the place that has probably not been present since well before the bankruptcy of the 1st Duke of Buckingham in the 1840s.

The way thinking has developed and has led into positive action can also be seen at Endsleigh, near Tavistock, in Devon. The great picturesque landscape created by Repton with its *cottage ornée* designed by Jeffry Wyatt as a holiday house for the 6th Duke of Bedford was acquired in 1962 by the Endsleigh Fishing Club, who used the house as a semi-private hotel. By the early 1980s it was clear that there was an increasing backlog of work to do on the place and at that time the Landmark Trust took on and restored the Dairy Cottage and Swiss Cottage. After Endsleigh was placed on the Register as Grade 1 and the 1987 storm occurred, it was chosen by English Heritage as one of 12

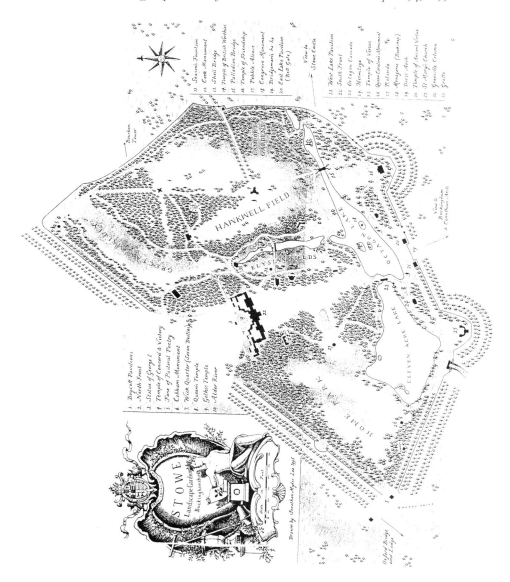

35. Stowe, Buckinghamshire. A 1995 re-interpretation of a mid-18th-century visitor's map showing the layout of the grounds and the monuments for use today.

places to take part in a pilot study of grants for outstanding parks and gardens. At the same time the Fishing Club decided to create a charitable trust for Endsleigh, granting it a 90 year lease, and that came into being in 1989. Work then went ahead on the Pilot Restoration Plan produced by the Colson Stone Partnership and by the end of September £400,000 had been raised including £113,500 from English Heritage. The following year the Trust launched a public appeal to raise another £100,000 and this was achieved by the end of the year.

The second element of the Endsleigh plan was to restore the house and a great deal was done in the years after 1989. However the Trust was short of £1.2 million to complete the work and endow the place, so in 1997 it applied to the HLF for £950,000 for capital works and £250,000 for endowment. It received about £1 million, and as part of the deal the Fishing Club gave to the charity the original furniture in the house that it had acquired in 1962. It is remarkable that so much of this survives and it was highly desirable that it should be tied to its setting in a formal way.

From the beginning the NHMF has been a generous supporter of the garden trust and garden and landscape restoration movement. One of its first decisions was to support the National Trust's acquisition of the Wimpole avenue, in Cambridgeshire. When the Trust was bequeathed the estate in 1976, it had 1 mile of the original 2¼ mile avenue of double elms, but these died in the 1970s. Then when in 1980 the Trust got the chance to buy the remaining 1¼ miles, the NHMF offered £47,000. In 1982–83 the NHMF promised the Trust £2 million so that it could acquire Studley Royal, which had been offered as a purchase by the North Yorkshire County Council. Among other Trust garden and landscape projects that the NHMF has contributed to has been Sheringham, in Norfolk, where, most unusually, in 1987 the Trust bought a notable country house and its landscape largely for the sake of the latter by creating a financial package also involving contributions from the Countryside Commission, Norfolk County Council and four bequests that it had received. In 1987–88 the NHMF contributed to the Trust's acquisition of Crom in Co. Fermanagh, an outstanding landscape covering part of Lough Erne that has remained largely unspoilt through its ownership by the estate and the lack of pressure from tourism due to the Troubles but is potentially very vulnerable. The Fund contributed to the restoration of several storm-damaged landscapes belonging to trusts, at Chevening, in Kent, in 1988–89, Petworth in 1989–90 and Arundel in 1990–91.

[203]

In 1993–94 the NHMF gave the Trust £309,000 to acquire more land at Gibside, in Co. Durham, a very decayed but once much admired 18th century landscape that is potentially of great importance in a heavily industrialised area. The same year it gave the Trust £200,000 towards the acquisition of the landscape at Prior Park running down from the mansion to the city of Bath. In 1995–96 the NHMF gave English Heritage a grant towards the acquisition of more land at Witley Court, Worcestershire, to protect the ruins of the house and its Victorian garden. The same year the HLF gave the Trust £4.9 million so that it could acquire the landscape at Croome Court, in Worcestershire, which was arguably the last chance for that early design by Capability Brown. It also helped the Trust with two other large grants, one of £792,000 to buy Home Farm at Stowe, and £825,000 to acquire land at Osterley with potential development value that slotted in with the Trust's restoration of the park.

However, garden and landscape making should not be just a matter of restoration and conservation and so it is encouraging that so many country house owners have made new gardens in recent years, particularly new formal layouts in walled gardens that are no longer required for fruit and vegetables.

Among them is one at Cawdor Castle, in Nairn. Three years after opening the place in 1976 the late Earl Cawdor found that visitors to the old walled garden, which was still planted as a vegetable garden, treated it as a picking ground. So he closed it and replanned it in two parts, one that he laid out as a maze in holly with a pattern taken from a Roman mosaic in Northern Portugal and the second that he gave to his wife to design. Lady Cawdor designed her area as three symbolic gardens, a circular Paradise garden with the sound of water and the smell of flowers, Purgatory with 32 kinds of thistle, and the Earth Garden. The last is laid out as a knot garden based on an old Scottish sampler hanging in the house and planted with a 16th century list of plants used in the still room, in cooking and medicine. And beside the three is an orchard planted as a Garden of Eden with old Scottish fruit trees. All the elements are new, but the thinking relates to the 16th and 17th century character of the place. In a sense the walled garden is a private fantasy, but from the beginning it was intended to be part of the visitors' experience of Cawdor, complementing the flower garden and the wild garden. It took about 12 years for the elements to grow up sufficiently for it to be opened in 1992.

A sense of history has played a similar role at Levens Hall, where to mark the 300th anniversary of the purchase of the place in 1694 by Col. Grahame, Mr and Mrs Hal Bagot have laid out an empty square of the formal garden with a design in pleached limes whose outline is shown on an unsigned survey of about 1735 that is a companion to the survey of the park. That does not provide sufficient detail for it to be regarded as a reconstruction: rather is the new garden a suggestion that pays tribute to the past, but with a new pool and fountain and a set of garden seats with scrolled backs based on a William and Mary chair in the house and made by the estate carpenter. Again, as at Cawdor, the garden is part of the visitor's experience.

At Burton Agnes Mrs Cunliffe-Lister, who runs the place for the charitable trust that now owns it, has taken the idea of an Elizabethan knot garden to create a new one in part of the walled garden to the south-west of the house. This she has replanned with a smaller formal kitchen garden, a maze and a jungle garden. In the knot garden she has created a series of rooms planted in different colours with a large-scale outdoor game in each one – chess, draughts, snakes and ladders, hoop-la, nine men's morris and so on. That is a pretty and witty place for children – of all ages – and for those watching them, who may want a respite from history and art. As a result more people are visiting Burton Agnes – and coming back again.

There is great variety in these gardens but almost all are based on a delight in formality ranging from the old-fashioned atmosphere of that at Hutton-in-the-Forest, which has been skilfully developed by Lady Inglewood in the spirit of a 19th century watercolour as a foil to the house and a contrast to the pleasure grounds on the other side of the house, to the ambitious layout created in the huge walled garden at Houghton and the new kitchen garden at Chatsworth.

In part these new gardens were intended to make the places more rewarding to visitors and in that they relate to the shift in the balance of enthusiasm from houses to gardens, parks and landscapes in the late 1980s and 1990s, which appears to be at every level from the academic and specialist to the popular, and to the ever-increasing demand for access to the countryside.

The specialist enthusiasm for gardens and landscapes has encouraged a new view of entities and of the importance of parks and landscapes in relation to houses that has slotted in with the emphasis on public benefit in several of the HLF's most complicated schemes. Certainly it influenced the HLF in its approach to Stoneleigh, where it was anxious to preserve more of the setting of the house, even if it meant reducing the amount of permitted development and buying out permissions to build in the walled garden.

More recently at Mogerhanger, in Bedfordshire, a Soane house that had been used as a hospital, the HLF has devised an ingenious scheme that has ended up with the house vested in the hands of a preservation trust, saved from a damaging enabling development scheme and being reunited with its landscape.

However while the HLF could still fund that kind of scheme in 1996–97, it is unlikely to be able to do so in the future. Even so the approach remains important, not least because it is a challenge to the concept of enabling development that can do, and has done, lasting damage to some historic houses.

7
◆
Tourism and Repair Grants 1974–1998

(a) *People and Places Open*

Every year when the figures for visitors to historic places are published, it is the totals and the top attractions that receive comment. Almost every year for the past 25 years, except for 1978–82, the total number of visitors and the number of places to visit have increased; and the number of places having 100,000 or more visitors has also gone up. According to English Tourist Board figures, between 1975 and 1978 there was a 14% increase in the number of visitors; then a drop of 18% in 1978–82; and a 30% increase since then, with a 33% increase over the years 1977–97.

However, the figures also show the increasing competition faced by houses from other categories of sites; and within their own category houses in private ownership, those owned by charitable trusts, the two National Trusts, English Heritage and local authorities, are all competing for visitors. According to the English Tourist Board's *English Heritage Monitor*'s table of trends in visits to places from 1984 to 1996, which started at 100 for all categories in the first year, the total growth is to 119. Within that the private sector dropped to 98 in 1986 and since then has increased to 110; English Heritage has increased to 119; local authority places have gone up to 120 and the National Trust's to 139.

In 1996 there were reckoned to be 70 million visitors to historic places, which compares with 65 million to museums and galleries, 44 million to country parks, 36 million to leisure parks and 18.7 million to wild life attractions. 15.2 million went to privately owned houses, 7.6 million to those belonging to the National Trust; 5.8 million to those belonging to local authorities; and 9.8 million to those in government ownership, including English Heritage. 436 historic places had more than 10,000 visitors, but no less than 47% of them had fewer.

According to English Tourist Board's *Heritage Monitor* 371 secular buildings have opened since 1977, and, according to Max Hanna's *Sightseeing in the UK 1996*, 45% of all tourist attractions have opened since 1980.

The following houses (excluding gardens only) are some of those that have opened since 1972. The list is impressive but the pace of new openings has reduced to two or three a year.

Allerton Park	Hartlebury Castle
Auckland Castle	Highclere
Belmont	Honington Hall
Belsay Castle	Hutton-in-the-Forest
Boughton House	Kelmarsh Hall
Bowood	Lamport Hall
Broadlands	Meols Hall
Brodsworth Hal	Norton Conyers
Carlton Towers	Orchard Wyndham
Chicheley Hall	Prideaux Place
Cottesbrooke Hall	Rode Hall
Dalemain, Cumberland	Scampston Hall
Dorney Court	Stanway
Duncombe Park	Stansted
Elton Hall	Stratfield Saye
Euston Hall	Tissington Hall
Fursdon	Ugbrooke
Grimsthorpe Castle	Winslow Hall
Hartland Abbey	

In addition since 1972 the National Trust has opened the following country houses, some of which were opened by their previous owners (as well as several other buildings including A La Ronde in Devon):

The Argory	Belton House
Avebury Manor	Calke Abbey
Baddesley Clinton	Canons Ashby
Basildon Park	Castle Drogo

Chastleton
Chirk Castle
Cragside
Dudmaston
Dunham Massey
Dunster Castle
Erdigg
Gawthorpe Hall
Hinton Ampner
Ightham Mote (garden)

Kedleston Hall
Kingston Lacy
Knightshayes
Mount Stewart
Newton House
Nymans
Plas Newydd
Standen
Wimpole

In Scotland the following houses are among those that have opened:

Bowhill
Brodie Castle
Castle Fraser
Cawdor Castle
Dalmeny
Drumlanrig Castle
Duff House

Floors Castle
Gosford House
Haddo House
House of Dun
Mount Stuart
Manderston

In Wales Picton Castle has been opened.

Naturally attention is always devoted to the new places open, but is also necessary to remember what have closed. Few of the houses were open more than 28 days; and some by appointment. Some are in institutional use. The list needs to be related to Max Hanna's figure of at least 566 attractions having closed between 1978 and 1996.

Among the houses closed are:

Acton Round
Allington Castle
Alresford House
Badminton
Barford Park
Barlborough
Beeston Hall
Belle Isle
Brympton d'Evercy
Callaly Castle
Came House

Carlton Towers
Castle Ashby
Chalcot House
Chicksands Priory
Chilham Castle
Compton Wynyates
Corby Castle
Creech Grange
Delapré Abbey
Denham Place
Ditchley Park

Doddington, Gloucestershire
Ebberston Hall
Eccleshall Castle
Eye Manor
Haremere Hall
Harrington Hall
Heveningham Hall
Hinwick House
Littlecote
Little Sodbury
Luton Hoo
Mereworth Castle
Moor Park
Naworth Castle

Nuneham Park
Pitchford Hall
Prestwold Hall
Prior Park
Rotherfield Park
Rudding Park
St Giles's House
Saltwood Castle
Sawston Hall
Sheriff Hutton
Stapleford Park
Thoresby Hall
Wardour Castle

Among the privately owned places sold have been Belle Isle, Brympton d'Evercy, Callaly Castle, Chilham Castle, Corby Castle, Doddington (Gloucestershire), Heveningham, Harrington, Hinwick, Littlecote, Little Sodbury, Mereworth, Pitchford, Rudding, Stapleford and Thoresby.

In 1996 21 houses in England and Wales that were privately owned or belonged to charitable trusts had over 100,000 visitors, headed by Warwick (820,000); Leeds Castle (598,714); Blenheim (419,902); Chatsworth (404,721); Beaulieu (386,352); Hever Castle (301,967); Harewood (254,000); Castle Howard (200,000).

After them came Arundel Castle (135,467); Blair Castle (152,402); Bowood (154,804); Dunvegan Castle (144,880); Glamis Castle (125,901); Hatfield (150,000); Knebworth (141,818); Newby (101,047); Scone Palace (102,783); Weston (164,256); Wilton (102,145).

The two most visited English Heritage houses were Audley End, with 116,698 visitors, and Belsay Hall, with 106,607.

In 1996–97 the National Trust had 15 houses and gardens with more than 100,000 visitors: Polesden Lacey, in Surrey; St Michael's Mount and Lanhydrock, both in Cornwall; Chartwell, in Kent; Cragside and Wallington, in Northumberland; Cliveden and Waddesdon, in Buckinghamshire; Lyme Park, Cheshire; Killerton and Castle Drogo, both in Devon; Belton, in Lincolnshire; Dunster, in Somerset; Plas Newydd and Powis, in North Wales; and Blickling, in Norfolk.

The two most visited National Trust for Scotland houses were Crathes Castle, with 16,561 visitors, and Culzean Castle, with 109,220.

What these figures do not bring out is the importance of children in places that attract over 100,000 a year. That can be seen at Newby and also at Bowood where there have been 50,000 children coming to the Adventure Playground ever since it opened, and it is they who bring many of the older visitors.

Nor do they bring out the increasing importance of gardens in house visiting. In *Sightseeing in the UK 1996* are some revealing comparative percentage figures. Taking 1976 as the base line at 100 for both houses and gardens, and taking a constant list of houses and a corrected one taking into account those that have newly opened and closed and the same for gardens, the percentages for houses only dropped below 100 in 1981 and 1982 and never for gardens. In 1990 for houses they stood at 118 and 128 and for gardens at 154 and 159; and in 1996 for houses at 121 and 132 and for gardens 188 and 198, which were all four the highest figures to date.

And that can be confirmed in visiting patterns at individual places. At Forde Abbey, in Dorset, for instance, instead of opening the house and garden for two afternoons a week for five months as happened until the mid-1980s, the house is now open on that basis for seven months, and the garden is open every day of the year from 10 a.m. The restaurant and shop are open for seven months from 11 a.m. and for the rest of the year there is an 'honesty' box. As a result the numbers, which had dropped from 33,000 in 1978 to 13,000 in 1985, have gone up to around 40,000, with 50,000 when Forde was the Garden of the Year and received extra publicity.

However, garden visiting figures do not bring out the difference between the number of visitors to houses and gardens on the one hand and those who make use of the grounds in the course of the year, probably taking in the gardens but not going to the house. Indeed the HHA believes that three times as many people visit private gardens as opposed to houses, and the total figure is as high as 45 million which is close to the figure for visits to country parks.

Also the figures do not reveal how houses are doing in terms of gross income and their costs (excluding capital repairs) and, since so many now make themselves available in other ways, it is dangerous to draw any conclusions. On the other hand it would appear that even the most successful operations cannot fund major programmes of repair out of income from opening: some cope with repairs when supported by grant aid, but others cannot even do that.

When considering numbers of people and houses, it is important to remember the high proportion of places which have under 10,000 – or even 2500 – visitors and those open by appointment that only attract a few hundred. Public discussion about access almost always concentrates on numbers of visitors and days open, and the political assumption is that places should be open more. However, both usually ignore the number of houses open in the United Kingdom. Surely what is remarkable is their vast number and their variety and what can be visited in one way or another, if a visitor cares to take advantage of the opportunities? In many of these cases there is simply not sufficient demand for greater opening that would make any kind of economic sense; and these places are available as long as the costs of providing access are minimal.

Here it is worth drawing attention to an imaginative scheme of visits to houses and gardens called *Your Private View* run by the Northamptonshire County Council through its Tourism and Conference Bureau (telephone 01604 671200). Northamptonshire is outstandingly rich in houses, many of them open to the public, but it is not usually thought of as a prime area for tourism. So it is a good idea to have lined up 21 country houses and gardens that can be visited on a number of days between early March and mid-October through a system of pre-booked tickets. The list ranges from a great house such as Boughton to fine lesser known houses like Courteenhall, Kelmarsh, Southwick and Weston. It would be interesting to know how many other counties run comparable schemes.

Such programmes could be valuable, because at the lower end of the visitor table numbers are not increasing, and in a few cases there seems to be a distinct pattern of declining numbers that is nothing to do with the interest and quality or the way places are shown but arises from increased competition. That can be seen in the following group.

	1991	1994	1995	1996
Dalemain, Cumberland	18,686	18,987	14,573	16,370
Leighton Hall, Lancashire	17,162	17,324	11,945	11,402
Hutton-in-the Forest, Cumberland	—	12,950	9,683	7,968
Doddington Hall, Lincolnshire	10,397	9,887	6,731	5,255
Stansted, Sussex	17,218	9,447	8,000	5,500
Squerryes Court, Kent	7,500	7,348	8,000	5,500
Burton Constable, Yorkshire	—	—	5,436	5,258
Stanford Hall, Leicestershire	45,358	40,461	26,657	25,718

Indeed it would be possible to do a most rewarding tour of places that attract fewer than 2500 visitors a year. It could start in Soho Square in the middle of London at the House of St Barnabas, 1 Greek Street, and then head south almost out of London to the Red House, Bexley, William Morris's first house. From there it could go on to Cobham Hall, a great Elizabethan house in Kent with its Gilt Hall combining rich plasterwork of the 1660s and decoration by James Wyatt. From there one might head north to Milton Keynes to look for Chicheley Hall, a superb house of the 1720s involving William Kent in an intriguing way, and then zigzag via the poetic Jonesian pavilions at Stoke Park, in Northamptonshire, and Vanbrugh with Pellegrini's decorations at Kimbolton Castle, now a school, to the Victorian Baroque splendours of Harlaxton Hall, Lincolnshire. From there the tour could take in Melbourne Hall with its wonderful early 18th century garden, and then head north for the endless riches of Yorkshire, going to the medieval manor house at Markenfield, to Hovingham for its learned amateur classical architecture, and end up with the thrill of Vanbrugh's Seaton Delaval, just north of Newcastle in Northumberland. Then it might be time to turn south and it would be possible to go to the Palladian villa at Rokeby and to Browsholme, a romantic antiquarian house in the Forest of Bowland, in Lancashire, before heading towards the Lancashire coast, to Meols Hall at Southport. On the way south through Shropshire it would be possible to go to Mawley Hall, one of the most remarkable interiors of the late 1730s and early 1740s, and then go via Moccas Court in Herefordshire to see its French neo-classical wallpaper in the circular drawing room, and Frampton Court, near Bristol, a perfect early Georgian manor house and garden with a gothick garden house. Many variations on such a tour could be planned and every one would provide an experience that would long remain in the memory. Without these houses our vision of England would be poorer, yet they tend to be undervalued because they do not cater for large numbers of people.

(b) *The Demands of Access*

It is essential to distinguish between the demands *for* access on the one hand and the demands *of* access on the other. Gone are the informal arrangements of the 1950s and '60s when the gate could be opened one afternoon a week and a trickle of people might or might not come.

Even with the simplest house opening operation the costs are now considerable, and they need to be related to the value of a single repair grant or conditional exemption and the likely income to derive from it. Most probably there will be investment in improving access to the place, providing car-parking, and lavatories. In addition there will be costs of conservation measures in rooms previously often kept in the dark, an improved security system and physical defences required by insurance companies as well as higher premiums, which may be impossible to meet.

Indeed, however good his security system, any owner who opens, even by written appointment, has to take into account the ever-increasing threats of theft, and not just within a house, but outside, with garden statuary and ornaments being particularly vulnerable. Theft has become the most serious deterrent to opening and it discourages people from applying for grants and seeking conditional exemption that would involve opening. Few owners can afford to fully insure the contents of their houses, and whatever they decide to do is a gamble that is increased by providing access. For the National Trust, because of inalienability, objects are deemed no longer to have a value because they cannot be sold, and so it never insures for loss, only reparable damage. For private owners, on the other hand, the contents of their houses, even taking exemption into account, are often their reserve assets and now often out of proportion to the value of their other property. So the whole equation of value, exemption, insurance and access is a much more complex one than is generally realised. How serious this is can be gathered from a recent HHA survey showing that

259 houses reported thefts in the course of the previous year, those from houses amounting to £1,837,850 and from gardens to £192,223, with lesser sums for thefts from tea rooms, restaurants and shops.

The income from smaller opening operations is likely to do no more than cover its direct costs and make no contribution to either annual running and maintenance or long-term capital repairs. And if the number of days is increased to attract more visitors, it is likely that there will not be enough of them to cover the extra costs.

However, if the opening proves to be a greater success than originally planned for, it is likely that more investment will be needed to improve the facilities, with hard surface car-parking that may need to be resited, a shop to be fitted up, stocked and run, a tea room to be equipped and staffed, somewhere where a school party can be received and inevitably ever more elaborate lavatories. The demands may provide uses for redundant buildings, but these may require planning permission, even listed building consent, as well as costing a large sum to put in order. If there is a drinks licence in connection with functions in the house, there will have to be extra fire precautions, with a dedicated line to the fire station.

In addition there are the fast-growing forest of regulations relating to health and safety, catering, and disability discrimination, instructions relating to training guides in first aid as well as the mounting risk of being sued because someone has tripped on a hole in a carpet that the family are used to. Also there is the rising tide of paper relating to tourism that is unrelated to the scale of opening of a great many places where even 28 days are a strain.

Of all this visitors remain blissfully unaware; and they have no concept of how expensive they are to receive.

On top of the costs and complexities are the demands on owners. Here it has to be remembered that most owners today live more simply than the previous generation. Certainly their parents had to make major changes in the way they lived after 1945, but they often managed to have a cook and so always ate in the dining room. The younger generation has had to rethink the pattern of life again, without a cook or any resident staff, who no longer seem essential or even desirable except on special occasions: the kitchen has become the fulcrum of life, and often the centre of family activity. Thus there is often no one to provide back-up if and when opening has to occur.

Here the situation has become more complicated in the past 15 years by the development of functions and the increase in the number of special parties. Thus a house open for 30 days may well have parties visiting it on another 35–50 days, an arrangement that suits the visitors and the owner. But owners are not allowed to count these extra days as part of any obligations they may have to open.

Also many of the smaller houses open for 28 or 60 days cannot cope with large numbers of day visitors, even if they could attract them. So they lay on a number of special outdoor events in the course of the summer that bring in more people usually to the garden or park – and more income – so that they provide a great deal more access than might appear at first.

The potential for functions, presuming an owner and his wife accept the idea – and some find it very hard or deeply unacceptable – depends not only on the scale and plan of the house but on its location. Moreover there can be a conflict between providing for visitors and providing for functions, as will be explained on p. 245, and this needs to be borne in mind in pressing for increased access to a house.

(c) *Competition For Visitors and Raising Revenue*

If the entries for houses open in the current edition of *Historic Houses and Gardens*, and even more in Hudson's directory, are compared with those of 25 years ago, it is immediately striking how many houses have broadened the ways in which they are available to the public, through special parties, weddings, social functions and business meetings, filming and so on. This has arisen from the need to raise a considerably higher revenue than is possible through conventional opening to the public on set days at set hours. In all this owners have shown themselves to have been ingenious and adaptable in the way that they have reacted to changing circumstances – and also remarkably successful.

Moreover there is a considerable public benefit from this great variety of opening, because groups and societies can often arrange to have special tours outside normal visiting hours, sometimes with specially arranged refreshments at a variety of prices. And that can suit a house too, because the group can be looked after by a minimum of staff and so overheads can be kept down.

The indoor functions business, which has developed since the late 1970s and early 1980s in many houses, has seemed like an answer to prayer to many owners, but success depends not only on their own talents and sense of style but on the location and plan of their houses and concentrating on what works best in them. At present, according to a survey of HHA members to which 270 replied, 91 houses were used for corporate entertaining and 57 could accommodate conferences. Fewer than might be imagined are really suited to conferences, large receptions or dinners, leaving aside the costs of investment in kitchens, lavatories and so on. In pre-1660 houses a great hall may not be as large as it sounds, and the Great Room or Saloon, which started to become fashionable in the 1720s, is not necessarily very big. Only in the early 19th century were plans made to open up houses for larger companies of guests, with double doors between series of rooms, so that just as London clubs became like country houses, country houses became like clubs. Thus a house like Leighton Hall, in North Lancashire, which is not large, can be used for functions, because there are double doors between the hall, library and drawing room. Later houses like Cliveden, Manderston and Sledmere as reorganised after the fire are really luxury hotels for house parties, and Cliveden, in fact, works well as a hotel. With houses of mixed dates the relationship of spaces may be good for large parties, but equally they can be unsuitable and some houses do suffer from over-use. Also there is always the risk to good furniture from moving it. Thus it may be that small conferences with 10–16 people staying for two or three days may be the best answer in certain houses where they can be slotted in with family life and limited regular opening. Also regular use may change the character of a house, and, as one owner's wife said, she would not want to do anything that so spoiled the place that it discouraged a successor from wanting to take it on.

There can be a middle way, however, with functions, because quite often what the organisers want is the setting and the sense of arrival. So it is quite acceptable to combine arrival at the principal entrance and greeting in the hall with a marquee attached to the house, as might happen for a reception after a family wedding. Alternatively, as happens at one house, the marquee is quite separate from the house, and the wedding guests never go inside it. Weddings now produce a steady flow of business for at least 79 houses out of 270 which answered the HHA survey, although not all those that make themselves available for receptions are, or wish to be, licensed for civil wedding ceremonies. So far, according to the HHA survey, 40 houses are licensed for these.

Sometimes there are problems in balancing regular opening to the public with accepting functions. A house open several afternoons a week, for instance, may have to turn down a profitable booking for a special three-day event that would have produced as much revenue as the whole opening season. In many cases the number of days open in a season is related to conditions attached to repair grants, conditional exemption or a maintenance fund, and so an owner may not be able to alter the pattern of opening in order to have more functions, perhaps being left with Mondays and Saturdays as closed days to the public and so free for other activities. On the other hand, provided there is heating in a house, functions can take place during the closed season, so spreading the earning capacity of the house through the year.

There is a steady demand for houses for filming, even if the producers hope to find an unknown and remote house within 30 minutes of Hyde Park Corner, and the HHA has done much to help owners make realistic agreements; a remarkable number are prepared to consider it. To some filming is a nightmare experience, while others accept it philosophically as a short sharp way to earn a useful fee, and a few even enjoy the excitement. Certainly films made at country houses have a special appeal as can be seen with *The Remains of the Day* in 1993 and *Pride and Prejudice* and *Sense and Sensibility* in 1995, which can bump up the visitor figures for the houses that are open.

How to strike a balance that makes financial sense is difficult. In the case of one house where the figures for day visitors were going down steadily and it was unrealistic to think that they could be built up again and sustained at the top figure, the owner reckons to more than double the total number of visitors through a limited number of special events, getting 40% more through the events in the house and 80% more through the events outside. As a result he hopes to generate about 50% of the running and maintenance costs, but this does not make any contribution to repairs.

Quite apart from functions indoors many houses have special events outdoors, such as car, caravan and mountain bike rallies, craft and antique fairs, clay pigeon shooting, grass skiing, firework displays and concerts. The range is now amazingly diverse.

The growth of functions, activities and events has been part of the fundamental change in the attitudes of many owners of houses and estates who have inherited since 1970. No longer can they look on them as providing a way of life that gives them the freedom to do other things: they have to be regarded as businesses involving agriculture and commercial activities.

At the same time the expansion in the ways houses, gardens and parks are used to generate income for themselves also means a corresponding increase in the contribution places make to the economy of the locality through providing full- or part-time employment and direct and indirect expenditure, direct through what is ordered locally and indirect through what visitors spend while they are in the area, on accommodation, food and drink, and shopping. According to a recent HHA survey 263 houses employ 7002 people, who are paid £65 million. Moreover they are a valuable focus for tourist promotion and attention, even when visitors do not go to them.

To show what has happened to house opening in the past 25 years, and how it has had to develop in order to increase revenue to meet rising costs, it would be difficult to find a better example than Ripley Castle, near Harrogate, in Yorkshire (Figs 36 and 37). It was first opened in a very low key way by the late Sir Joslan Ingilby, because he received a grant for repairs from the HBC in 1958, after he succeeded, and 100 people on a Bank Holiday was considered a busy day. Then about 1966 Yorkshire Television filmed *The Flaxton Boys* at Ripley and as a result at the first opening in 1967 the Ingilbys were overwhelmed by 1000 people. So the amount of opening was increased. Sir Joslan died in June 1974, nine months before his transfer of the estate to his 18-year-old son, Thomas, was complete. That led to a CTT liability that caused the sale of half the estate. Even so it took six years to clear the CTT, CGT and interest charges, and during that time everything ground to a halt on the place, with no repairs done. The house opening was immediately extended in 1974, but Sir Thomas, who was still a student, did not return to live at Ripley until 1978, and then on a part-time basis; and it was only after 1980 that he was able to devote all his time to it. Then it began to be possible to plan positively for the present and the future.

It was the opening of the Harrogate Conference Centre in 1981 that was to offer a new and unexpected potential, because that prompted people to ask Sir Thomas whether it would be possible to hold functions at the castle. So what started as an *ad hoc* arrangement snowballed in three years to such a degree that it had to be put on a commercial basis, with proper kitchens and a professional catering staff.

36. An aerial view of Ripley, Yorkshire. This shows the relationship of the castle to its landscape and to its village which still mainly belongs to the estate. The new hotel faces the square.

That in turn stimulated the idea of establishing a small high-quality hotel in the village, which had been 'dry' for 70 years. The idea was that those attending functions could stay within walking distance of the castle, and at the same time the catering in the hotel and the castle could be planned as interlocking operations.

All might have been well with this thinking, but the hotel opened in 1990, just at the start of the recession that led to the rapid decline of

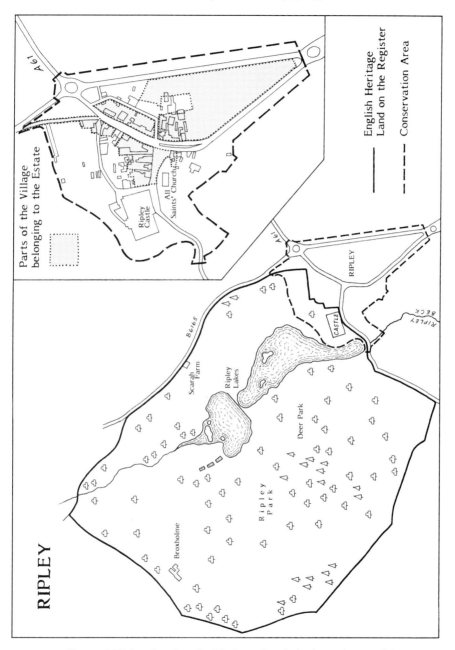

37. Plans of Ripley showing the Heritage Land, the boundaries of the Conservation Area and Estate ownership in the village.

the conference trade and the cut-back in functions. So for three years it was a matter of trying to keep the hotel going without bringing down the whole Ripley operation. Even so more of the estate had to be sold. In 1993, however, business began to pick up, and now the hotel has 25 bedrooms and employs 45 people – and has been awarded four stars. So it has become the key to success.

Even before the function business started, Sir Thomas began to convert the castle outbuildings, forming two shops that are now in operation all the year and can be visited without going to the castle. Also he began to organise outdoor events. In the early 1980s he began to repair and modernise the estate houses and cottages in the village, which hitherto had been let on uneconomic rents. He financed that through selling off building plots in the village and derelict farm buildings and applying for grant aid. So he has been able to turn the village round both physically and as a community.

Thus what had been an agricultural estate, which could never have supported the place and the family, has been turned into a totally different kind of economic enterprise with much greater returns. However the non-financial price has been a high one in that it has been so demanding of Sir Thomas and his wife, and also of their family of five children: they live on the upper floors of the castle and so are surrounded by the buzz of the functions and have no private garden. Also there is the physical strain on the castle, because, like many pre-19th century houses, it does not have large rooms, and a permanent marquee is up in the courtyard. However there are plans for repairs and conversion of the outlying parts of the castle that will not only bring the rest of it into use but take some of the pressure off the main building and enable the marquee to be removed – and so some of the pressure off the family as well. Meanwhile a situation that most people would regard as impossible is making well nigh impossible demands.

If Ripley demonstrates a revolution in thinking brought about by one owner on one estate since 1974, another Yorkshire estate, Broughton, near Skipton, represents another brought about by two generations since 1970 (Figs 38 and 39). In 1970 Henry Tempest inherited from his elder brother a large house on a neglected estate of 3000 acres producing a negligible income, 80% of which came from farmland. Today Mr and Mrs Tempest continue to live in the house, of which they rent part from their elder son, Roger. The latter retains 2000 acres, with 75% of a much more considerable income coming from office rents and only 10–15% from farmland.

The situation on the estate in 1970 was not unlike that which many owners had faced in 1945. Henry Tempest applied experience gained in Africa, accountancy, and computers in Oxford to pulling it round. He also continued repairs on the house, which his brother had begun in the late 1960s, but before he started on them, he went on an SPAB repairs course so that he would know what he was talking about. He always saw development potential in the mill complex half a mile to the west of the house, and in the mid-1970s, when the main road that runs close to the house was improved, he accepted the closure of one access road to the estate on condition another was made to the mill. Then in 1982 he converted part of the stables into offices, while retaining some loose boxes and the harness room for use.

Five years later the Home Farm became vacant, just when he was preparing to hand over the estate to his elder son, who wished to return to Broughton. So it was the latter who masterminded the conversion into offices of the farm buildings, which are close to the house, and, when they were completed, he tackled the mill complex. Now the estate has 25 office buildings ranging from 10,000 square feet downwards and has 30 tenants employing 300 people. When Mr and Mrs Henry Tempest gave an estate party to mark the 400th anniversary of the building of the house, their own 40th wedding anniversary and 25 years at Broughton, 600 people came, a remarkable demonstration of the economic vitality of the place today.

From the mid-1970s the house was open to a limited extent because of its HBC grant, but that condition lapsed on the transfer of ownership. So the house is now only open on Bank Holidays and by appointment for groups, many of whom come in the evening. Also it is used to a limited extent for corporate functions and for occasional wedding receptions. The result is that there are events on about 44 days in the summer months. Opening never made any real contribution to the costs of the house, but the new policy is giving the whole place a sound financial basis as well as making a new kind of contribution to the life and economy of the district.

The developments at Ripley and Broughton have been particularly intensive, but there are numerous comparable schemes on other estates that have been devised to increase revenue and also to provide uses for farm buildings made redundant either through changes in farming

38. An aerial view of Broughton Hall, Yorkshire.

methods or by the amalgamation of farms. In the 1970s preservationists suddenly woke up to the challenge of a whole range of buildings in
the country that were decaying because they had lost their traditional
uses, and the desire to see them preserved coincided with the desire of
some landowners to find new uses that not only maintained them and
produced an income for the estate but provided work places and
employment.

One estate that took this up early was Alscot near Stratford-on-Avon
in Warwickshire, which had been reduced from 14,000 acres in 1880 to
3000 in 1960 and reflected not only the agricultural but the industrial
decline of that period and the losses in opportunities for employment.

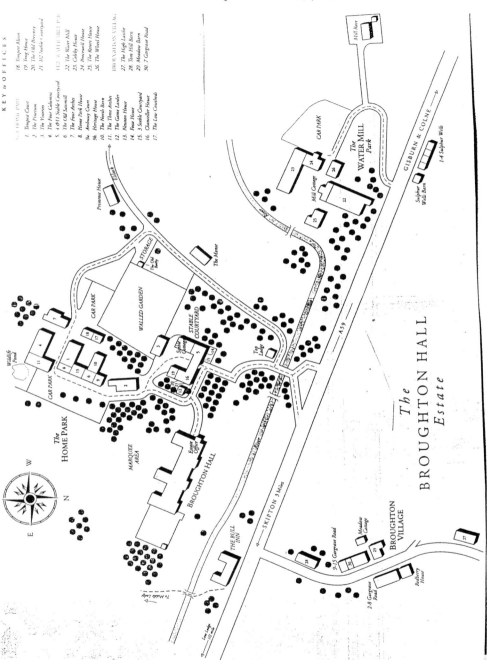

39. A plan of Broughton showing how buildings close to the house have been converted to new uses.

[225]

What has happened since the mid-1970s has been a determined campaign by the late Captain James Alston-Roberts-West and his daughter Mrs Andrew Holman-West to reverse that. The first workshop in former farm buildings was taken in 1976 by a furniture restorer, who wanted to return to Stratford but did not want to work in an industrial park and had been unable to find premises that were congenial and affordable and not discouraging to clients. On another farm taken in hand by the owner the buildings became redundant but they provided space for a potential eight businesses. By 1982 there were two there, and altogether there were 15 new enterprises on the estate and 51 people had found new employment. Sixteen years later there are about 45 businesses in old buildings on the estate employing 247 people; and all the time not only are standards of what is required going up but there is a healthy demand for premises on the estate, because of its atmosphere, ease of parking and convenient location not far from the motorway at Warwick. Thus the economic base of the estate and so support for its important Gothick Revival house has changed.

At Squerryes, in Kent, a policy of converting buildings to workshops and offices began about 15 years ago. First two workshops were made in the old stables near the house and after that, in the mid-1980s, a set of redundant farm buildings were let to a sawmill business and now to a timber business, while another set of farm buildings were made into four sets of workshops. Since then the Home Farm buildings have been converted into offices and that is still continuing. The problem is always the shortage of capital to do the conversions and some of the work is done by tenants, so it may be up to 10 years before buildings are producing full rents. However, the process together with rents from houses and cottages means that the income of the estate has changed: 25 years ago 75% came from agriculture and agricultural rents; now 66% comes from non-agricultural sources.

The conversion of redundant buildings on estates leads on to two other interlocking subjects that have developed in the past 25 years, vernacular buildings and agricultural buildings, in particular barns. Thus what has been done at Broughton, Alscot, Squerryes and elsewhere needs to be related to research on vernacular buildings to be found in books like Ronald Brunskill's *Vernacular Architecture of the Lake Counties* (1978) and *An Illustrated History of Vernacular Architecture* (1987) and to the SPAB's campaign that started with its Barns Day in 1980 and led on to its national survey of 1984.

(d) *The Role of Repair Grants 1984–1998*

In 1994 the Historic Houses Association became concerned about the drop in repair grants from English Heritage for privately owned houses; as a result of its researches and making its case to English Heritage in 1995–96, the allocation for individual grants was increased in 1996–97 and, according to English Heritage's Corporate Plan for 1997–2001, it hopes to continue to make further increases in that period.

The 1970s saw the rapid expansion of the work of the Historic Buildings Council, with the grants for individual outstanding buildings, which included country houses, being extended to cover first grant-aided schemes in conservation areas, then grant aid for historic gardens (under the Town and Country Amenities Act 1974) and outstanding churches and chapels in use (promised in 1975 and introduced in stages starting in 1976–77). In addition it had new responsibilities for advice on matters relating to conditional exemption for outstanding buildings and amenity land.

However, the reports give the impression that a fair balance was maintained between the claims of the different categories of buildings.

In 1973–74, the HBC's allocation for grants to individual buildings (a category which is considerably broader than historic houses let alone country houses in the sense the term is used here) was increased from £1 million to £1.5 million; that for conservation grant was increased from £500,000 to £750,000 and to £1 million in 1974–75.

In 1981–82 Council reported that from an initial £250,000 in 1953 (in fact for Scotland and Wales as well as England) the total allocated to individual buildings had grown to over £35 million by 1 April 1982; and the £6,759,000 offered to them in 1981–82 represented a third of the total sum offered in the course of the year. However such had been the pressure on funds that the normal rate of grant had been reduced from 50% to 40% in 1979. Of the total, £500,000 went to the National Trust and nearly £400,000 to local authorities. 'The proportion of grant funds going to private individuals has therefore fallen.'

In its last full year, 1983–84, the HBC offered grants to the value of £21,113,556, with total expenditure coming to £13,534,831. As far as individual buildings were concerned, 376 grants worth £8,636,636 were offered (and 201 applications were rejected), £1,071,632 going to the National Trust (including £246,069 as maintenance grants for the six houses) and £1,177,100 to local authorities.

In many cases these grants were part of programmes of repair spread over several years, two of them relating to the longest running schemes at Blenheim and at Knole. In the case of Blenheim grant-aided work started in 1957 and that has been the longest running programme. However, the figures of grant aid for Blenheim give little idea of total expenditure or what that represents in present-day figures. Some idea of the increase in prices can be gathered from the fact it received £15,000 in 1957 and £223,998 in 1986–89. In the case of Knole the first programme of work began in 1954 and lasted for 20 years.

When English Heritage was set up, there were natural worries that there would be a conflict between its management of and expenditure on its own properties and its responsibilities towards buildings in other ownerships. Certainly owners soon noticed a difference in approach and atmosphere as well as in the way business was handled by the new organisation, which seemed to lose the sense of personal commitment that had existed hitherto.

In order to understand the complicated financial picture since 1984, it is necessary to divide the period into two, the years 1984–94, when the full grant figures for the years up to 1992 were published for the first time and the HHA became concerned about the drop in repair grants, and since 1994; and to consider six main points, four of which relate mainly to the first part of the period.

The first is that English Heritage's annual grant-in-aid from the Government grew from 1984 to 1995/6 and so did its expenditure, both on its own properties, which increased in number, and also on grant aid, which had to cover wider fields and meet greater demands.

Second is English Heritage's response to this increasing pressure, which included cutting back on grant aid for country houses. This was first mentioned in its reports for 1985–86 but was not fully clear until all the grant figures were published in 1994.

Third, in 1995–96 English Heritage's grant-in-aid started to be trimmed back and, much more serious, the Government made no allowance for rising costs. From £105.7 million in 1995–96 its grant was trimmed to £103 million in 1996–97; then to £101.1 million for the following three years. But what its Corporate Plan for the years 1996–2000 estimates is an overall loss of £44.7 million over the four years.

It would be interesting to be able to show the pattern of English Heritage's expenditure over the years and in particular compare what it has spent on its own properties in relation to grant offers and expenditure. However the figures for its own properties are not available before 1992–93. Total expenditure went up every year until 1996–97 and in that time it went up more than 2½ times, whereas grant offers went up by only 50% and grant expenditure, at its highest that year nearly doubled, offers having peaked in 1994–95. Yet expenditure on its own buildings has gone up by more than a third while its offers of grant aid and expenditure on grant aid has declined.

Year	Total Expenditure	Expenditure on Own Properties	Individual Grant Offers/Expenditure	
1984–85	£49.016m		£13.044m	£10.620m
1985–86	£56.499m		£11.313m	£10.063m
1986–87	£62.763m		£14.524m	£12.488m
1987–88	£71.036m		£15.469m	£11.284m
1988–89	£78.373m		£15.480m	£12.450m
1989–90	£86.959m		£15.811m	£14.425m
1990–91	£90.186m		£16.721m	£15.860m
1991–92	£100.538m		£17.651m	£19.019m
1992–93	£113.307m	£29.445m	£21.525m	£18.775m
1993–94	£115.962m	£33.069m	£26.196m	£18.670m
1994–95	£126.123m	£38.535m	£31.262m	£18.257m
1995–96	£126.200m	£37.085m	£21.142m	£19.814m
1996–97	£129.713m	£36.374m	£19.800m	£20.548m
1997–98	£127.713m	£39.861m	£18.024m	£15.949m

In 1988–89 the individual grants were divided between commercial owners who received 8.2%; charitable trusts, 4.1%; local authorities, 12.6%; the National Trust, 17.6%; private owners, 37.5%; and other bodies 20%.

In 1989–90 the proportions changed, partly reflecting the Buildings at Risk thinking. Commercial owners' share went up to 19.3%; charitable trusts' to 11.6%; local authorities' to 14.3%; while the National Trust's share dropped to 15.2%; and private owners' to 24.8%; other bodies' rose to 24.8%.

In this period English Heritage took on a number of extra commitments including the three houses formerly owned and run by the Greater London Council – Kenwood, Marble Hill, and the Rangers House at Blackheath – and later the restoration of the Albert Memorial. It has also accepted responsibility for Eltham Palace and the repair of Danson Place, Bexley. In addition it accepted the gift of Brodsworth Hall, near Doncaster, without endowment and restored it at the cost of £4 million. Since then it has taken on Downe House, Kent, the former home of Charles Darwin. Moreover it would have liked, but failed, to take on Kedleston, Monkton House, Sussex, a highly individual small 20th century house that had belonged to Edward James, Pitchford and Stokesay Court, both in Shropshire.

At the same time the fields covered by grant aid were broadened to cover cathedrals, which were offered grant aid for the first time in 1991–92, and Buildings at Risk. Once churches had been brought within the grant aid system, it was clearly right that the cathedrals, many of which were involved in large appeals for repairs, should also be included. Buildings at Risk was a natural development of the Town Scheme and Conservation Grant systems, being intended to deal with buildings that could not be handled through them. English Heritage, having become aware of them about 1988, began to look at them systematically in 1990, and the Buildings at Risk policy was published in 1992. Also English Heritage has had to consider help for a great variety of historic buildings given up as a result of cuts in the defence and health services.

It is not that country houses and historic houses are regarded as less important, but rather that a great many other kinds of buildings are seen to be more significant than they were before and in more urgent need of help; and since the cake has ceased to grow and has even shrunk – because of lack of commitment on the part of past and present Governments – its slices have to be cut thinner.

In the report for 1985–86, when the number of applications for individual grants went up by 54% to 770 and 241 offers worth £6.1 million were made (as opposed to £7.2 million the previous year), there were the ominous words: 'A number of pre-eminent houses are known to need major repairs which, in many cases, will not be undertaken without the offer of a substantial grant. The steady demand from this type of house severely limits the Commissioners' ability to respond to other claims.'

In 1986–87, when grant aid increased by £1.5 million, the number of applications for grants for individual secular buildings fell by a third to 511, 'probably as a result of the more stringent rules we have had to introduce, but the average value of offers rose'. 245 grants worth £8.05

million were offered, but one was of £1 million to the National Trust for Calke Abbey.

In 1987–88 again there was a decrease in the number of applications to 402. There was also a 22% drop in the number of offers, to 186, 'partly due to a decision to defer a number of offers until after the end of the financial year, because of resource restrictions', and also in their value, to a total of £7.8 million.

The report for 1988–89 did not give the numbers of applications or offers of grant.

In 1989–90, when an extra £3 million was promised by the Government for 1990 for church grants, there was a shift in balance between church and secular grants, with a total allocation of £8.2 million compared with £7.1 million the previous year. The report said: 'The continuing squeeze on secular grant funds meant that we had to further tighten our criteria for grant offers, with a move away from some of our more traditional customers, such as the major country houses, to buildings more immediately at risk . . .'

In 1989 English Heritage decided to change the old informal means test, which had been used in the past, to a more formal Needs Assessment Procedure. That has had the unexpected result of showing the needs of some applicants to be greater than realised and so led to a higher percentage of grant. Also it has contributed to the unlocking of certain old problems like the mansion at Stowe.

In 1991–92, surprisingly, there was no mention of individual secular buildings in the annual report.

The details of all the grants offered to individually outstanding buildings between 1984 and 1992 were not published until 1994 and there is no clue as to the present uses of buildings or their ownerships. On the other hand it is striking how many grants went to historic houses in different kinds of adaptive use as well as those belonging to the National Trust.

It is impossible to list all the figures here, but it is important to recognise that there continued to be a number of large grants made to houses in this period. Among grants over £90,000 there were:

Arley Hall, Cheshire, 1984–89 £158,000
Avington Park, Hampshire, 1984–86 £99,677
Belvoir Castle, Rutland, 1987–89 £176,877
Berkeley Castle, Gloucestershire, 1986–87 £109,000

Blenheim Palace, Oxfordshire, 1986–89 £223,998
Broughton Castle, Oxfordshire, 1987–92 £246,049
Burghley House, Lincolnshire, 1984–91 £480,000
Cawood Castle, Yorkshire, 1986 £143,000
Chiddingstone Castle, Kent, 1988–90 £115,478
Corsham Court, Wiltshire, 1984–85 £220,000
Duncombe Park, Yorkshire, 1985–87 £166,947
Eastnor Castle, Herefordshire, 1987–91 £227,588
Farnley Hall, Yorkshire, £217,000
Hawkestone Hall, Shropshire, 1986–87 £149,311
Knebworth, Hertfordshire, 1984–89 £113,360
Ledston Hall, Yorkshire, 1987–90 £175,000
Orchard Wyndham, Somerset, 1985–88 £131,500
Pitchford Hall, Shropshire, 1984–92, £195,523
Raby Castle, Durham, 1984–92 £121,815
Rode Hall, Cheshire, 1986–88 £121,000
Rokeby, Yorkshire, 1985–86 £186,955
Rotherfield Park, Hampshire, 1987–91 £180,078
Shotover Park, Oxfordshire, 1985–91 £169,210
Syon Great Conservatory, Middlesex, 1986–88 £394,522
Ugbrooke, Devon, £200,000
Wilton House, Wiltshire, 1985–91 £646,000

It is natural to draw attention to these large grants, but they only suggest part of what has been going on. Many of them relate to work spread over many years, with some grant-aided programmes like that at Blenheim covering more than one generation; and almost all of them could make interesting reading.

However the smaller grants can be just as crucial, as at Norton Conyers in Yorkshire (Figs 44 and 45). Two years after he inherited in 1982 Sir James Graham commissioned a surveyor's report that revealed serious problems with the roof, which is hardly surprising since little had been done to the house for 60 years. However that year only a small grant was offered for the repair of the Orangery. It took until 1986 to win a more substantial grant for the repair of the house. Since then, work has gone ahead without major problems over the rate of grant and there have been consistently constructive relations between the owners and their architect and English Heritage's officers. By 1990 work on the roof was complete, and now there remains about another three years' work to do on related repairs to the stables and other structures. Here grants need to be related to the conditional exemption of the house and park and the setting up of a maintenance fund, both of which had been planned but not established by Sir James's father before he died, the latter's opening of the house in 1976 in anticipation of that, and then the *in situ* deal over the Beechey portrait in the Great Hall. Without that total package Norton Conyers could not have survived the past 16 years: as it is, it shows how well the English Heritage system has worked for one private owner of a country house in recent years.

Among the larger grants one that stands out is the £121,815 offered to Raby Castle in the years 1984 to 1992 (Fig. 40). Raby is a great moated castle dating from the late 14th century onwards and almost continuously inhabited ever since, with important 18th and 19th century interiors. Lord Barnard inherited in 1964 and, when in 1971 he began to consider how to tackle the buildings, he asked Donald Insall to do a complete report on the castle and what needed to be done, but without costs attached at that stage. The report, which is an elaboration of that produced for Burton Constable, has been the basis for everything that

40. Raby Castle, Co Durham, from the air in 1972. This shows the extent of the roofs and stonework that has had to be repaired since 1976.

has been done to the castle over the past 26 years. In 1976 the architects worked out with Lord Barnard an eight-year programme of repairs totalling £184,000 to put to the HBC with a view to starting work that summer. By 1984 the first four phases were completed at a cost of £155,000 with grant aid at variable rates having come to £81,500; a fifth phase that summer brought total expenditure to £185,000. The vast scale of the place combined with its historical and physical complexity demanded a clear vision; it is a remarkable tribute to Lord Barnard and his staff at Raby, to Donald Insall's office in London and particularly Alan Frost, who has been in charge of the project from the beginning, and to the support of, first, the HBC and since 1984 English Heritage that all the major repairs to the roof and stone work of the main building have now been tackled.

Alongside the programme of repairs to the structure and the interior, in particular Carr's hall and the Octagon Drawing Room (Plate IV), Lord Barnard has also rewired the whole castle and installed a computer-operated gas heating system that copes with problems of humidity in those parts not used while being able to bring any part in use to comfort level. Lord Barnard only occupies a small part of the castle, and some areas with fine 18th century interiors have not yet been brought back into commission, but now that the structure is in good condition and with power and temperature control installed it will be possible to tackle them too.

A more recent development has been Donald Insall's preparation of a maintenance manual for the castle. That was introduced in 1992 as a 'guide to the Estate for daily, monthly, yearly general items of maintenance that should help in keeping the fabric in good order. It is arranged to cover a period of 5 years to co-ordinate with the recommended Quinquennial Survey of the condition of the fabric by the architect.' It lists all the jobs with their frequency and is countersigned by those responsible for carrying them out.

In 1992–93 among grants in excess of £50,000 there were only two to privately owned houses – £76,800 for the stables at Ragley; and £56,421 for Broughton Castle; £80,000 was granted towards another phase of work at Burghley, a charitable trust.

However, there were a number of other significant grants to houses. Those to the National Trust included £282,000 towards the restoration of Ightham Mote, which had been bequeathed to the Trust in 1985; £88,655 for Lindisfarne Castle; £85,941 for Claydon; £58,000 for

Ickworth; £61,116 for Lacock; £83,500 for Beningbrough. £20,000 was offered for Pell Wall, an important small Soane house which at least looked as if it was at last going to be saved; £39,340 to Woodchester Park, in Gloucestershire, a most remarkable unfinished Victorian house that also had looked as if it had no future; £50,000 to Westonbirt, in Gloucestershire, an important Victorian house long in use as a school; and £93,550 to Smithills Hall, Bolton, a local authority historic house museum.

The most significant grant was one of £216,478 to the mansion at Stowe, which was in addition to the £214,796 given to the National Trust for the buildings in the grounds. In all the years when the HBC had been trying to save the garden buildings, it had always been politically unacceptable to ministers to get involved with the mansion because it belonged to an independent school. However when the School gave the grounds to the National Trust and the financial enquiries were put on to an official basis, it was possible to prove the School's need for support in looking after the house and also to see the mansion as part of the whole. That was a most important breakthrough.

In 1993–94 grants of £50,000 or more went towards the repair of six houses in private ownership. They were £204,683 to Combermere Abbey, in Cheshire, a house that had been a worry since the early 1980s; £75,000 to Ugbrooke, in Devon; £111,000 for Castle Howard; £70,133 for Somerhill, Kent; £51,009 for Broughton Castle; £63,309 for Norton Conyers, Yorkshire; £211,000 for Harewood, a charitable trust.

But again more grants went to other categories of house. The National Trust, for instance, received £351,000 for Hardwick; £274,000 for the clock tower at Cliveden; £142,000 for Ightham Mote; £99,400 for Attingham; £58,464 for Packwood; £53,600 for Lacock; and £188,800 for the garden buildings at Stowe.

Among large English Heritage grants to houses in institutional use were two for Stowe totalling £367,000, £86,000 for Kings Weston, £275,000 for the gymnasium at Prior Park, £135,196 for Dartington Hall, £97,500 for the stables at Ston Easton, now a hotel, and £151,858 for Cound Hall, a baroque house in Shropshire now divided into flats. In addition £698,500 went towards the saving of Iron Acton Court and £249,606 to Highcliffe Castle, while £1 million went towards saving part of the Royal Crescent at Buxton.

The editorial entitled 'Grants – Targeting A Limited Resource' in

English Heritage's *Conservation Bulletin* stated, that it was decided to move away from private owners 'towards bodies which are more directly concerned not in maintaining buildings that they already own, but in acquiring historic buildings at risk and securing [them] for the future through repair and the establishment of a use . . . This is a much more limited scale of activity than is good for the buildings, since a long-term repair plan based on a thorough knowledge of the structure and some certainty about financing is the ideal. It reduces our ability to work in partnership with owners, and it may well mean that some out-standing buildings will only be saved at the expense to their owners of other highly desirable objectives – be they the retention of an historic collection associated with the property, continued occupation or type of use, or development of other cherished plans.' The remark about the expense of the retention of a historic collection seems to run counter to everything that English Heritage and the HBC had been trying to do since 1953 and against almost all current preservation thinking.

It was the publication in 1994 of all the grant figures for the years 1984 to 1992 that revealed what had happened to individual grants, particularly to houses in private ownership, in those years, and led the HHA to commission Saffery Champness to investigate. Whereas the number and value of grants had increased between 1984 and 1988, rising from 33 to 69 houses, both had dropped after that; in 1993 their value was only 25% of the 1988 figure and they were offered to only 12 houses.

In the autumn of 1995, following the Saffery Champness report for the HHA, Sir Jocelyn Stevens, the chairman of English Heritage, speaking at the HHA's AGM said: 'At English Heritage we regard England's historical houses, great and small, as the corner-stone of England's heritage . . . We acknowledge that you, the owners and/or occupiers, [are able to preserve them] more efficiently, at greater sacrifice and a lower cost to the nation, and to a greater benefit to the nation, than we or any other conservation body could achieve. 'He went on to promise 'to extend the amount of work which can be grant aided . . . Now that private owners have been specifically and inexcusably excluded from benefiting from Lottery funding, English Heritage long-term funding for private owners is more vital than ever before, and we intend to make the system work more effectively for you.'

The following year at the AGM William Proby, the president of the HHA, spoke of the recent improvement in relations with English Heritage: 'I believe that last year marked a watershed in our relations with English Heritage and I would like to pay a special tribute to the role that Sir Jocelyn has played in reversing the considerable degree of mistrust that private owners have had in the past. There is still more work to be done, both in the area of grants and listed building consents; however we have made a step forward . . . and altogether we are seeing at all levels of English Heritage a much more owner-friendly approach.'

As a result of that, the HHA, English Heritage and Saffery Champness held a seminar on *Repair Grants for Historic Buildings from English Heritage*. One striking remark made at the seminar was from Tony Sannia, the Finance Director of English Heritage, who said: 'English Heritage is firmly committed to the conservation of historic estates. Fundamental to our approach to "historic estates" is the belief that an estate should remain a going concern in the hands of current owners. English Heritage has no wish to jeopardise the longer-term ability of an estate to maintain its historic property and we wish to avert the danger that an owner may be forced to sell important historic contents.' That kind of thinking is encouraging and a correct development of the experience that has come from English Heritage's involvement with conditional exemptions and maintenance funds.

In 1997 the HHA published a study, *A Stitch in Time*, which was their Case for Capital Support from the Heritage Lottery Fund. On the basis of a survey of 10 houses throughout the British Isles, it 'estimated that privately owned properties would require a total of £130 million for essential outstanding capital work over the next ten years – the equivalent to £13 million per annum.'

In Saffery Champness's 1998 revision of *A Stitch in Time* for the HHA it found that out of the 32 houses it looked at, 15 had undertaken repairs with the assistance of English Heritage in the preceding 10 years, with the English Heritage contribution usually ranging between 20 and 50%: eight out of the 32 houses indicated that they should be spending more on maintenance. The report also showed that in its survey of nine houses the large ones were underspending on repairs by £20,000 a year and smaller houses by £11,000.

In 1994–95, apparently as a result of the HHA's discussions with English Heritage, the situation began to improve a little for privately owned country houses. Grants of £50,000 or more went to four houses, £159,610 to Elton Hall; £263,622 for Capesthorne, Cheshire; £60,000 for Somerhill, Kent; and £61,561 for Norton Conyers, Yorkshire.

Burghley received £111,525. Stowe School received £292,560 for the mansion. £157,643 went to Hall i't' Wood, one of the earliest historic house museums, at Bolton. Among other large grants were £748,000 for Highcliffe; £1 million for Pell Wall; £621,810 for the stables at Stoneleigh; £225,000 for Laxton Hall, Northamptonshire; and £269,342 for Barlaston, Staffordshire.

However in 1995–96 English Heritage had to reduce by 25% the total amount of money it had originally planned to offer for the repair of outstanding buildings because of problems of balancing allocation and future take-up and spend. So again there were few large grants to country houses, with Muncaster Castle, Cumberland receiving £450,000. Two charitable trusts received substantial grants, Burghley getting £91,400, and the stables at Harewood £97,903. In the public sphere the Buxton Assembly Rooms, which form part of the Crescent, received £431,000; Stanmer House, Sussex, £400,000; Mogerhanger House, Bedfordshire, £160,000; the Great Tower at Buckden, Huntingdonshire, £60,000; Vale Royal Abbey, Cheshire, £200,000.

In 1996–97 grants of £50,000 or more to privately owned places included £150,000 to Croxdale Hall, Durham, £76,000 for the gates at Elmore Court, Gloucestershire, £51,480 for Forde Abbey, Dorset, £70,650 for Duncombe Park, Yorkshire, and £125,117 for a range of repairs at Castle Howard. Stowe School received £89,092 for the house. Barlborough Hall, Derbyshire, received £200,000, Temple Newsam £50,000 and Lydiard Park £72,930.

Clearly English Heritage is under great pressure, but evidently it has also been listening to the case made by the HHA and trying to devise a scheme to help hard-pressed private owners, because as recently as September, 1998, it announced a pilot project for a year to target help for outstanding smaller country houses with roof and related structural repairs. That offers assistance in two stages, first with grant aid for condition surveys and repair proposals that will be up to £5000 or 80%, whichever is the lower, and then with help over repairs to be carried out within two years, offering grants of 50% up to a maximum of £200,000. Both the emphasis on speed and the type of building are welcome, but, of course, going to press as the scheme is announced, means that it is impossible to know what the response will be and whether English Heritage will be able to meet it. Hopefully, however, the initial year will soon be extended, because it usually takes time for any grant scheme to get going and few owners are likely to have their share of the costs immediately available, unless they have already been considering a repair programme.

It is natural that some private owners feel that the National Trust absorbs too large a proportion of the grant cake, but in fact English Heritage grants to the National Trust houses have to be looked at in two ways, first as individual grants to houses alongside those in private and other ownerships, as was partly done in the last section, and then as a special category, because since 1990 part of the allocation for individual buildings has been earmarked for the National Trust. In 1990 that was set at £750,000 and was to cover capital repairs to all its buildings including the six houses acquired by the Trust through the Land Fund with an extra allowance for their annual running costs. (When the arrangements were made originally the understanding was that the Government would continue to refund all the running costs and also meet the costs of repair, but it is many years since it has met either in full.) The allocation was increased to £1.6 million in 1993–94 and 1994–95, but since 1995–96 it has been reduced to £1.3 million. That is shared out by the Trust among all its English regions, which make annual bids for repair projects, put into orders of priority. Most of the time the Trust is able to meet the first priorities of the individual regions with grant aid, but if there is a particularly big job going on in a region that may mean that there is little grant money left for others. For instance, the repair of Ightham Mote, in Kent, which is due to be completed in 1998, has proved so expensive that there has been little left for Knole.

So in looking at the larger grants to individual Trust houses they have to be seen as part of a broader picture. For instance, in 1993–94 there was a great deal of work going on at Hardwick costing just over £800,000 and there was grant aid of £367,000; Ightham Mote received £130,000 towards a total expenditure of £613,000. That year work on the temples at Stowe came to £472,000 and grant aid to £188,000. There was also a large grant of £274,000 towards the costs of the clock tower at Cliveden that came to £402,000. The gross costs of the year came to nearly £5 million and the grants to £1.75 million. In 1996–97 the repairs at Hardwick cost £429,000 but there was no grant aid, because the money had gone on large contributions to Ightham Mote (£523,000), the Temple of Concord at Stowe (£207,000) and the chapel at Petworth (£88,000). So the Trust gets nothing like 40% grant on all eligible work, but it reckons it gets fair treatment given the constraints on English Heritage.

That still leaves unsolved the Trust's three greatest problems of Hardwick, Knole and Petworth. In 1995 the Trust prepared figures to submit to the HLF for desirable work at all three houses and the totals came to £19 million for three phases at Hardwick, £14.2 million for Petworth and £19.4 million for Knole. The HLF hopes to make a start on Hardwick, where the first phase was costed at £8.9 million, but, because of its own position and English Heritage's responsibility, it envisages a more modest programme, producing £900,000 to match a grant from English Heritage that would have to be in addition to the annual allocation, with the Trust producing 20%. That would be a start. However, even when Ightham Mote is complete and money can be allocated to Knole once more, it is hard to see how the outstanding work there and at Petworth and Hardwick is going to be financed.

Since 1995 the other new element has been the unexpected success of the National Lottery and so of the funds that have been available to the Heritage Lottery Fund. However, as was explained in Chapter 4, its direct contribution to the country houses in private ownership has been disappointing. On the other hand the HLF has taken some of the strain off applications to English Heritage for large grants for the repair of individual secular buildings and also landscapes not in private ownerships. Moreover, and more important, it has taken over a considerable amount of responsibility for the repair of churches and for conservation schemes in urban areas, including some of the Buildings at Risk, and the intention is that English Heritage should be able to devote more help to individual outstanding buildings, including country houses. However until the reports for 1997–1998 and 1998–1999 are published it will be impossible to see how that is going, but even they will not reveal anything about those who have not applied for help and why.

It is right that English Heritage should remain responsible for individual buildings, and not only for political reasons: those buildings often involve programmes of work spread over several years, with phasing of grants and the need for the advice and supervision provided by the English Heritage professional staff, who often get to know buildings very well over a long period of time and so provide a complementary service to that of owners' own architects. While their expertise is available to the Lottery organisation, the purposes and priorities of the HLF are different; and it cannot get involved in running long-term programmes of work. An essential element in English Heritage's approach is being able to use grant aid to focus attention on the right priorities for repair, including stonework, which owners often put off until there is more to do at greater cost and renewal has to take the place of earlier conservative repair.

However, it has to be realised that English Heritage faces the new century with a great many more responsibilities for buildings in care as well as buildings in a wider range of ownerships, and is in an ever-weakening financial position. No amount of shuffling the pack of grant cards can hide that deteriorating situation.

8

❖

Public Benefit, Access and Education

The idea of the right of public access to privately owned houses and gardens, as opposed to the long-established privilege of access, dates from the introduction of repair grants in 1953 and agreed access as a quid pro quo. Then it was extended by conditional exemptions of outstanding buildings, land and works of art from Capital Transfer Tax, and now Inheritance Tax, and the establishment of maintenance funds, both introduced in the mid-1970s. All these arrangements have brought more access to gardens, parks and landscapes as well as houses, almost without people realising it.

The introduction of the Heritage Lottery Fund emphasised the concept of public benefit, and that, followed by the change of Government in 1997, has drawn attention once more to the whole subject of access to privately owned country houses, gardens and parks.

Here it should be remembered that part of the glory of the British Isles lies in the variety of its landscape, with the lowlands owing a great deal to the centuries of modelling through enclosing, draining and planting and the creation of estates and the building of houses by landowners. Today part of the pleasure of travelling through the country is being able to enjoy that legacy, which only survives because it is still being looked after in a positive way. Yet few houses face a public road as deliberately as Blickling, in Norfolk, or Sudbury, in Derbyshire, or Attingham, in Shropshire, which was designed to look as impressive as possible from the high road that is treated as a drive through its park. But think of the way that the castle at Arundel or the great house at Hatfield stand over their towns. A view of a country house and a church in a park or a house at the end of an avenue is as good as a fine English landscape in an art gallery. Also there are surprises like suddenly coming on the huge house of Burton Constable lying in its park without lodges or gates. Often, however, a house is hidden in its park, and so the pleasure lies in the suggestion made by lodges, park walls and belts of trees as at Burghley, and in the way one can be sensed for miles because of its woods, spinneys and belts, with monuments just appearing as at Castle Howard. At other times the clue is provided by a village being kept up by an estate, as at Rockingham, where it looks up to the castle and church on the ridge (Fig. 64). A well-run estate confers great visual benefits for all to enjoy simply by being there. Think of driving through the valley in which Chatsworth stands or through the Yorkshire Wolds near Sledmere, where in the late 18th and early 19th century Sir Christopher Sykes created one of the three greatest agricultural estates in Eastern England and where, according to the monument to him in the village, he 'made the desert smile' (Fig. 17).

Those are benefits that cannot be measured and certainly not costed, but they soon become apparent when an estate gets broken up and the landscape starts to lose its cohesion, or when a new road cuts through it.

And they should be borne in mind in considering demands for access, which are increasing all the time. Since the Second World War the developments in education, the increase in mobility through the number of cars, as well as in leisure, have created demands for access to gardens and parks that could never have been foreseen. Nor could the increase in the number and variety of the places open. That can be seen from the annual publications *Historic Houses, Castles and Gardens* published by Johansens and *Hudson's Historic Houses and Gardens*.

In the 1950s and '60s the regular opening of an increasing number of houses seemed to be broadly in step with, or possibly ahead of, demand. However in the early 1960s there deveoped a new demand for access to the countryside; this was recognised in the Goverment's White Paper *Leisure in the Countryside* published in February 1966 and in the concept of country parks and the Countryside Act 1968. That in turn stimulated criticism of the National Trust for not opening some of its houses more; and as a result opening was increased at a number of places. Sometimes, however, the Trust was bound by the terms of a lease to a donor family, who were not prepared to revise it despite the great change in public attitudes, perceptions and demands.

Access reared its head again a few years later when the Labour Government considered it in relation to Wealth Tax and CTT and the introduction of the principle of conditional exemption.

Now virtually all the greatest houses and historic collections are open to the public on a regular basis, even if there is no obligation to do so. A very few, like Drayton, in Northamptonshire, a very fragile house, are open by appointment. And every year one or two houses open for the first time, usually as a result of having received a repair grant from English Heritage or taken conditional exemption or set up a maintenance fund. Thus in 1997 Scampston Hall, Yorkshire, opened for the first time, and in 1998 Tissington Hall, Derbyshire; but the pace of new openings has slowed down to a trickle. The great houses formerly open and now closed include Badminton, in Gloucestershire, and Longford Castle, near Salisbury: but it is hard to think of others. In addition there are a fairly small number of important houses without large parade rooms that are not open, among them Melbury, in Dorset, Raynham, in Norfolk, and Dumfries House, in Scotland. However the fact that a house is not advertised as open does not mean that its owner will not show it to occasional specialist groups or those with particular reasons for asking permission. Very few are resolutely closed.

The usual reason for buildings being open by appointment is that they have received grant aid for repairs and are of special interest, but comparatively few of these are country houses. Among them are Frampton Court, Gloucestershire, Hoveton House, Norfolk, Courteenhall Hall, Drayton House and Weston Hall, all in Northamptonshire, and Broughton Hall, Yorkshire (Fig. 38). In addition there are many interesting and surprising buildings belonging to the Landmark Trust, which are let by the week to people who wish to stay in them. They include Woodspring Priory, Avon, Swarkestone Pavilion in Derbyshire, the Library at Stevenstone, the Gatehouse at Shute and Wortham Manor, all in Devon, Woodsford Castle, in Dorset, and Tixall Gatehouse in Staffordshire. There are also a number of houses that are now in institutional use such as Bisham Abbey, Buckinghamshire, Mersham-le-Hatch in Kent, Staunton Harold Hall in Leicestershire, Harlaxton Manor in Lincolnshire and Hengrave Hall in Suffolk.

The other important point, discussed in Chapter 7, is the financial one of a house and garden generally not generating sufficient income from opening and so having to combine opening with functions. That raises questions about degrees of use and the strain on the fabric as well as the occupants.

Thus a political enthusiasm for public benefit and access that sounds attractive and simple needs to be viewed with caution. All places where there are official doubts about the degree of access and there is opportunity to review them need to be considered individually, relating demand, financial costs, conservation demands and human costs. Crude directives could have the opposite effect to that intended, leading owners to say that the balance is no longer acceptable for themselves or their successors and there is no point in carrying on.

Also it is important to remember that access has come about not just through legislation and tax concessions or even economic reasons. A great many landowners believe, as their predecessors have done before them, that they have a duty to share what they have inherited and let others enjoy their houses, gardens and estates.

In the 1950s and '60s when the opening of houses was a relative novelty, a tour of the house was generally seen as complete in itself; visitors were expected to be able to enjoy their visit and understand what they were looking at with the aid of a guide and/or a guidebook and nothing more.

One exception to this was in the use of houses for concerts, recitals and in recent years operas on a variety of scales; these continue to be part of the annual diary of many houses. They are a particularly happy aspect of modern country house life, because not only do they enable people often living in remote areas where there is still little live music to enjoy music in special surroundings but they provide opportunities for young musicians to perform and gain experience and also they bring life and excitement to a house.

However in the late 1960s and early 1970s, partly as a result of work being done on education in a few British museums and a growing awareness of the role of 'interpretation' at historic sites and historic house museums in America, it was realised that more could and needed to be done to inform visitors, particularly young people, and that there was a role for places that combined a new social purpose with a new market. Indeed that has been one of the most significant developments of the past 28 years; and, as with so many subjects relating to country houses, it should be remembered that the first steps were being taken before the tax crisis of 1974 and the emphasis on public benefit in the Government's proposals at that time. On the other hand the crisis, and the way it coincided with European Architectural Heritage Year in 1975, stimulated thinking and activity in the field of what came to be called Heritage Education. The concept of EAHY was itself educational in the broadest terms, in that it sought to increase awareness of the architectural qualities of towns; it had its own Heritage Education Panel chaired by Lord Briggs which prepared the way for the Heritage Education Group set up with D.o.E. support by Lady Birk in 1976. It was building on that mood in 1975 that the HHA proposed the idea of 1977 being designated Heritage Education Year, with the Sandford Awards to historic places with imaginative educational programmes being given for the first time in 1978. A list of early country house winners demonstrates the spread of the idea: Beaulieu, Doddington and Sudbury in 1978, Harewood and Tatton in 1979, Castle Ward and Rockingham in 1980, Hagley in 1981, Blenheim, Holker and Leighton in 1982, Bickleigh Castle and Hopetoun in 1983, Combe Sydenham and Culzean in 1984, Holdenby, Lamport and Sheldon Manor in 1985. The Heritage Education Trust was established in 1982 and it remained active for about the next 10 years.

The first privately owned place to set up an educational programme was Beaulieu in 1970. It was then that Lord Montagu established contact with the chief officers of the local education authorities and out of that came a pilot project. Teams of teachers worked on various aspects of the estate and packs were produced on Palace House, the Motor Museum and Beaulieu Abbey. The first education officer was appointed in April 1972, and in 1975 the education department was established as a charitable trust. Groups now come at every age from pre-school to A level, but the majority are in the seven to eleven age group at primary schools, when it has been easier to relate visits to the national curriculum and all subjects are taught by one teacher, who has control of the timetable. With children at secondary level visits do not fit in so well and also it is harder to programme them, because a number of different teachers are involved and so timetables are less flexible. There is no charge for the educational part of their visit, but they pay the normal group entrance price. Between 10,000 and 15,000 children come in the course of the year, but numbers are dipping, partly because of the costs for schools and parents and partly because it is more difficult to relate visits to schools' programmes.

Probably the most ambitious programme is that at Harewood House (Fig. 41), which started about 25 years ago when Leeds City Council subsidised teachers for school groups. That arrangement came to an end, and Harewood, which is a charitable trust, now aims to cater for children and young people from pre-school age, through primary and

41. Harewood House, Yorkshire. A new angle on the terrace steps during a photographic workshop in 1998.

secondary stages to further and higher education; altogether about 10,000 children come every year, paying a nominal charge. In recent years alongside that it has been developing programmes for adults and also specialist BA and MA courses in collaboration with Leeds University, when Jane Fellars, the principal curator, does much of the teaching herself. She is assisted by two people who organise the schools education and the adult programmes, but how much can be done depends on their abilities and that of the Trust to raise extra money through grants, subsidies and sponsorship. Last winter, for instance, thanks to sponsorship by Tennants Auctioneers, it was possible to arrange for the third year running a group of three talks, this time on Italian Renaissance and Spanish pictures in the collection given by outside specialist lecturers, and also to arrange two-day art history workshops for 35 A level students from five schools in the area. Throughout the year there is a programme of special events, with a particular emphasis on music, that are advertised through a mailing list supported by a booking system.

42. Education at Boughton House, Northamptonshire. Children dancing on the
lawn to the north-east of the house.

This new thinking, related also to the attitudes of owners, can be
seen with the decision of the Duke of Buccleuch, who succeeded in
1970, to open Boughton House, in Northamptonshire, Bowhill at
Selkirk and Drumlanrig Castle, in Dumfriesshire. In his father's day,
although the houses were not open, there was a constant stream of visitors with special reasons for seeing them, and loans were always being
made to exhibitions. Moreover, when he had been a Member of
Parliament, he had become concerned that townspeople knew so little
about the way of life of those working in the country and making their
livelihood there. So in 1975 and 1976 he held Family Days at Boughton,
which is within easy reach of the Midland conurbations, so that people
could get an idea of the working life of an estate and how agriculture,
forestry and land management fit together. However those days were
complicated to organise, and since 1977 he has held two annual School
Days when up to 2000 children come from schools in the surrounding
area. He has established the Living Landscape Trust at Boughton (Fig.
42) to develop a mainly outdoor educational programme but also
organise the opening of the house and special educational visits.

The director's calendar of events now has a booking almost every
day of the year, and the programme runs to capacity with about 10,000
children. Any more would involve taking on more staff, and even for a
professional educationalist like Gareth Fitzpatrick, who runs the trust,

it is a challenge to keep up with changes in the curriculum. About 10 schools come every year, so a child may come once a year for three years; and two or three local schools use the house for history, geography, biology and art teaching. Unusually there is no charge made for school visits, and schools only have to pay for their transport.

In addition Boughton has about 100 groups a year, and 90% of these could be classed as educational. It is the only country house that has been the subject of a monograph on its contents as well as its architecture in recent years. That is invaluable for more advanced teaching, such as the courses that Sotheby's runs every year in the house. As an unexpected spin-off, Boughton is also the first country house to go on to the Internet, as a result of co-operation with De Montfort University at Leicester. Since 1997 it has been possible to do a complete tour of the house and the estate on a computer: not only those considering visiting the house but students all over the world can have images of its architecture, interiors and works of art.

According to a recent survey of its members the HHA found that of 251 replies (not all of which would count as country houses in the sense used here) 45 places had educational programmes, 22 of them having special staff, and they cost £97,760 to put on; they were attended by 113,480 children. On the other hand 104 believed that their places had a potential for programmes and 11 said that funding was needed to enable them to establish a programme.

The National Trust took time to enter the field of education, and, indeed, one of its principal developments in the past 25 years has been its taking up of the idea and establishing what has become a wide-ranging programme that is planned by a central and regional staff. In the late 1960s the Trust was opposed to the concept of education as being part of its responsibilities; Robin Fedden, in particular, was strongly against the use of the Trust's houses for educational purposes. However it was clear that was an untenable position, and the way forward was shown at Sudbury, in Derbyshire, by John Hodgson in the early 1970s. He had become interested in the education of children through his work at the Geffrye Museum, in East London, where he was deputy curator to Molly Harrison, a pioneer in the field; in 1967 he wrote to Robin Fedden suggesting applying what he had learnt in the National Trust, but got a polite rejection. However, when in 1970 he heard of the impending opening of Sudbury, he decided that might be the opportunity he was seeking, because it involved both the main part of the 17th century house in which the Trust was interested and the establishment of a museum of childhood in the Victorian wing of the house as part of Derbyshire County Council's contribution to the partnership with the Trust. It was initially for the museum that he devised a programme for schools, and gradually he infiltrated it into the house, almost without the Trust being aware of what was going on. By the year from June 1974 to July 1975, 189 school parties with 10,616 children visited the house. By that time he was gradually persuading the Trust of the point of the work. Lord Montagu and Lord Sandford who was Parliamentary Under Secretary in the D.o.E. in 1970–73 and in the D.E.S. in 1973–74 visited Sudbury to see what he was doing there, and so he was invited to become director of Heritage Education Year, the Trust seconding him for the year. After that he became the Trust's first education adviser, a post he held until 1989.

What he started from a modest office in Lacock has become so successful that in the late 1990s the Trust welcomes 600,000 children a year on booked educational visits – an unknown number go to open space properties – and has a full-time education staff of 17 people, five in London and 12 in the regions, who are mainly responsible for planning, with a further 40–50 education officers attached to individual properties who do the teaching. The houses most used are Shugborough, in Staffordshire, and Tatton, in Cheshire, both run by their County Councils, with about 35,000 children each in 1995–96. There is a special schools membership scheme by which they pay a moderate subscription on a sliding scale that enables them to bring parties of up to 60 free, and about 6000 schools belong to that. The Trust produces a guidebook arranged by regions to all properties that have educational facilities, listing what they are, how they relate to the national curriculum and whether there is an education officer on site. It also produces special resource books for teaching for about 25 houses, among them Hardwick (1995), Belton (1997) and Canons Ashby and Rufford (1998).

In recent years, as at Harewood, the Trust has been devoting more thought to adult education, and in 1998 for the first time it correlated details of events going on all over the country. Those at houses ranged from 'Elizabethan Life' at Chirk Castle and an 1890s garden party at Lanhydrock to sessions of putting a house to bed for the winter in five houses, which are always popular, a series of four lectures on aspects of the picture collection at Upton, a textile study day at Knole organised in association with the University of Kent and also a WEA course of

10 lectures on the development of the house, three week-long seminars as part of the Local History Summer School organised by Oxford University Department of Continuing Education for the first time in collaboration with the National Trust, a seminar on aspects of recent research at Osterley, and a post-graduate study week at Ickworth for students doing the MA course on Gallery Studies at the University of Essex. Such a range is surely encouraging.

Part of the difficulty for houses planning education schemes, particularly those in private ownership, is the need to relate what they offer to what schools want; since the national curriculum was established in 1990, there have been a number of changes in it that affect houses, and more are in the pipeline. One problem for houses of the classical period has been that the 18th century has not been one of the options for history courses in primary schools: the choice has been between the Tudors and the Early Victorians. Now, as a result of further revisions in the curriculum, with its new emphasis on literacy, history will become optional, and, if a school chooses to continue it, it may take smaller, more focused subjects. So at present it is not clear how the contribution of houses will relate to the new demands, although visual aspects of learning will be just as important as they have been in recent years, if not more so.

In order to cope with school parties a house needs to have somewhere where the children can assemble, but it does not need to be elaborately equipped. What is much more important is the enthusiasm and skill of whoever receives groups at a house, and the time they have to devote to making contact with schools and teachers and plan visits with them. That is expensive, as can be the setting up of a school project.

It is a matter of balancing costs and income. Presuming that a school party, consisting of a coachload of 50 children, pays the price of a group's entrance plus 50p that means the income per group is £175. So 5000 children in 100 parties bring in £17,500; and at £2 per head £10,000. However that is not the total cost of visits for schools and parents, because there is the hire of a coach, generally £100–£150, the equivalent of another £2 or £3 per child. Also parents are not obliged to pay for their children's visits and if a number of parents refuse that may mean that a class has to cancel its visit.

Ideally school parties need to come at other times to the general public, either in the mornings or on days when the house is not open. Then a house that can cope with up to 500 visitors taking themselves around during a four-hour afternoon can cope with 180 children during a school day. Therefore unless a house can build up and sustain a steady programme of visits, the costs are likely to outweigh the income.

Any educational project at a house has to take into account staffing on site and the costs, the outside organisation, schools' curricula and their cost in coming, and behind that the attitude of the local education authority. As one owner explained to me: 'This, in the 20 years we have operated a Schools Project, has varied enormously according to the political background. We are finding a great resurgence of interest in the house now, particularly as the school curriculum is sorted out. This has been a protracted process, but the attitude currently is a great deal more helpful and the LEA is making small overtures towards us.'

Thus a marvellous idea that looks very good in reports and studies and can also sometimes be politically effective – one owner said that his programme was valuable in attracting a level of grant aid for repairs in the 1980s – is actually difficult for many private owners to provide.

However, as we have seen, education is not just for schoolchildren. What is done for students in higher education and for adults can be very rewarding.

How much higher educational use is made of country houses as opposed to their archives in record offices is hard to say, but one of the most interesting early projects was the BA course run at the University of Leeds by the Fine Art Department in collaboration with Temple Newsam, which started about 1969 and continued until 1995 to teach the history of the decorative arts from the collections at Temple Newsam and Lotherton Hall. Leeds University now runs a variant three-year BA course on the History of the Fine and Decorative Arts as one of four options in its Department of Fine Art, concentrating on Harewood in the second year. Also since 1996 it has run a one-year MA course in Country House Studies, which makes full use of Harewood and also visits Castle Howard and Chatsworth. The 1997–98 course attracted 22 students, six full-time and the rest, most of whom have already started work in the field, doing it part-time over two years.

Since 1994 Burton Constable has been involved with a course in Country House Studies that has been organised with Hull University. That is a two-year part-time course forming part of an undergraduate degree programme.

Where those courses must be for the few, adult education can be for the many. Here NADFAS has become important, having grown to

66,000 members in 300 constituent societies in 30 years and still expanding, with waiting lists for existing societies and new ones being formed all over the country and now abroad. NADFAS' aim is 'the promotion and advance of the aesthetic education of the public, the cultivation, appreciation and study of the decorative and fine arts, and the giving of aid to the preservation of our national artistic heritage'.

The secret of its success lies in its unique combination of give and take. All its societies lay on programmes of lectures with study days and visits, and about 175 of them have volunteer groups who do practical work in places open to the public including country houses, mostly privately owned but some belonging to the National Trust (Fig. 43). For some houses they provide guides and stewards, including Chenies, in Buckinghamshire, where they started, and Euston Hall, Suffolk, where there is a roster of 150 volunteers.

NADFAS groups also do a variety of conservation work, which has grown out of the concerns of the late 1960s and early 1970s. The main field is in libraries, where there are 51 groups involving 415 volunteers working in houses belonging to HHA members. Generally a group, which has been trained by a professional book conservator, works once

43. NADFAS volunteers remounting embroidery on curtains at Blair Castle, Perthshire.

a week until the job is complete, which may take two years or more. At Elton, for instance, in the late 1980s, when the British Museum provided a grant for conservation and cataloguing, two librarians worked for a year and five NADFAS volunteers worked twice a week for two years. The society in Ayr, which is more ambitious than most, now sends a group of seven people for four days and three nights once a month to the library at Mount Stuart on the Isle of Bute, going over on the ferry and staying in the house.

A second field that NADFAS groups work in in country houses is textiles, where there are 20 groups with 184 volunteers. Again the teams are guided by professionals, who are careful to give them tasks that can be tackled by amateurs. Much of it is conservation of old materials, but in some houses they make sun curtains and clothes for use in educational programmes. Among the houses they have worked in or are working in are Arundel Castle, Blair Castle, Petworth, and Harvington Hall, Worcestershire, where they are involved in a project to make a new set of crewelwork bed hangings in 17th century style for a bed of that period.

Thus many houses benefit from work that might not be done at all being carried out at remarkably little cost. At the same time those doing the work develop all the satisfaction of a constructive regular activity that brings them in contact with like-minded people and gives them a sense of involvement. Not surprisingly a library that they have worked on becomes 'our' library rather than the owners', and the house becomes 'our' house, to which they enjoy taking other people to see. However one difficulty for NADFAS is that since more women work than 25 years ago, they cannot join the afternoon groups until they retire, so the average age of the volunteer groups is going up.

What is so astonishing about country houses today is the range of activities that they offer, both outside and in, and the flexibility of owners and administrators in working out new ideas for attracting people – and business – and making visits individual and memorable. As visitors become more sophisticated in their responses, they become more demanding, and, while that in turn encourages a healthy spirit of competition among owners, it adds to the challenge that the houses themselves make, for there are always questions about the costs of improvements and new ventures and whether they will even pay for themselves.

[254]

9

♦

The Significance of Smaller Houses

Many people express their sympathy for the smaller country house, probably having a vision of a gabled manor house in the Cotswolds, like Sheldon Manor or Owlpen, or Sandford Orcas Manor in Dorset, or a timber-framed house within a moat in Suffolk like Otley Hall, or a Yorkshire house like Norton Conyers with its 17th century Dutch gables disguising its medieval origins. However what they usually forget is its historical roots in the land, as the centre of what was probably always a small or medium-sized estate. In fact, it is an extraordinarily difficult category to define precisely, particularly if its estate still survives and is taken into account. It depends partly on the size and plan of the house; partly on the social standing of the family or families who created the house in its present form; partly on their means in the past as well as in the present; and partly on the survival of historically associated contents.

Norton Conyers represents their undramatic intensity supremely well, a medieval house that was altered probably more than once in the 17th century and then again at the end of the 18th century, a house of romance and legends, of a Royalist owner whose horse brought him home wounded after the battle of Marston Moor so speedily that his iron shoe burned the bottom step of the staircase and of a mad lady kept in the house in the 18th century whose story was told to Charlotte Brontë and helped to suggest Thornfield in *Jane Eyre*. Its Great Hall (Figs 44 and 45), classicised in the late 18th century, is hung in a deliberately Romantic way with a long series of family pictures from that of Sir Richard Graham, the purchaser of the place in 1626 who fought at Marston Moor, which is still surrounded by contemporary armour, to Sir Bellingham Graham, a figure of the Waterloo period who seems to

44. and 45. The Great Hall at Norton Conyers, Yorkshire. Mid-17th-century armour surrounding the portrait of Sir Richard Graham, whose horse is supposed to have carried him home wounded after the battle of Marston Moor and brought him back into the hall where his hot hoof burned the step of the staircase.

have been enamoured of his fancy uniform in Beechey's full-length portrait, a portrait which was the subject of an in lieu *in situ* deal with York City Art Gallery. Norton Conyers is a place of suggestion, evocation and allusion, and as such very vulnerable today, depending on the family's will to soldier on. If they went, the house would now doubtless survive in other hands, but that would not be the point: in the process of change it would lose its contents and so the evidence of its history and much of its significance.

Such houses are closely tied up with one of the great joys of British architecture and building, its extraordinary regional variety. That partly grows out of the geological complexity of the island that has given us such a range of materials within a comparatively small area, as is shown in Alec Clifton Taylor's *Pattern of English Building*. That is reflected in all kinds of buildings, churches, farmhouses and agricultural buildings, in towns and villages, and industrial buildings as well as, of course, country houses. Thus a building proclaims where it is through its materials and the way that they are worked, and smaller country houses in particular often speak a strong local language, because when their owners built or altered them, they tended to employ the architects, master builders and craftsmen at work in the district.

This sense of place also emerges in the way their monuments and hatchments fill the parish churches, just as their arms still give their name to the village pub, and this leads on to a very important point about English landscape, the ancient link between manor house and parish church that still provides the visual key to many English villages and to the patchwork of rural England.

Stanford, on the borders of Leicestershire and Northamptonshire, is a particularly good example of this partnership expressing the antiquity of the place. It tells much of the story of the ups and downs of English history since the place was granted by King Stephen to the monks of Selby Abbey in 1170 – the grant is on display in the library at the Hall. The involvement of the Caves begins with Peter, who arrived as tenant of the Abbey in 1430, and his brother, who was vicar of St Nicholas's Church in the corner of the park, a fine building that was already more than a century old. The Caves then farmed the land until Sir Thomas bought the place from Henry VIII in 1540 at the dissolution of the monasteries; his great-grandson, the 1st Baronet, was a staunch Royalist, who among other things saved the outstanding 14th–early 16th century stained glass in the church, which was only put

46. Cave family monuments in the church at Stanford.

back in the 1930s after it was rediscovered at the Hall. All the early Caves are commemorated by fine monuments in the church (Fig. 46), and these combine with the portraits in the house to form a complete family gallery in stone, marble and paint (Fig. 47). The 2nd Baronet, Sir Roger, began the present subtly handsome and eminently sensible house, employing Francis Smith, the architect and builder, whose family made such a major contribution throughout the Midland counties in the first

[259]

47. Cave family portraits on the main staircase at Stanford Hall.

half of the 18th century. The house and stables (Fig. 7) were completed
by the 4th and 5th Baronets, the last working with Francis Smith's son,
William. The result is the beau ideal of an early 18th century squire's
place with hall and spacious stables set in a park that combines late 17th
century formality with a mid-18th century naturalism. In the early 19th

century the 6th Baronet's daughter, the redoubtable, unsuitably married and romantically minded Sarah Otway-Cave persuaded Queen Victoria to call out of abeyance in her favour the Tudor barony of Braye that had appeared to die out so swiftly in 1557; and it was she who bought in Rome the portraits and relics of the Stuarts from the estate of Henry Cardinal Duke of York that make such an unexpected appearance among the rows of Caves and their kinsmen. Thus Hall and church are part of a whole, giving a particular vividness to the sweep of English history through the intimacy of scale and the character of the place and also because of the sense of family continuity extending into the future.

In recent years both buildings have benefited considerably from grant aid, and the churchyard adjoins what could be exemptable land. The repair grants may have come out of different allocations of government money, but the reasons for giving them are the same. And just as it is vital that the small congregation with an electoral roll of 10 keeps the church alive, it is important that the family keeps the house going too, for the one without the other would be the poorer, and so would the whole area. Thankfully both places are now in sound physical condition – which they weren't 40 or even 25 years ago. Surely this is an aspect of entities worth pondering on?

Houses and places like Stanford are now much rarer than is generally presumed. There are a great many manor houses that have passed by descent for two or three generations and even more than have changed hands fairly regularly and without any contents that are 'outstanding' as buildings in English Heritage terms; but there are not many that are 'alpha' in terms of architecture, historic contents, and setting. Without attempting to compile such a list even from the places at present open on one or two days a week or by appointment, their variety is suggested by the following examples taken from different parts of the country and conveying the character and history of their regions.

Hutton-in-the-Forest, in Cumberland (Fig. 48), has a northern strength and spans 500 years of Border history. It grows from a medieval pele tower that is still visible on the entrance front, although partly hidden by the still Jacobean Long Gallery range built in the 1640s: it adjoins the Charles II version of an Inigo Jones design that forms the centrepiece of the house, and that in turn is overshadowed by Salvin's new pele tower built about 1830. Within, 17th century woodwork, mid-18th century plasterwork and 19th century decoration give it a strong character. Hutton is an intensely romantic place where Border raiding

48. Hutton-in-the-Forest. A house of Northern strength that has grown from its medieval pele tower to Salvin's new pele tower of about 1630.

still seems a possibility, and suitably, when the present owner's father, whose ancestor had bought the place in 1606, was made a peer in 1964, he chose the title of Inglewood from the medieval forest in which Hutton stands. The present Lord and Lady Inglewood have not only added to the collection of historical portraits in the Gallery, but they have commissioned for the Victorian drawing room a successful family group painted by Anthony Eyton (Fig. 49). At a first glance the room appears all of a piece, but then when the visitor turns round, the big picture is seen reflecting the window against which the figures stand. Thus there is a strong sense of the past looking into the future.

From the Midlands I have chosen Doddington, between Newark and Lincoln, partly because it has kept its estate (Fig. 51), which is more or less the same size as it was in 1749 when it was laid out in its present form; and in Lincolnshire terms it is a great rarity, because in that vast county there are remarkably few houses that have survived intact and even fewer that still retain their historic estates. The house consists of an Elizabethan shell of great distinction which was most carefully restored and remodelled within in a simple classical style in the middle of the 18th century (Fig. 50). It is a combination that is invariably sympathetic, but here the controlled geometry of the house with its three

49. Anthony Eyton's recent portrait of Lord and Lady Inglewood and their family in the Victorian Drawing Room at Hutton.

cupolas makes its attribution to Robert Smythson convincing, while Sir John Hussey Delaval's tactful handling of it sets it on a high plane. Moreover it is a house rich in texture, of tapestries, damask and needle-work, and has excellent mid-18th century wallpapers and papier mâché, so it feels a place to which people have always brought things rather than taken them away. In recent years good modern pots have been added and they look particularly well in the Hall, particularly now that it has a long table designed by its present owner, Antony Jarvis, and made out of Doddington oak that was dried for six years before it was made by Herbert Palin of Croxton-Kerriel in 1991 to mark the Jarvises'

50. An aerial view of Doddington Hall, Lincoln.

51. The Hall at Doddington refitted about 1760 with the new table designed by Antony Jarvis and made of Doddington oak to mark his and his wife's silver wedding.

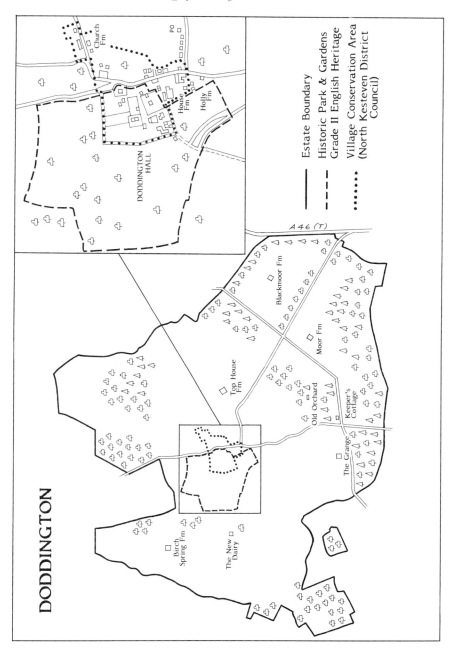

DODDINGTON

Church Fm

PO

House Fm

Holly Fm

DODDINGTON HALL

Estate Boundary

Historic Park & Gardens
Grade II English Heritage

Village Conservation Area
(North Kesteven District
Council)

A 46 (T)

Blackmoor Fm

Moor Fm

Top House Fm

Old Orchard

Keeper's Cottage

The Grange

Birch Spring Fm

The New Dairy

52. The Doddington estate today. An estate that largely retains the form and character given to it by John Hussey Delaval in the mid 18th century.

silver wedding in 1987 (Fig. 52). This sense of continuing to add to the house makes the evidence of the earlier centuries all the more vivid, and it is right that the house should have received several bouts of grant aid for repairs since the first year, 1953, and been the test case for the in lieu *in situ* arrangement, worked out over Reynolds's portrait of Lord and Lady Mexborough in the Gallery at the top of the house. Here it looks down on those who come to the regular concerts and recitals held on summer evenings.

Part of the delight of Doddington is the way it is still tucked away in a rural area; the woods suggest that there might be a house in the vicinity and then there are glimpses of the distinctive three cupolas on the roof. It stands in the centre of the village besides its gothicised church, and together they are the key to the conservation area that interlocks with the land round the Hall, which is graded 2* on the Register of Historic Parks and Gardens. Antony Jarvis suggests that John Hussey Delaval adopted the same approach to the estate as he had to the house and, being influenced by the writings of Stephen Switzer, looked at it as a visual as well as an economic entity. Unusually he never formed a park, which could have been created to the west of the house, but instead concentrated on the landscape as a whole, planning vistas and avenues in the woods, and increasing the number of farms on the estate from two to the seven that still remain on the estate. It was he who planted the shelter belts on former heathland on the east and south sides of the estate, and they have become vital protection for the whole area round the village, defending it against the spread of Lincoln, whose cathedral lies about five miles from the boundary of the estate and can be clearly seen from the Hall through the arch of the gatehouse.

Lincoln is expanding westwards all the time towards the bypass, which has sheered off the most easterly corner of the estate and would have cut right through the belts if its line had not been moved slightly to the east. The bypass is both a barrier against the pressure from the east and a magnet for development up to it; already limited develoment has been allowed within the belt on land that no longer belongs to the estate.

As can be seen from a modern estate map, it contains not only the conservation area and the area on the Register but sites of special scientific interest, semi-natural ancient wood recognised by English Nature, and woods managed under woodland Grant Schemes and so on.

If the estate had to be sold, it would almost certainly be broken up

53. Squerryes Court, Kent. 'To many people the most desirable type of English house.'

so that the qualities of the entity would be destroyed: even if the house with its contents survived for a time, it would be unlikely to be for long, because there would be no point in soldiering on in a place threatened by development. Thus it is interesting to see how John Delaval's thinking 250 years ago has such relevance today, linking history, amenity and community arguments with those of sound planning.

Squerryes Court, near Westerham, in Kent, is a felicitous example of a late 17th century house that is to many people the most desirable type of English house, an essay in warm brickwork with white paint that always seems to smile (Fig. 53). Since 1731 it has belonged to the Wardes, a family originally of successful London merchants and bankers. Over the generations the interior has been considerably altered and Squerryes is now particularly notable for its pictures and furniture mostly collected by the family in the years immediately before and after they acquired the place. The first John Warde, the purchaser, evidently brought a good deal of fine furniture with him, possibly acquired when

[267]

54. The Tapestry Room at Squerryes. Joshua Morris tapestries of the late 1720s hung soon after they were acquired.

he was married to his wife, who died after seven years of marriage in 1727. This included the set of Joshua Morris tapestries bearing their arms that form what must have been a Tapestry Drawing Room on the first floor (Fig. 54). It was his son and namesake who acquired most of the pictures between 1747 and 1774, and over half his well-documented collection is still at Squerryes, happily complemented by an unusual group of 18th century family pictures. Today it is rare to find a house on the scale of Squerryes with so many things of high quality.

In any attempt to convey the varied character of country houses in Britain, and particularly those of gentry families, the special history and atmosphere of old Roman Catholic houses needs to be borne in mind. They have an intensity to their history that comes from their owners having been cut off from public life, office and service from the mid-16th century until after Catholic Emancipation in 1829, a sense of having been under siege for many generations when they had to marry within narrow circles, send their children abroad to be educated and often make complicated arrangements to hang on to their property. The way that sense of the past comes down to the present can only be maintained by the families themselves who continue to maintain a chapel. A few country house chapels that are Roman Catholic are well known, with that at Wardour being arguably the finest, but there the house has lost its family; and it is the chapels that are part of family houses that keep up that particular strand of history, at Stonor, Leighton and Broughton.

Not surprisingly the National Trust has a number of good examples of manor houses, among them Baddesley Clinton, Canons Ashby, Clevedon, Cotehele, Farnborough and Gunby. These houses that depend on continuity in the past for much of their character need to be seen as being different from those that have been carefully restored by 20th century purchasers creating visions of the past, as at Great Chalfield, in Wiltshire, Lytes Cary, in Somerset, Packwood, in Warwickshire, and Westwood, in Wiltshire.

In considering what houses have survived, it is also important to note where they are, because they have become rare in the counties that have been heavily industrialised. Many of their estates have been swallowed up, although a few of the houses survive in alternative uses in urban areas. The process of swallowing up still continues as happened recently with The Oakes near Sheffield from which the Bagshaws withdrew to live in another house they owned. Houses close to the edge of urban areas are highly vulnerable when they come up for sale in that they may find purchasers but there is no way of ensuring that they retain their protective land. That was part of the argument for the use of the Land Fund in 1980 to secure Baddesley Clinton, in Warwickshire, which Mr Ferrers-Walker wanted the National Trust to acquire. If the house had been in a remote part of Norfolk or Suffolk, the place would not have seemed vulnerable, but the proximity of Birmingham threatened the seclusion of the ancient manor house and church protected by its remaining fields.

In recent years a number of these squires' houses like Hinwick House, Bedfordshire (Fig. 55), and Shoteshan Park, Norfolk have been sold and lost their contents, as can be seen from Michael Sayer's lists, and usually that happens without preservation circles being aware of it and without even a full record being made. It is often difficult to know, or at least to say, why these houses have been sold up. Taxation is always presumed to be the reason, and it may well be the determining one, but there are probably other reasons to do with family situations or decisions that are just as significant.

55. Hinwick House, Bedfordshire. One of a number of squires' houses that have been sold and lost their contents in recent years.

In thinking of what can be done for these houses that have retained their contents, the first question is who else other than their traditional owners can do anything. Here the National Trust's position has to be understood. In the past it acquired a considerable number of houses on that scale, by gift or devise and sometimes in combination with a tax deal. However the element of gift remains the key. And now the value of such houses and their settings and their contents is very high and endowments have to be very large.

Also it has become more difficult for the Trust to attract support from the NHMF or the HLF for houses, because the perceived element of public benefit has become a much more significant consideration. In the 1970s and '80s it was the quality of the place that was the paramount consideration; little account was taken of how many people might wish to come. Now, however, merit, cost and benefit have to be looked at together.

That changing view emerged particularly clearly at Pitchford Hall, Shropshire, in 1992. If that had been offered as a gift or in lieu in the 1960s or 1970s, the Trust would have accepted it on merit. But in the 1990s when there was no element of gift and the interior seemed disappointing, merit and cost were out of balance. And the answer had to be No. It was a difficult decision for the Trust, because in a sense it was a new one.

The problems of these houses are distinct from those of great houses on large estates that can be run as show places. Yet they are an integral part of the heritage of houses, and they need to be considered as a group, and as a highly vulnerable one, so that some improved framework can be worked out that resolves the problem of private and family interests.

10

◆

A New Direction: The National Trust's
Country Houses Scheme 1974–1998

If the mid 1970s stand out as crisis years for private owners, it was a time of change for the National Trust in its attitudes to historic houses and its management of them. Thinking began to become more professional and the number of the staff involved in their care began to be increased. However in order to understand what has happened in the past 25 years, it is necessary to understand how the Country Houses Scheme has grown over the past 60 years.

By 1973 the National Trust held 94 substantial houses in England, Wales and Northern Ireland. Of these 76 had come as gifts or devises, 12 through the in lieu procedures and the Land Fund, and only two as direct purchases; of the Northern Ireland houses only one was a gift, Florence Court.

However in the last 25 years the growth has been at a slower pace. In 1977–86 20 houses were acquired, 14 as gifts or bequests, and four through the Land Fund, while the Ulster Land Fund and the NHMF contributed to seven of the acquisitions. In 1987–97 five houses were acquired, three as gifts or bequests, with the NHMF giving Chastleton and providing most of the endowment for Kedleston, and two as purchases using bequests.

In 42 cases there was no son to inherit a house, in some cases because of deaths in the two World Wars. 19 of the houses were acquired by the donor or transferer rather than being inherited by them.

27 of the houses given, bequeathed or transferred through the Treasury came with estates in excess of 1000 acres (Wallington, Blickling, Gunby, Killerton, Stourhead, Arlington Court, Sizergh, Penrhyn, Attingham, The Vyne, Mottisfont, Croft, Tatton, Erddig, Wimpole, Hinton Ampner, Dunham Massey, Buscot, Ickworth,

Sherborne Park, Lyme, Cotehele, Kingston Lacy, Calke, Belton, Felbrigg, Cragside, Dudmaston, Hardwick). With only three estates that came as gifts or devises did the families have sons – Wallington, Killerton and Sizergh: in the case of Kingston Lacy there was a son but he was not married. Of the places bought by the donor, only three had estates in excess of 1000 acres (Buscot, Mottisfont and Wimpole).

In many cases the family has retained the estate and/or the contents. According to a 1996 survey carried out by the Trust, there were 146 houses of all kinds with significant collections of indigenous contents and in 51 a proportion were privately owned.

The majority of those who gave inherited places were members of the country gentry rather than the higher aristocracy. Thus only one belonged to a ducal family (Hardwick); and that came in lieu of tax. Three belonged to Marquesses (Blickling, Ickworth, Plas Newydd); and Ickworth was the first case where objects were accepted in lieu of tax. Blickling was a bequest and Plas Newydd a gift. Nine belonged to the families of Earls (Ashdown, Castle Coole, Clandon, Cotehele, Dunham Massey, Osterley, Powis, Saltram and Shugborough).

This pattern confirms the impression that the great houses belonging to the higher ranks of the aristocracy have survived best, and it suggests that comparatively few of the houses that have come to the Trust would have survived in private ownership, either because there was no son or obvious heir to inherit or because there was not sufficient land to support them in the future.

Moreover it is often forgotten that in the majority of Trust houses where there are donors and their families they continue to live in them, in the whole or in part depending on the way they are open and how many visitors come. Remarkably few families have moved out later, to get away from the Trust and opening. Indeed, in some cases the family or a member of it has returned. At Charlecote, for instance, Sir Edmund Fairfax-Lucy lives in the family wing, the first person to do so on a permanent basis since his grandfather, Sir Henry, died in 1944. And at Stourhead there is once more a family presence in the house.

Not surprisingly some think very hard about following the previous generation, wondering whether it would be easier to continue in a smaller house rather than cope with the restrictions caused by opening, and a few decide that revised opening arrangements make it an unacceptable proposition; or they may wonder whether they can really afford to move in, even if they are not responsible for the roof.

Inevitably in some cases relations are perennially delicate and now and again become bad; but is it not worth remembering that relations can be poor, or worse, in a family where there is no National Trust involvement?

Just occasionally things can come right again after many years, as has happened recently with Florence Court in Northern Ireland. In 1997 the Dowager Countess of Enniskillen gave to the National Trust a collection of over 250 family pictures and historic items which had belonged to her husband, the 6th Earl, and which he wished to go back to the house. Ever since Lord and Lady Enniskillen left the house in the early 1970s the Trust had battled with the problem of furnishing it, and so it was a wonderful surprise when Lady Enniskillen informed the Trust that she was about to send back to the house its historic contents.

Part of the reason for the relationship between families and the Trust being potentially difficult is that few of the arrangements are clear cut, with ownerships often overlapping. While the Trust has the fabric of a house and the garden, it is unlikely to own all or even the greater part of the contents; and in some houses it owns very little: the contents remain the property of the family. Or at least that is how things are at the beginning. Then over the years a family may find itself with capital tax debts to settle and wishes to offer contents in lieu; or it may need to raise capital for its own purposes and so again wishes to sell contents, which the Trust regard it as essential to acquire. So gradually the balance changes, with the Trust's responsibilities increasing and the family's sense of ownership declining. Also the family's means may decline too, and with that their ability to live comfortably in a house that is really too big for them. And with the best will in the world this can lead to uneasy relations, with an inevitable feeling of resentment that the Trust can do things which the family can no longer afford. Often relations work best when the Trust has sufficient funds to look after a place, and the family has the means to enjoy living in it. Such problems probably occurred to no one in the early years of the Country Houses Scheme.

The Country Houses Scheme has now been in existence for over 60 years, which is the equivalent of two generations in many families, and in the case of a few houses and gardens, such as Wightwick, the Trust has owned the place for as long as or even longer than the creators' or donors' families. Thus as the years pass it will be increasingly seen that the Trust's ownership of a house and a garden has its own history, which is just as relevant as the previous history under private ownership: it is just a different kind of history, a point that has become much more apparent during the last 25 years.

Indeed if the years 1973–74 stand out in the post-war history of country houses in private ownership, they also serve as a marker for the National Trust in its approach to country houses. First, in 1973 Robin Fedden retired as Historic Buildings Secretary after 23 successful years and handed over to St John Gore, who was to play a crucial role in the professionalising of the Trust's historic buildings work. For many years he had combined being the Historic Buildings Representative for Surrey and Kent with being the Trust's adviser on paintings, and it was through his care of paintings that he was so aware of the need for proper care and conservation of everything to do with houses; and that was to have a profound influence on the presentation of houses to the public.

The second change was also personal, the establishment of Gervase Jackson-Stops as a full-time member of the staff in 1975. After Oxford he had gone to the Woodwork Department of the Victoria and Albert Museum as a trainee, and there, through his work on Daniel Marot, he had developed an unusually broad approach to the fine and decorative arts, both benefiting from and contributing to the lively atmosphere in the Department at that time.

With his main responsibility being for research in support of the Historic Buildings Representatives' restoration schemes and writing guidebooks, he brought the Trust into much closer contact with others working in the field, particularly in the Victoria and Albert Museum, and in the process gave it a new authority. He came to work across the whole field of country houses in a most remarkable way, and that was to bear fruit in *The Treasure Houses of Britain* exhibition in Washington in 1985–86.

Thus St John Gore and Gervase Jackson-Stops looked at the Trust's houses differently from Robin Fedden and James Lees-Milne, whose approach was anyway already being challenged outside the Trust. The earlier idea of the Trust showing houses on lines as close as possible to those of private houses, as lived-in places with the family having gone out for the afternoon, was becoming an unsustainable illusion. It could still work in those houses that were not open a great deal and did not attract many visitors, and where the donor family continued to live in all or most of the house. But in houses with rooms of parade where there was no family in occupation the atmosphere was becoming false.

Moreover the illusion was being challenged in the Victoria and Albert Museum's rearrangement of the rooms at Osterley and Ham on historical lines.

That caused great unhappiness to the Trust, which was anxious to hang on to its established approach and, particularly with John Fowler's help, suggest that rooms were still lived in or at least could be. That can be seen in what was done in the drawing room and library at Sudbury Hall, Derbyshire: there a wall removed in the 19th century to form one large room was rebuilt to divide the spaces again because of the conflict between the two richly decorated 17th century plaster ceilings and to restore the original rhythm of the plan; and since the rest of the house was short of furniture, with no seat furniture in the adjoining saloon, it was decided to give the two smaller rooms a soi-disant lived-in character with what furniture was available.

However, with the growth of research on interiors, with more use being made of documents, such as inventories, bills and old photographs, it began to be seen that some rooms could only be shown in a way that made better historical sense and provided more vivid experiences if the clock was turned back in a carefully thought out way. What happened can be seen if the Trust's approach to Wallington, in Northumberland, is compared with that at Clandon and then Erddig. When Wallington was rearranged in the late 1960s, its mid-18th century character was emphasised, and the rooms were rearranged on lines very similar to those found in a private country house of the time. Most traces of what seemed unsympathetic 19th century furnishing by the Trevelyans were removed from the mid-18th century saloon, and it was carefully repainted, leaving the old pale blue colour with white on the cove and reversing it on the walls. A generation later that approach would be unacceptable, but a less attractive ensemble might be the result.

At Clandon the challenge was quite different, as has been explained already, because it involved creating a new synthesis out of the Onslow possessions and Mrs Gubbay's bequest, but John Fowler spent many hours poring over the inventory made in 1778, one of the few documents relating to the interior of the house. As a result the early 18th century embroidered state bed with its related chairs was removed from the Green Drawing Room to the room where it had been in 1778; and, when the damask hangings in the former were taken down, a complete mid-18th century green wallpaper was discovered behind them. Both the hall and the saloon were partly restored and partly repainted following careful scrapes. Thus the result was a combination of historical and empirical thinking.

This process of developing approaches to houses has gone on, with each house being looked at on its own and without any definite overall policy decisions being taken. However, the tendency has been to make houses look less worked on, even when a great deal has been done, as at Canons Ashby, in Northamptonshire, Calke Abbey, in Derbyshire, and most recently at Chastleton, in Oxfordshire.

It is easy to see how the untouched look has gained ground, but there is a real difficulty in that it has developed not in places that have been well maintained but in those that had already gone into marked decline. Erddig was pulled back from an advanced state of decay, and the justification for so doing was the high quality of the contents of the house. In almost every category there are objects of great interest and rarity.

A few years later Dunham Massey was first viewed by the Trust as a time capsule, largely because the last Lord Stamford had so discouraged visitors, but on closer examination it proved to be largely an Edwardian reinterpretation of the past and that has come to be regarded as of increasing interest.

Calke was also seen as a time capsule, but it seems to me that while the park is very fine the house lacks the quality to justify the effort and money put into saving it.

Chastleton also came to the Trust after many years of decline, with significant losses of contents in recent years, and to many people it seemed a house on its last legs. The challenge was whether or not to take that low state as the starting-off point for showing the house; and a great deal of trouble and expense was involved in keeping the house as it was while carrying out essential repairs and conservation on interiors and contents. Most visitors have accepted that approach.

Paintwork, carpets and upholstery in any building have to be renewed, and also attitudes change to earlier Trust schemes of restoration and decoration in country houses, as can be seen in work now going on at Ickworth, in Suffolk, and The Vyne, in Hampshire. When that happens, more research is done on colours and paint, patterns and materials, the evidence of photographs and archives and on subjects such as picture hanging and frames, as can be seen at Stourhead and Petworth. Very few houses and rooms are candidates for complete freezing.

[277]

The most frequent criticism of Trust houses is that they tend to appear the same, but I suspect what visitors register is the high standard of presentation and upkeep of houses and a similarity in approach in the way that visitors are received rather than the look of the rooms. But inevitably the signs of family life that give individuality to houses as well as the small objects that a family usually takes away with them have gone from rooms that are hardly ever used. There are no longer coats, hats and boots in halls or papers in sitting rooms, except on rare occasions such as Mr Straw's House at Worksop, because they feel false when not used. Thus the Trust's houses often have a positively different character to those of private owners.

It is worth considering whether the Trust's developing approach is also a response to the changing way private houses are lived in. The way of life of most owners today is simpler and more informal than that of the previous generation, and, although a remarkable number of houses are in a better state and better presented, fewer of the rooms shown to the public are used, even rarely, and very few of those in regular use that are shown are as complex as or have the brio of the rooms that are memorable from the late 1950s – like those created by Mrs Lancaster with the help of John Fowler – and had such an influence at the time.

What is also significant is the effect of the huge increase in visitor numbers to Trust places partly as a result of the growth in membership. In 1945 there were only 7850 members and by 1965 that had increased to 157,581. After that the numbers went up rapidly, to 539,285 by 1975, and in 1985 they passed the million mark to reach 1,322,996. Now it stands at just over 2½ million. Constantly rising costs and visitors' expectations exert a double pressure on houses, encouraging schemes not only to attract more people but to persuade them to spend more, particularly if they are members with free entry. It is a situation that makes the preservation of an intimate lived-in feeling in a not very large house increasingly hard for the Trust to achieve.

Where the Trust has a great advantage is as a charity with special powers given it by Parliament, particularly relating to inalienability. Also it has been asked by successive Governments to take on certain places and receives favourable treatment in various ways (even if successive Governments have failed to honour their promises to continue to carry the full burdens of the places it has asked the Trust to take on). Moreover as a charity it has an ability to appeal for money and attract gifts and bequests. Also in the past 35 years its staff has built up a very considerable bank of knowledge as well as having access to the knowledge of members of its committees, while outside experts are generous with their time.

Here it is important to recognise the contribution of the Historic Buildings Representatives, who are responsible for the appearance of houses, and the way they respond to the challenges that face them. Those who started in the 1960s were strongly influenced by James Lees-Milne's approach and, being familiar with country houses as living places, found no difficulty with the lived-in look. Also for them the 18th century was the central period and the Rule of Taste a basis for judgement. However, Lord Crawford always saw that future generations of Representatives could not have that experience and would come to see houses as places to study. And he has been proved to be right.

In the 1960s the Historic Buildings staff was tiny; in 1970 there were still only five Representatives and five who were honorary. Five years later that had only grown to seven full-time and four who were honorary. By 1980, as a result of Lord Gibson's insistence that the whole country must be covered, there were 12 full-time with two assistants. In 1997 there were 15 with 13 Assistant Representatives. As well as 14 area or regional conservators, the handful of regional housekeepers have grown into 11 full-time conservation advisers for paintings, painted surfaces, wall painting, ceramics, glass, textiles environmental control, organic matter, archaeological artefacts, archaeological sites, and the housekeeper. Thus the Trust has become one of the principal employers of people involved with historic buildings, and it has become a training ground from which people move on to work elsewhere.

Most of the younger generation have moved on from the enthusiasm for the 18th century to later periods, and it is interesting to see how then they respond more happily to work of the 1850s onwards than the 1750s. Just as privately owned houses reflect the tastes and priorities of different generations, so do Trust houses, one difference being that the generations of Trust staff, like those in museums, are much shorter than those in families. And just as each generation in a museum wants to turn it upside down, some of those pressures build up within the Trust, although brakes are kept on by a combination of shortage of money, the amount of consultation that goes on – a process no private owner would go through – and good housekeeping that now makes everything last much longer.

In a recent talk Anthea Palmer, the Representative now responsible for, among other houses, Claydon, Grey's Court, and Osterley, said: 'In many cases the donor families remain, providing continuity of occupation and approach . . . Donors are traditionally land agents and Representatives, and potentially public affairs managers, regional enterprise managers, regional volunteer co-ordinators rolled all into one. In the running of its houses, the Trust has the luxury of employing individuals in each of these roles. The hazard that comes with this is the loss of an individual view, or choice, on what is to be done. While the Representative also has the potential to create a very particular relationship with the donor based on mutual regard for a house as a *place* rather than as a piece of *property*.'

Rising standards and the existence of the National Heritage Memorial Fund since 1980, which gave the Trust a new initiative that it had not had up to then, have made it more selective about houses it will accept in terms of both merit and financial arrangement. Thus it sees itself much more clearly as a solution of last resort, and has been relieved when some prospective offers have not been pursued or have collapsed, and owners have followed the charitable trust route or found other solutions. However, it has invited a few owners to come back if they cannot find a solution. Several of the houses recently put into charitable trusts might have come to the National Trust either as gifts or devises or through the in lieu mechanism. Indeed in a number of cases there were discussions with the Trust, which came to nought usually because the donor considered the requirements for endowment to be beyond the family, or excessive, or both.

Thus it was surely a healthy sign that in the same year that the Trust took on Chastleton, an early 17th century house of great beauty and romance whose future had long been a matter of concern, it also received 2 Willow Road, Hampstead, the house designed by Erno Goldfinger for his own use in 1937. After Mrs Goldfinger died in January 1991, the first thought had been that the house and its contents would be sold, but soon the family had the idea of offering the house and its contents in lieu of tax so that it could pass to the National Trust. That was a marvellous opportunity to preserve a Modern Movement house for the future and to show a fine collection of 20th century European art in the kind of setting for which it was intended. But it was not quite as great a surprise move on the Trust's part as some might presume. For at least 15 years the Trust had been discussing what it ought to do about preserving examples of 20th century architecture and particularly those representing the Modern Movement, but suitable offers or opportunities to make acquisitions are exceedingly rare. So it was entirely right that the Trust should have responded so positively to the offer of the house and its contents.

But it is good that the National Trust has not taken on any major house since, because it has had to concentrate on a number of major building as well as landscape projects: considerable work has been going on at Ightham Mote, Ickworth, The Vyne, Osterley, Petworth and Ham, as well as the restoration of Uppark after the fire, and that has been in addition to what has been involved in taking on Kedleston, Belton and Calke – surely enough challenges for any organisation?

On the other hand there is a case for saying that any institution depends for some of its dynamic spirit on growth, and, if there are not fresh challenges, there is a loss of pace and direction. With the Trust there is never a lack of challenges, but I detect a change of direction among the staff as a whole away from houses to gardens, parks and landscapes, and a desire of the younger generation, who have a more sociological and less art historical approach, to consider other cate-gories of buildings such as the workhouse at Thurgarton, in Nottinghamshire.

Thus there is a certain, but quite incorrect, feeling around that the Trust will not take on any more houses. That is not so. Rather is it that most of the houses that it has been asked to consider in recent years have come too late so that the entity has been compromised, or they have not been worth the huge amounts of public money required to acquire and endow them. When the Trust was considering Appleby Castle, in Westmorland, which was on the market, it recognised its immense appeal in the locality, partly because of the extraordinarily vivid personality of Lady Anne Clifford, one of its 17th century owners, but the interior let it down. The Trust was looking at a building a genera-tion too late. Also the castle had lost control of its setting, and it was likely to continue to suffer from development. Moreover there was no element of gift, which was not only contrary to the Trust's policy, but made it a difficult project for the NHMF or the HLF to support to the degree that would have been necessary.

In 1997 Trust committees discussed an Acquisition Policy Review, which contained a section on partnerships. This may well be important for the future given the huge expense of accepting a major house like Kedleston and the out-of-proportion costs involved in a middling large

gentry house. The Trust had become unhappy over the old arrangements made over Lyme, Osterley and Ham and the short-term one over
Heveningham, but even so the paper pointed out that 'it should be
recognised that they have all resulted in very substantial financial
resources being made available by outside organisations, without which
the Trust could not have afforded to maintain the properties involved,
or indeed acquired them in the first place.' And it attributed many of
the problems that the Trust encountered to the lack of good agreements and leases. Indeed it says, 'Equally we can see no reason at all
from our examination of these cases to reject properly organised,
formal partnership agreements.'

Recently the Trust has been considering again the future of
Godolphin, in Cornwall, a romantic place with a manor house of
medieval origin with a remarkable early 17th century entrance front,
gardens and estate of 623 acres. It was first offered to the Trust in 1969
by Mr and Mrs Sydney Schofield and accepted on merit, but it could
not go through for lack of finance. However in 1972 and 1977 the
Schofields gave covenants over most of the property. Then in 1991
Mrs Schofield approached the Trust again and again Godolphin was
accepted on merit but once more the acquisition did not go through
for lack of money. The family then explored the possibility of establishing a charitable trust with the support of the NHMF, but that body
felt unable to become involved. Mrs Schofield approached the Trust
for the third time in 1995, and, since then, as a result of new research,
particularly on the significance of the garden adjoining the house,
which has led to exciting discoveries about its Jacobean form, and the
archaeological significance of the estate, Godolphin has proved to be
a much more important place than was realised before. However at the
same time due to the decline in the Government's support for the
NHMF and the pressures on the HLF it is no longer possible to con-
struct a financial package for the whole property. So the Trust has had
to reduce its plan to hoping to acquire the estate from the family, partly
through regional funds but with some support from the HLF, and
leaving the ownership of the house, garden and some amenity land
with the family but so enabling them to repair it with the aid of English
Heritage. The family and the Trust's long term hope is that it will be
possible to reunite the property in the Trust's ownership, but meanwhile some of the pressure will be removed and the Trust will secure
the sensitive land surrounding the house that has its own high historic

significance. So it must be counted as a success if it goes through.

However in the context of country house saves made by the Land Fund, the NHMF and the HLF since the Second War, it should be seen as a dire warning of how the last and present Governments have betrayed the concept of the Land Fund and how that has led to a situation in which it is no longer possible to take on even a medium-sized house, let alone a great house with a collection like Kedleston. So is Godolphin the first of a new round of country house casualties?

Godolphin is thus a much more important case than it might appear at first, and a great deal will depend on how persuasively the Trust can present the broader case to the Government, because it will affect the private sector as well as itself. And if the Trust is seen to falter or be thought to be faltering in this sphere of activity, that would be extremely damaging to the cause of country houses.

II

◆

The Role of Charitable Trusts for
Country Houses

One of the surprises of recent years is that the National Trust has not taken on any country houses since 1991. That prompts the question 'Why?' The answer is partly that owners have not needed to turn to it, because of a combination of lower rates of tax, the introduction of Inheritance Tax which enables property to be handed over, conditional exemption and maintenance funds, and partly that those who have needed to find solutions have been able to establish charitable trusts. Without anyone being aware of the spread of the idea, there are now over 30 set up for important houses. At least five are for houses that were the subject of earlier serious talks with the National Trust that came to nought.

In England there are charitable trusts for Allerton Park, Yorkshire; Arundel Castle, Sussex; Belmont, Kent; Blenheim Palace, Oxfordshire; Boughton House and Burghley House, both in Northamptonshire; Burton Agnes and Burton Constable, both in Yorkshire; Chambercombe, Devon; Chatsworth, Derbyshire; Chavenage, Gloucestershire; Chiddingstone Castle, Kent; Endsleigh, Devon; Godinton, Kent; Grimsthorpe Castle, Lincolnshire; Harewood House, Yorkshire; Hellens, Herefordshire; Hoghton Tower, Lancashire; Kelmarsh Hall, Northamptonshire; Knebworth House, Hertfordshire; Lamport Hall, Northamptonshire; Leeds Castle, Kent; Parham and Stanstead, both in Sussex; Stoneleigh Abbey, Warwickshire; Stratfield Saye, Hampshire; Sutton Place, Surrey; Titsey Place, Surrey; Weston Park, Shropshire; Wilton House, Wiltshire.

In Wales there is a trust for Picton Castle, in Pembrokeshire.

In Scotland there are trusts for Blair Castle, Perthshire; Bowhill, Selkirk; Castle Leod, Berwickshire; Castle Menzies, Perthshire;

Hopetoun House, Midlothian; Mellerstain, Berwickshire; Paxton House and Thirlestane Castle, both in Berwickshire.

In addition there are several trusts for gardens, parks and landscapes, among them Exbury, Hampshire; Painshill, Surrey; Painswick Rococo Garden, Gloucestershire; Spetchley, Worcestershire; Wentworth Woodhouse, Yorkshire; West Dean, Sussex.

Although the practice of setting up charitable trusts has developed since the 1975 Finance Act included what it called Gifts for Public Benefit, the idea had been around since the Gowers Report; the Duke of Devonshire, for one, had been interested in the concept ever since he inherited Chatsworth in 1950, but he was not able to pursue it until after 1974 when the estate duty and the interest on it was finally settled.

The first house to become vested in a charitable trust was Hopetoun House, near Edinburgh, for which the arrangement was made by the 3rd Marquess of Linlithgow in 1974 after the failure of negotiations with the National Trust for Scotland on endowment. However, with the encouragement of Basil Skinner, who had originally gone to the house to make a survey of the pictures for the Scottish National Portrait Gallery, Lord Linlithgow developed the idea of a trust, which was already possible under Scottish law. The trust was given the house but hardly any of the contents, and the endowment was modest. However, largely thanks to generous grant aid for repairs from the Historic Buildings Council for Scotland and the NHMF, the trust was able to keep going for several years after Lord Linlithgow's death in 1987.

By the early 1990s, however, more capital was essential if the trust was to carry on. Also it was vital to secure the contents of the principal rooms that remained the property of the family. The only hope of achieving either or both lay in the support of the National Heritage Memorial Fund; and how a new solution was arrived at is considered in the context of the Fund's involvement with other charitable trusts.

Soon after it was established in 1980 the NHMF began to consider whether alternatives to the National Trust and the National Trust for Scotland could not be worked out, in particular finding one that involved much smaller endowments. The first Secretary, Brian Lang, had been secretary of the Historic Buildings Council for Scotland and so was well aware of the problems of private houses and those belonging to the National Trust for Scotland as well as the Hopetoun solution; and it was no accident that the first charitable trust set up by the NHMF was for Thirlestane Castle in Berwickshire (Fig. 56). There the family

56. Thirlestane Castle, Berwickshire. The first charitable trust for a house to be set up with the support of the National Heritage Memorial Fund.

gave the main part of the house and its contents to the trust, but not the family wing, which they continue to own and occupy. And occasionally they use some of the main rooms. The funding for the trust was provided by the NHMF. There are seven trustees, four initially nominated by the NHMF and three, including the chairman, by the family; after six years the NHMF trustees became self-electing but still subject to agreement with the family nominees.

Since then the NHMF has been involved with four more trusts for houses – for Weston Park, Shropshire, Paxton House, Berwickshire, Burton Constable, Yorkshire, and Stoneleigh Abbey, Warwickshire, as well as Hopetoun.

Since the matter of endowments is crucial, it is interesting to see some of the NHMF and HLF endowments for houses and gardens set down together: Thirlestane (originally £668,505 and £250,000 added in 1988–89), Belton (in the region of £2.76 million), Calke, Chastleton (£2 million), Burton Constable (in the region of £3.3 million), Hopetoun (£1 million), Canons Ashby (£1 million), Kedleston (in the region of £6.31 million), Newhailes (£6.4 million).

The result is that the charitable trust tends to be seen in some quarters as a preferable solution to the National Trust, but this may prove to be an over-simplified view, because the NHMF may find that it has to top up more of its endowments. It always knew it might have to do this at Thirlestane and has already done so in 1988–89. Also it involves the nature of the houses and what property goes with them, the position of the donor family and questions of management.

In terms of tax treatment there are obvious advantages for the family in choosing the charitable trust route in that a trust has all the benefits of a charity, and, if its funds are skilfully invested, it should be possible to increase them very considerably; a trust may also be eligible for money from other sources and grants. That, however, is not the complete picture.

Houses and estates invariably need periodic injections of capital and that applies whether they are in a trust or in private ownership; and a family, having established a charitable trust, may be unwilling, or unable, to inject any more funds later if the original endowment has not grown sufficiently. Thus putting a house into such a trust may be like launching a ship on an uncertain voyage without hope of future supplies. And when a house in a charitable trust gets into difficulties, it is very difficult to keep it afloat; the costs of trying to refinance it from the sale of constituent elements such as exempt works of art can be daunting.

At present there are four main groups of charitable trusts, with the family in two of them retaining a large measure of responsibility for management.

The first group consists of places where a trust has been set up because there was no son to succeed and the heir was a nephew or a cousin. The most obvious example is Arundel Castle. There the late Duke of Norfolk had negotiated an arrangement with the National Trust that did not go through after his death in 1975. Much more satisfactorily, the present Duke and his family then established a charitable trust to hold the castle; the executors of the late Duke carried out a major programme of repairs that had been delayed, and endowed it with a capital sum. That was a fifth of what was required by the National Trust but acceptable to the Charity Commission. Since then the endowment has been built up satisfactorily and the castle opening operation, which has been kept as simple as possible, works well. The contents remain the property of the family, except for the group of historical portraits that were the subject of one of the first in lieu *in situ* deals. The Duke is the chairman of the trust, and, although he and his son, the Earl of Arundel, provide the lead, the family have to be in the minority on the trust.

In 1988, soon after the birth of their son, Lord and Lady Arundel decided that they should live at the castle in order to give it a sense of life, which they felt was draining away since no one had lived in it permanently since the late Duke and Duchess had moved into a new house in the park completed in 1960. However, whereas they had lived in the main part of the castle, which was also open to the public, the Arundels decided to move into the nearly derelict east wing, which had been planned in the 1880s as the family wing. Since the whole castle had been given to the trust in 1977 Lord Arundel has a long lease and pays rent for the wing, which he and his wife have restored, modernised and decorated in a spirited way. If and when they want to use the principal rooms or any of the bedrooms in the trust's part of the castle, they rent them on a business basis, the arrangements being made by two different firms to avoid questions about personal benefit. In this the arrangement parallels that at Hopetoun and it does not appear to cause any mental blocks.

What is so encouraging about the arrangement at Arundel is Lord and Lady Arundel's sense of commitment to a place where he had not been brought up and their seeing it as a joint personal challenge. Even now with the enthusiasm for late 19th century architecture established, most young couples might feel daunted by the castle's aggressive architectural interiors and the configuration of its family wing, with everyday life taking place on the ground and second floors. However the castle makes great demands on Lady Arundel, and, whereas the wife's role in a privately owned house is recognised, it could be taken for granted in the structure of a charitable trust. All works well here, but clearly anyone considering establishing a trust needs to think of the position of a wife and how she is able to have a role that benefits the place as well as being satisfying for her: if a trust does not work for her, the idea of family commitment will cease to work too and a place will lose its family feeling.

At Burghley the charitable trust was set up by the 6th Marquess of Exeter, who had daughters but no son to succeed to the title, and it came into being on his death in 1981. He vested in the trust part of the house and part of the estate, reserving the private apartments on the ground floor for himself and future generations of the family. Lady Victoria Leatham, his youngest daughter, runs Burghley for the trustees of the charitable trust and lives in the private apartments with her husband, Mr Simon Leatham. These are visited by many specialist groups during the year and by those with specialist interest in their contents, which are also loaned to travelling exhibitions that raise money for the upkeep of the state rooms. Moreover she frequently uses the private rooms for the benefit of the charity when it comes to fundraising – and she lives literally under the shop, acting as principal administrator and curator for the building. Thus before the lead on the roof was renewed in the course of the 1980s she described hers as an Eight Bucket Family. The governors of the trust have placed great emphasis on the restoration and improvement of the house and encouraged her direction of Burghley during the past 17 years through funding major structural works as well as a great deal of much-needed redecoration and conservation of pictures and furniture, as is explained on pp. 000–000. If she had provided the inspiration and the driving force, the broad success of the operation owes a great deal to John Culverhouse, who has been the house manager for 14 of those years.

Burton Agnes, near Driffield, belongs to this group of family-funded trusts and contradicts the hunch that the charitable trust idea is best suited to great houses that naturally divide into rooms of parade and private apartments. It is a large manor house rather than a great house. The place has passed by descent, but through several families, since 1173, and the late Marcus Wickham-Boynton, having abandoned the idea of bequeathing the house to the National Trust, decided on his own variant of the National Trust Country Houses Scheme by dividing his inheritance into two main parts in 1977. For the house and garden, which had been open since 1946, he established a charitable trust; and to that he gave the house, an endowment in cash and 600 acres of land, with the proviso that the house should be lived in by his chosen heirs. The rest of the estate and the contents of the house he left in another trust to those heirs, the family of the Hon. Nicholas Cunliffe-Lister, the younger grandson of Mary, Countess of Swinton, who was a Boynton, thus maintaining the connection with his own mother's family and so with the line of descent. On his death in 1989 the trust's running of the house, which is open every day from the beginning of April to the end of October, was taken on by Mrs Cunliffe-Lister, and she lives in it, paying a rent for the private rooms that strikes a balance between her contribution to the running of the place and the benefit she and her family get from living there. The rent is an essential ingredient in the equation as far as benefit is concerned, because the house is not large enough to permit a division into public and private parts, and the family needs to have daily use of the dining room, which is across the hall from their sitting room as well as being one of the rooms always open to the public. Mrs Cunliffe-Lister also runs the estate and the farm for the family. Thus the arrangement has all the advantages of the security of the National Trust (except for inalienability) and the advantages of personal management and sense of continuity of life in the house, in the creation of new gardens, which are increasingly important in the visiting pattern, and the addition of new works of art to carry on Marcus Wickham-Boynton's enthusiasms as a collector.

Mrs Cunliffe-Lister takes the brisk view that the charitable trust protects the place from the uncertainties of modern life as well as taxation; and that it is better for the place to be secure, even if individual members of the family have less as a result. Perhaps because of the way her family have come into the estate, she does not think of it as their place. In 1990 the family trust gave the porcelain in the house and the carpets to the charitable trust; and presumably in the future, when need be, in lieu *in situ* deals could be done over the contents, as has happened over the portraits at Arundel.

The Burton Agnes trust has now been in existence over 20 years, and it will be probably some years before her younger son takes over the running of the estate or the management of the house, but Marcus Wickham-Boynton's plan appears to have much to commend it. So it would be interesting if other families with less complicated patterns of descent followed Mrs Cunliffe-Lister's line of thinking.

The second group of places are those where the direct succession appears assured, there are substantial estates and the house or part of it is leased to a charitable fund for a period of years, with the majority of the contents leased or on loan. The arrangements for Chatsworth, Boughton and Bowhill work in this way. They have the advantage of not creating an alienated hole at the heart of the estate, which would be unsatisfactory for the estate and in preservation terms.

The idea of the Chatsworth House Trust, which was established in 1981, went back to the 1950s when the Duke of Devonshire realised that it was essential to take the strain of the house and gardens off the estate, and so he asked his lawyers to devise what he described to them as his own National Trust for Chatsworth. It could not be set up until the trustees of the Chatsworth Settlement were free of death duties. The Duke's heir, the Marquess of Hartington, became the first chairman, and non-family members are in the majority on the board. The trustees of the Chatsworth Settlement leased the structure of the house, the public rooms and their contents together with the gardens to the house trust and gave it an endowment raised from the sale of Poussin's *Holy Family* (which is now shared by the Getty and Norton Simon Museums in America). The Duke hopes that the scheme will see the house through at least the next 50 years and that the family will continue to live in it.

However, the creation of the house trust should not be seen in isolation, because it related to the change in public perception of what had come to be called the heritage, with its greater appreciation of such places. That made it seem more worth soldiering on. Also the appearance of a younger generation who were prepared to work for it has been a great encouragement.

Luton Hoo was intended to work in a way similar to Burton Agnes, although the family ceased to live in it. However it was only partly endowed, the intention being to increase the endowment later out of the profits of develpments on the estate, which belonged to the family. Unfortunately there were major problems with those developments which put an end to that intention, and eventually led to the family's decision to sell the whole estate. Moreover the problems on the estate led to the sale of a number of major objects that were lent to the foundation by members of the family, and the foundation itself had to sell objects from the collection that it owned to meet deficits that arose when the endowment could not be replenished. And now the foundation has had to find a new home for the collection. Thus a charitable trust cannot always provide the secure future that was hoped for.

The third group of places consists of those where succession is definitely not assured, and now or at the end of the present generation there will be no one in the immediate family to provide the motive force. Here the Grimsthorpe and Drummond Castle Trust established by the late Earl of Ancaster is the outstanding example.

In this group comes Belmont, Godinton, Kelmarsh, Lamport and Blair. In the case of Lamport Sir Gyles Isham, who was unmarried, had considered leaving the place to the National Trust, with which he had been involved for many years, but because of the size of endowment required by the Trust he decided to create a charitable trust, which he set up in his lifetime and endowed on his death in 1976. He left the house, its contents and the estate of about 2225 acres including a farm of 300–400 acres in hand to the trust. But in the early years there were considerable financial problems partly because of the need to complete the repair of the house after a series of battles with dry rot that had forced Sir Gyles out of it. The trust now operates in four parts, with the house, park and contents in the Preservation Trust, and the remainder of the estate in an endowment charity to support and feed the Trust; and there are two trading companies, one for the farm, and one for the opening of the house and related enterprises.

The difficulty with Lamport is that it is a house of specialist interest that needs the personality of Sir Gyles, who had been an outstandingly handsome actor before he became an antiquarian squire passionate about all things to do with Northamptonshire. So it does not attract a great many visitors, about 3–4000 a year, and it is reasonable that it is not open a great deal, on Sunday afternoons and Bank Holiday Mondays from Easter to early October and for a single tour on weekday afternoons in August; it concentrates on special parties and educational groups.

At present Lamport is fine with committed local trustees including Sir Gyles's nephew, but I wonder how long houses like it will be able to maintain a head of steam and whether in the long term it might have been safer if a way could have been found of transferring it to the National Trust, into an established and evolving system, even if that meant that the endowment had to be topped up. However given the run down in the NHMF and the direction taken by the HLF that possibility seems more remote than five years ago.

It is this group of squires' houses in trusts that causes concern. In the past they have depended for much of their character on belonging to families committed to them, and now trustees have to face all the problems the National Trust has with smaller houses that are no longer lived in. They need the kind of enthusiasm that Lady Victoria Leatham has brought to Burghley, and that is so difficult for a committee of trustees to maintain over a long period.

The fourth group consists of places where trusts have been established through the initiative of the National Heritage Memorial Fund. The first of these was Thirlestane Castle and since then variant arrangements have been made for Weston Park, Paxton House and Burton Constable.

In the case of Burton Constable (Fig. 8) in 1991–92 the National Heritage Memorial Fund contributed £5,417,284 towards the establishment of a foundation for the house, park and scientific instruments. The furniture, pictures and most of the rest of the contents were given to Leeds City Art Galleries to remain on permanent loan in the house. It is a satisfactory solution for the problem of a huge house in a remote area which has great difficulty in achieving a substantial number of visitors and for which John Chichester-Constable and his late wife had fought valiantly for 30 years. However the interior still presented a major conservation challenge; the support of the Leeds Museums and the personal commitment of the staff at Temple Newsam are crucial for the success of the project. The practical side of that can be seen in the grant from the HLF towards the conservation of the huge Wyatt-Chippendale pier glasses in the drawing room, which had reached a near dangerous state but whose repair had hitherto been beyond the means of any public funding agency.

In addition in these four groups there is a small sub-section of places which had been set up as charitable trusts and have received help later from the NHMF. So far only Hopetoun, Endsleigh, which was discussed on p. 000, and Stoneleigh come into this category.

Hopetoun House was the first trust set up by a family where this has happened; and here the Fund contributed £4 million, £1 million for endowment; £700,000 for repairs and £2.3 million for the purchase of contents. The refunding of the trust has coincided with a new approach to management by the present trustees who run the place on commercial lines to maximise revenue while minimising the strain on the house. Being so close to Edinburgh the house has not attracted more than 35,000 visitors a year. On the other hand its situation close to the city and airport is an advantage for functions of different kinds; and in the ballroom, converted in the late 19th century out of the riding school and originally planned as a library, it has the largest room in the district, where it is possible to give dinner to 160–180 people.

57. The Saloon at Stoneleigh Abbey, Warwickshire, as it was in 1984. The house and setting, which were threatened after the collapse of a charitable trust, have been saved by the Heritage Lottery Fund and other bodies collaborating to establish a new trust for it.

The management aims are being met by the establishment of two trusts and an operating company, and profits are now being made that will be crucial to future phases of repair. It is realised that stonework repairs will need to start about 2002 and these are estimated to cost about £6 million over the following five years.

In the case of Stoneleigh (Fig. 57), which lies in the heavily pressurised area between Coventry, Kenilworth and Leamington Spa, the charitable trust established by the Leigh family in 1980 had run out of funds and into debt. That meant that the huge house with its great front range by Smith of Warwick and its contents, which belonged to the trust, and what remained of the wider setting were all at risk. So the HLF had to decide whether to step in at the eleventh hour and go in with English Heritage, the European Regional Development Fund, both of which agreed to contribute £1.35 million, and Warwick District Council to establish a new trust that would buy out the old one and enable it to settle its liabilities. The HLF's contribution came to £7.37 million of which £2.6 million was for the cost of the house and its contents. It was a brave decision, because the problems of Stoneleigh were so daunting and went back a long way, to a bad fire in 1960, then via all the difficulties the family had in the 1970s finding a suitable commercial use for the house, and death duties on the death of the late Lord Leigh in 1979 before the first trust was formed. The new trust is the best arrangement that could have been made in the circumstances, but without the contents and the threat to the setting, an important amenity in the area, the decision to back it might not have been taken; and even two years later the HLF might be unable to find so much money. So it cannot be regarded as a precedent for baling out other similar operations that get into difficulties.

Almost inevitably the concept of charitable trusts has had to become more formalised since the first ones were established in the 1970s and early 1980s, not least because the whole business of charities has been under review with new Acts of Parliament in 1992 and 1993. Not only has there been a review of charity law, but the Charity Commission is reviewing its register of charities and considering what ought to be charitable; also it is visiting all houses that are in such trusts. And when a scheme for a new one is presented, the Commission wants to know more about how it will be managed and looks harder at questions of benefit. If it is considering what should be charitable, perhaps it could also think about what could be done to make a charitable formula work for smaller houses where there is still a strong family involvement and it is likely to continue and the house cannot be divided into two distinct parts. Given the difficulties of devising alternative arrangements through the National Trust, particularly in view of the run-down of the NHMF, it is the less than great houses that need a more secure framework than exists at present.

Owners and their advisers are naturally cautious of the idea of charitable trusts, because they do not like surrendering control. Also they are concerned about conditions in the future being made more onerous by the Charity Commissioners, with family benefit becoming increasingly sensitive and demands for access increasing. However, I have been surprised to find their thinking about trusts changing as they worry about primogeniture, future matrimonial problems and the need to take the strain of the house off the estate.

Thus, as with conditional exemption and maintenance funds, a concept that has been developed for one reason may develop in rather broader directions and become a 21st century equivalent of the 18th century strict settlement that worked so well for so long.

12

⸻ ◆ ⸻

The Entity of the Country House
Today and Tomorrow

(a) *Country Houses in the Late 1990s: Public Attitudes and Private Problems*

If the country houses situation in 1998 is compared with that in 1974 or in 1948, the two lowest points in the past half-century, it is striking that not only do many more owners seem more optimistic about the present and the future, but many more houses have come through the past 25 years than seemed possible in the dark days of 1974–78 and, partly thanks to repair grants and the standard of work insisted on, most are in a better physical state than they were 50 years ago.

The optimism can be seen not only in those country houses that have passed by descent, but in other ways. In recent years there has been unexpected demand for large country houses, and some have commanded very large prices. That, however, depends on character and location, with houses of liveable size and within two hours of London selling for very high prices; those that are either more difficult or in remote places take longer to sell and often fetch lower prices. Tythrop Park, Oxfordshire, was put on the market at £4.5 million in 1994; Wilbury Park, in Wiltshire, is rumoured to have sold for £8 million in 1996. In 1997 Hackwood and its Hampshire estate of about 2400 acres was put on the market for £15–£20 million. In 1997 Pusey House, Berkshire, with 1500 acres, was put on the market in two lots inviting offers in excess of £8 million and was sold for a sum approaching £10 million. Moynes Park, Essex, with 417 acres, fetched the guide price of £4 million. Culham Court, Oxfordshire, with 840 acres, which was put on the market at a price in excess of £6 million, reputedly fetched a sum in the region of £12 million–£14 million.

58. Duncombe Park, Yorkshire. In the late 1980s, after being let to a school for 60 years, the house was restored for family use and opened to the public.

A surprising number of houses that were in institutional use have returned to private occupation. Allerton Park, in Yorkshire, and Brancepeth Castle, in Co. Durham, for instance, have found new owners. Others, like Farleigh House, in Hampshire and Duncombe Park, in Yorkshire, which were schools, have been taken back by those who have inherited them. Farleigh had been let to a school in 1954, after the Earl of Portsmouth had gone to Kenya in 1950. His grandson, who had hated his time there, was determined to drive it out and make it his home; he took the house back in 1983 and finally went to live there in 1989.

The return of the family to Duncombe Park (Fig. 58) is an even more remarkable story, because it had been in occupation by a school for 50 years. The house had been let in 1926, during the minority of the 3rd

Earl of Feversham, whose father had been killed during the First World War, the year after he succeeded his grandfather. The present Lord Feversham inherited Duncombe (but not the earldom) from the 3rd Earl, his fourth cousin, in 1963, and he lived outside the park. That was frustrating enough since the splendid park is the key to the estate, but what made it worse was that the school did not have a full repairing lease, so that the estate was going to have to shoulder most of the burden of a looming repair programme. So when a break in the lease came up in 1986, Lord Feversham decided to exercise it and take the house back, restore it for his own occupation and open it to the public. It is a huge building and the task was a daunting one, but what is surely so interesting is that Lord and Lady Feversham were prepared to tackle what is essentially an Edwardian house restored by the 1st Earl after a fire in 1879. Would that have happened 25 years earlier?

Country houses, happily, arouse surprisingly deep feelings in people, especially if they have some family connection with a place, and they are prepared to stretch themselves to a quite remarkable degree to bring a house back to life. That can be seen at Winkburn, in Nottinghamshire, which Mr and Mrs Richard Craven-Smith-Milnes bought back in 1979 when it was virtually derelict.

Other houses with uncertain futures have become successful hotels, among them Ston Easton, in Somerset, Middlethorpe Hall, near York, and Hartwell House, near Aylesbury. Brocket Hall, which had been developed for conferences by Lord Brocket, was sold in 1997 for £9 million for a 60-year lease.

Several notable houses that had lost their contents have found new lives through being subdivided into apartments. Here a remarkable contribution has been made by Kit Martin, who has tackled what has become a fleet of distinguished houses, with Callaly Castle, in Northumberland, Cullen House, in Banffshire, Dingley Hall, in Northamptonshire, Hazells, in Bedfordshire, Keith Hall, in Aberdeenshire, Tyninghame, in East Lothian, and Burley-on-the-Hill, in Rutland.

Local authorities, on the other hand, have taken hardly any new initiatives in the historic house field in recent years and often find their historic house museums, like Heaton Hall, Manchester, and Temple Newsam, Leeds, expensive undertakings for which they have been looking to the HLF for assistance to catch up with the backlog of work and the funding of improvements. The exceptions to that are Newport

Borough Council's taking on of Tredegar House in 1974 (Fig. 23) and the development of the house into one of the most successful historic house museums, and Birmingham Museum's taking on and restoring Matthew Boulton's much smaller house, Soho Hall.

Indeed it has been more symptomatic of the time that public authorities have withdrawn from places. That seems to have started in 1983 when North Yorkshire County Council sold Studley Royal and it was acquired by the National Trust with the aid of the NHMF. Since then the Victoria and Albert Museum has retreated from Osterley and Ham, and Stockport Council from Lyme Park, Cheshire, and all three have been taken into full management by the National Trust. In the case of Lyme the house, which had been run by Stockport since the late 1940s, was taken over by the Greater Manchester Council in 1975 but, when that was abolished in 1986, it went back to Stockport; in 1993 the Trust was asked whether it would take over management, provided an annual sum continued to be paid by the Borough. Similarly Speke, which had been leased to Liverpool City Council in 1943 when it was acquired by the Trust, was taken into direct management by the Trust in 1986 supported by an annual grant from the National Museums and Galleries on Merseyside.

It is surely worthy of note that neither the NHMF nor the HLF has funded any acquisition of a historic house by a local authority. So they cannot be looked on as providing possible solutions to problems as they did in the years before 1970.

However, despite the successes in the private sector, there can be no room for complacency. There have been collapses of families and houses and dispersals of contents, as we have seen, as well as a great deal of draining of objects from houses – many sad stories for families – and also there are a number of houses with uncertain futures. That is partly because of the shortage of supporting assets, usually reduced by several lots of death duties during the last 100 years, and the need of houses and estates for periodic injections of capital; and partly because of the uncertainties hanging over the future of agriculture; but it is also because of the demands these houses make on their owners if they are to be kept going. So no one can predict how many will survive in 25 and 50 years time.

At the same time it is worth drawing together some of the positive threads examined in this study and considering the position that has been reached. What strikes me – and I stress that I write as a non-owner who is spared all the worries – is how much more sophisticated has become the approach to houses and their settings in the last 30 years. That is partly the result of the development of specialised knowledge and thinking about a whole range of subjects fully represented in country houses – the histories of architecture, collecting and patronage, decoration and furniture as well as of gardens, parks and landscapes that, of course, involves flowers, plants and trees. In addition there has been the development of conservation thinking and a much greater awareness of the educational contribution that places can make.

Thinking has developed in depth in all these separate directions, and at the same time it has fanned out in breadth, and the multi-faceted aspects of a country house, garden, park and estate has become much more widely appreciated in terms of its contribution to life and leisure today. Thus the entity has much greater meaning and a much higher value than it did 25 years ago.

It is that very English step-by-step progression of thinking that has given much broader meaning to the concept of conditional exemption of outstanding buildings and their settings underlining the value of estates in terms of conservation planning. Conditional exemption of a setting of a house is in one sense inward-looking, in that it provides a protective band for a building, but also protects as far as possible views from it. However, what is also so encouraging is to see how conditional exemption can be complementary to a conservation area, providing positive management as opposed to passive or merely negative planning protection.

So while the entity is perceived to have a higher value than it did a generation ago, the framework within which it survives and flourishes has also become much more complex. Inevitably at times exasperated owners feel that they have to work within not only a set of guidelines but a series of strait-jackets imposed by different departments and agencies of central and local government: to them the concept is one of control rather than partnership. Yet the latter must be the aim of Government. Certainly there was a sense of partnership between owners and the HBC in the 1960s, '70s and early '80s, and it is on that kind of approach that it is necessary to build in the future.

The other essential point is that husbands and wives remain as loyal to their places as the immediate post-war generation, and there is no sign of this faltering. Owners of smaller estates realise that they and their heirs can no longer look to their property for a full income for themselves, and that they will only be able to keep their land and their houses if they pursue careers with success. Then, when they take over management of the property, they will either have to carry on with their careers or provide their own professional management.

But it has to be faced that heirs may not be so able or hard-working, or may have doubts about wanting to be so committed to a place or prefer to continue to follow their chosen career. And, if that happens, it is only fair to understand their doubts and accept their decision not to follow on. In the past a house and an estate could survive a weak generation or many people living off it. Today that is much more difficult, and no official preservation system can – or can be expected to – cope with that.

In considering family attitudes, it is also important to bear in mind what seems to me to be a new problem, that of the future of primogeniture. Whereas in the early 1970s it was just assumed that it was one of the corner-stones of the British system and would continue unchallenged, now it crops up quite frequently in conversations with owners about how they see the future. It is a system that has always been tough on younger sons and daughters, and that seems increasingly less acceptable to both parents and children. Not only do daughters feel that they should be treated in the same way as sons, but careers and the instability of modern marriage have dented the idea of a wife's dependence on her husband.

Thus, although there is no legal definition of how estates should be divided, and the presumption is still in favour of the eldest son having the lion's share of the property and the contents of the house in order to keep the entity together, particularly if there is a title involved, there is evidence of estates having to find larger portions for younger sons and daughters. Those portions siphon off capital that can be difficult to raise and can be ill afforded, particularly if there are taxes to be paid on transfers. Thus estates are weakened.

Moreover an increasing number of owners do not automatically assume that the eldest son will inherit. Some realise that they cannot decide their children's lives for them and that their children will not have such decisions taken for them; they consider whether a daughter might do the job better than a son, and also wonder whether they are handing on an opportunity or a life sentence.

When owners think about primogeniture, they also have to consider the risks of future divorces and the threat they pose to houses and estates. That seems to be leading a few to think again about the role of trusts and charitable trusts as a defence against the risks.

Quite apart from broken marriages, settlements and divisions are almost certainly going to create more problems in the future, and it is going to make it more difficult to hold together houses and their contents if there are several heirs involved. And it will be the smaller country houses that will be hardest hit, simply because the smaller the cake the more difficult it is to divide without destroying it.

Those who are offered and accept the challenge of running an estate with a house open to the public are given an opportunity for a working partnership between husband and wife that is rare today. Yet a house is likely to be as demanding as a third person in the marriage, always there and always in need of attention. As one owner said to me: 'The house does not belong to me: I belong to the house;' or as a wife said, she always feels as if she is 'being run by the house'. Both, however, must believe in the future, and that what they are doing is worthwhile for themselves, their family and the wider community as well as for the house; here the family is the most important element, because that involves a long historical perspective that looks backwards and forwards. In this they are surely being challenged by their ancestors, not to be the generation that fails the family, past, present and future, and breaks the chain of descent. Or as James More-Molyneux has written of his house, 'Each generation of the family is called upon to serve Loseley in its own particular way.'

Obviously some owners enjoy opening and sharing their houses more than others, but almost all get satisfaction from the pleasures that they provide for their visitors and from feeling that what they do has public support. If their contribution cannot be costed in normal terms, it is important to recognise that there has to be a balance between the satisfaction of carrying on and doing something that is of public benefit, and the burden involved in it. That is not just a matter of money and taxation, but problems of staffing, maintaining security and coping with increasing bureaucracy extending from listed building controls to health and safety regulations: all these add many weights on the downside of the scales.

Privacy, convenience, the quality of family life and also the price paid by the children need to be taken into account. Owners are reluctant to include these matters in any public assessment, but anyone used to the freedom of their own house will soon be struck by the demands and restrictions imposed by a country house open to the public today and of the surprising lack of privacy. It is important for the family as well as for the house that they should be able to use most of it occasionally; it is also good to give the house its own sense of life and purpose, not least because visitors quickly sense if all the life has been drained from the rooms that they have come to see.

For most owners and their wives who are directly responsible for a house-opening operation, it is a job that is best done for a term of years, and not for life. When they reach 60, they often find they have less steam for keeping going and thinking progressively about the yearly programme; but a husband and wife may look differently at giving up and handing on, perhaps not being ready to do so at the same moment. The matter of handing on, however, will have been in their minds for quite a long time.

In this thought needs to be given to three generations rather than the two that are generally thought of. Most owners now in their 50s would say that the ideal age to take on a place is 40 or a little more, but less than 45, and that the children of the incoming generation should be over six, so that they are able to look after themselves in a big house and grow up enjoying it so that they develop their own deep commitment to it. By their late 50s many owners are thinking not only about when and how they can hand over, what they will do afterwards, and where they will live, but whether the son and daughter-in-law are going to be ready and willing to take over.

Thus the ideal time for an owner to be in the saddle seems to be about 25 years, from about 40 to about 65 as the outside ages. Theory and practice, of course, turn out to be very different, because there are so many variables due to age, marriage and its stability, when children are born and how many there are, and times of inheritance. Quite a number take over earlier, when they are about 30, before their children are born, and they tend to have a longer innings, of 35 rather than 25 years.

In all this the wife and daughter-in-law are crucial, because much of the detailed, day-to-day work falls on the wife, and she has to be willing to take up the challenge. Arriving from outside she may find it takes five or six years to come to terms with a house and make it come to terms with her and her family; and naturally she will want to place her own stamp on it. That will involve not only her husband's attitude – and probably means – but the appearance of the house and her in-laws' attitude to it. And equally in some places husbands and sons-in-law should also be remembered.

While an estate may maintain itself and contribute to the support of a house and indirectly the family, few can support two generations of a family over a long period. So one of the practical problems of handing over is slicing the cake in such a way that it can provide for both the generation that is handing over and the one coming in. Moreover two generations are likely to have different attitudes to property and may have problems discussing their ideas and worries with each other, and that makes things more difficult. The immediate post-war generation of owners were remarkably tough and puritanical – they had to be – and talking to present generations about their predecessors reveals how determined they were. Most of the present, younger, generation, whether they are owners or heirs, have had a much easier time, and, although they often work harder, they expect success sooner and greater financial rewards with higher spending power. Also they are less used to the historical discipline of trusts and settlements, which have been broken up for tax reasons, and they expect to have greater freedom to decide how they manage their estates.

Only those directly involved with such transfers know what a strain they can prove to be, even when both generations set out with the best intentions and the highest hopes. No two situations and no sets of experiences can be the same, but anyone interested in country houses should have a sympathy for families having to work things out – and not be totally surprised when one occasionally turns to the National Trust and presents it with at least some of their personal problems as well as their property.

All this means that, in spite of all the developments in thinking, in legislation and improvements in taxation, many owners and their wives and their families are still like trapeze artists on the high wire.

(b) *Changing Perceptions of Country Houses*

Undoubtedly some places have gone down in interest and significance during the past 25 years, particularly through the loss of contents, either major works of art or general furnishing. The converse is that other

59. Rodmarton Manor, Gloucestershire. Begun in 1909 to the designs of Ernest Barnsley, it is one of the houses that is more highly valued than 25 years ago.

places have become a great deal more important and are stronger candidates for preservation now than in 1970. 19th and 20th century houses are more highly valued than they were 25 and 30 years ago. Here houses that stand out include Sandon, in Staffordshire, one of the few surviving complete houses by that master of early Victorian planning, William Burn; Knebworth, in Hertfordshire, a Victorian novelist's fantasy, with a remarkable drawing room by Crace; Somerleyton, in Suffolk, which represents much more solid manufacturer's taste; and Rodmarton, in Gloucestershire, which is arguably the finest Arts and Crafts house (Fig. 59).

The change in attitudes can also be seen with Stokesay Court, in Shropshire. When Mark Girouard wrote *Victorian Country Houses* in 1971, he was not impressed by it, including it only in his catalogue, where he described it as 'very large, unoriginal and unlovable'. The owners were understandably rather offended, but when some years later

I went there with James Lees-Milne who asked whether he might write about it in *Country Life* as an example of manufacturer's taste, they refused, because they did not like that emphasis on trade. It was only after the death in 1992 of Lady Magnus-Allcroft, whose house it was, that it was discovered that most of the original contents had never been unpacked after the Second World War and so it was an unusually complete document. Evidently Lady Magnus-Allcroft had never envisaged anyone being interested in the house after her time: indeed she made any preservation scheme virtually impossible because of the division of her estate laid down in her will. English Heritage would have liked to have acquired the house for preservation, but could not get the support of the NHMF. Whether or not one regrets the dispersal, the change in attitude in a little over 20 years is worth remembering.

When in 1976 the Marquess of Anglesey offered Plas Newydd to the National Trust, it was accepted not only as an early 19th century gothic house in a superb position, but even more because it represented country house taste between the two wars through its transformation by Lord Anglesey's father. It was he who commissioned Rex Whistler to paint the dining room, one of the most remarkable painted rooms in England.

Even before Plas Newydd came up, the National Trust was concerned about how to preserve 20th century country house taste for posterity, and how to balance the classical tradition with the Modern Movement, because there is an increasing awareness of the fact that what is being done now is for future generations. In 1978 Lord Iliffe offered the Trust Basildon Park, Berkshire, which he and Lady Iliffe had saved in the 1950s and filled with fine pictures and furniture. While at the time it was viewed as an important 18th century house by John Carr, it is the Iliffe period that is already the more interesting one and will surely seem significant to future generations because it illustrates so well the enthusiasms of the post-war years.

Not only do views of what should be preserved move forward, but attitudes change to what has already been accepted for preservation. That is to be seen with a number of National Trust houses. Charlecote, for instance, was originally accepted in 1946 as an Elizabethan house with Shakespearean connections, but all too soon James Lees-Milne considered it 'too drastically altered in the 1850s. The strange thing is that Mrs George Lucy, who perpetrated the abominations, was the one member of the family who most loved Charlecote, and revered its

Shakespearean associations.' Yet by 1952 Christopher Hussey was able to write; 'The Elizabethan house built by Sir Thomas Lucy in 1558 is equally notable for the romanticism of the early 19th century restoration.' Since then it has been increasingly seen as a fascinating example of early 19th century Romantic taste and response to the past.

Lanhydrock, in Cornwall, which was given to the Trust in 1953 by the 7th Viscount Clifden, was originally seen as an early 17th century house, but after the family connection came to an end with the death of the 7th and 8th Viscount's sister in 1969, the Trust had to think about how it was going to show the house. It decided to concentrate on the house as it was rebuilt after the fire of 1881, as a late 19th century social document revealing how life was organised on both sides of the green baize door.

A more recent illustration of changing attitudes is to be seen at Treasurer's House in York, which was set up as a historic house museum by Frank Green between 1897 and 1914. When he gave it to the National Trust in 1930, he left fierce instructions about how nothing was to be changed or moved. By the 1960s, however, the house looked very dejected without yet being a period piece, and so, when the Trust had to do some repairs, it made some changes to the colours of rooms that seemed right at the time. However within a few years they were felt to jar with Frank Green's taste, which was coming to be seen as of interest in its own right; and so in the 1980s a drive took place to put the house back to what it had been in 1930.

Two examples of gardens with houses also come to mind, Knightshayes, in Devon, and Nymans, in Sussex. At Knightshayes Sir John and Lady Heathcoat-Amory began to develop the garden soon after the Second World War and in 1955 Sir John created one of the first charitable trusts for it. Ten years later he began to talk to the National Trust about the future of the whole place and the Trust agreed to take on his garden trust after his death. Not surprisingly, and quite understandably, neither he nor his wife had cared for his grandfather's house begun in 1869 to the design of Burges and completed by Crace, and over the years they modified much of the interior. After Sir John died in 1972, Lady Heathcoat-Amory moved out of the main part of the house, and that left the Trust with the problem of what to do with a building that still seemed a monster to most people, a monster because of Burges and Crace but equally unsatisfactory to admirers of Burges and Crace because of the modifications. The Trust decided to open it to the public and gradually to reveal and restore original decoration that could be uncovered and recreate other parts of the scheme. In the late 1970s it started with the dining room, morning room and upstairs corridors, using Campbell Smith who had done the original painting, and since then it has tackled the drawing room and the library, which was completed in 1998. The most ambitious operation has been to restore the Great Hall, which has involved putting back the screen and restencilling the roof; a start has been made on revealing the stencilling on the walls and redoing that. It is an amazing story, but, if the Trust had ever thought in the mid-1960s that it would have to face up to the house, it would surely have refused to get involved. In the mid-1970s the restoration seemed the only way forward. But if the decision had had to be taken a generation later, in the mid-1990s, would anyone have had the confidence to choose that route?

At Nymans, the West Country manor house created by Mr and Mrs Leonard Messel in the 1920s had been gutted by fire in 1947, and in 1954, again not surprisingly, no one took the ruins very seriously or imagined that in the longer term anyone would want to live in what remained of the house. Certainly no one could have foreseen that some 40 years later the Trust would want to open the surviving ground-floor rooms to give visitors a sense of the relationship of house and garden and of the personalities who created the garden.

With these threads in mind, it is surely important to consider the preservation of country houses by architects working in this century. Lutyens is an obvious candidate. It is good that the National Trust owns Lindisfarne Castle, in Northumberland, and Castle Drogo, in Devon, but it is highly desirable that some of his early Surrey houses should survive intact. Goddards was given to the Lutyens Trust and leased by it to the Landmark Trust, but that is furnished by the latter and has none of its original furniture. And what should be done about a major Raymond Erith house and a complete house by Francis Johnson? It would be interesting for posterity to be able to compare these with Meols Hall, Southport, designed for his own use by Roger Fleetwood Hesketh in the early 1960s and exempted on his death in 1987 (Fig. 61).

Also it is desirable that a major scheme of private country house decoration by John Fowler should be preserved, but that is much more difficult, because of the transitory nature of decoration and the difficulty of faithful renewal. Radburne Hall in Derbyshire may well be the best example.

[309]

60. The view from the Ballroom to the Drawing Room at Manderston, Berwickshire. The finest Edwardian country house in the British Isles.

The Scottish situation has to be looked at separately, because the history of houses is different and so has been the interest in them. The antipathy to the 19th century has been very strong and a great deal has been lost, but that was a great period for Scotland and so it is important that complete examples of houses by Burn and Bryce should be preserved. The National Trust for Scotland owns Kellie, the home of Robert Lorimer, but there are very few of the houses that he designed and furnished left. John Kinross was never so successful, but he was a highly skilled architect, and Manderston, in Berwickshire, is arguably the finest house of its period in the British Isles (Fig. 60). The most recent house in Scotland to cause concern is Gribloch, in Perthshire, one of the most interesting country houses of the 1930s to survive with most of its original contents. It was designed by Basil Spence in a style that spans the Regency Revival and the Modern Movement, and in terms of merit and rarity it is a house that would be a highly desirable acquisition for the National Trust for Scotland. However it is also a house that would be desirable to a private purchaser and so cannot be regarded as under threat. On the other hand there is no way of tying the contents to the house, and all will depend on the sensitivity of the purchaser – may it be as lucky as it was in 1984. The Trust discussed the case with the HLF but, understandably, received no encouragement to pursue it, so all depends on market forces.

This changing perspective also affects private owners, as I have sensed in the course of working on this study. Going back to houses 25 or 30 years after I wrote about them in *Country Life*, I find younger generations having a much more positive attitude to the 19th century aspects of their houses, and this will continue.

All this means that a list of country houses worthy of preservation cannot ever be closed, and finite lists are dangerous, because they are bound to become out of date and create unnecessary hurdles and barriers. Meols Hall (Fig. 61) is a particularly good illustration: in 1960–64 Roger Hesketh designed and carried out the transformation of an undistinguished fragment of a 17th century house into what is in my

61. Meols Hall, Lancashire. It was largely designed by the late Roger Fleetwood Hesketh and built in the early 1960s to contain family pictures and furniture. It was accepted as suitable for a maintenance fund and for conditional exemption from CTT.

view the most successful country house formed in England since the Second World War, partly because of the way that he planned the interior round the family pictures that had been left to his branch of the family. Meols was greatly admired by Sir John Summerson as a work of architecture – he was not normally drawn to country houses as living entites. In the late 1970s or early 1980s Roger Hesketh applied to set up a maintenance fund for Meols and for that the house had to be accepted as outstanding by the Historic Buildings Council. It was, the fund was set up and after Mr Hesketh's death Meols was exempted from Capital Transfer Tax – surely an admirable illustration of why history does not and cannot stop.

Changing attitudes do not just mean whole houses; during the past 25 years there has been a marked change in attitudes to alterations and reductions of houses that perhaps has not received as much attention as it might. After the war many houses only survived because they were reduced in size, with large late Victorian and Edwardian additions being eagerly removed, but with the growth of interest in later periods and the increasingly historical approach to architecture the way houses have grown is seen as an important part of their value, so there has been an increasing reluctance to accept reductions. Here the listing system and those who operate it come in for a great deal of criticism from owners unable or reluctant to spend large sums on parts of houses that are beyond their requirements, but in fact the listing system only reflects a way of thinking that needs to be understood. Here there is not the space to go into the whole subject of listed building consents and country houses, which has come up most recently over the application to remove the late 19th century wings from Barrington Park, a fine house of about 1740.

How thinking changes in this field is particularly well represented by the demolition of the ballroom at Deene Park. It had been added on to the house in the early 1860s by the 7th Earl of Cardigan and by the mid-1970s it was the only remaining part of the huge house unrestored after a programme of repairs that had started in 1947 and had absorbed all available resources. In about 1975 Mr Edmund Brudenell applied to the HBC for grant aid but it was rejected on the grounds that the building was not of sufficient interest. That view led him to apply for permission to demolish it; after that was refused, he appealed, and the case went to a public enquiry. There the application was hotly contested, but in 1979 the Inspector finally came down in Mr Brudenell's favour; and demolition took place in 1984. If the case had come up in 1965 rather than 1975, there would surely have been no serious problem and the loss of the ballroom would have been seen as a reasonable price to pay for the restoration of the rest of the house. But by 1979 attitudes had changed both to the architecture and to the historical significance of the building, and the decision was finely balanced. By 1989, by which time the bill for restoration would have doubled or tripled, it is hard to believe permission would have been granted. The temptation is always to see preservation issues as being absolute, but the Deene ballroom shows how attitudes are in a state of constant change.

(c) *The Contribution of Estates to Conservation*

Well-managed estates have always been natural units for what has come to be recognised in recent years as conservation, but the new word has brought with it a fresh perception of their value to those outside the circles of owners, their agents and advisers, or who live on them, particularly to those professionally concerned with preservation and planning who see estates as outsiders. Thinking about areas, and conservation areas in particular, started to change attitudes and under-standing, but arguably it was the introduction of conditional exemption of land from Capital Transfer Tax and its inclusion in maintenance funds alongside the influence of garden and landscape history that brought planners face to face with the importance of estates as agents for positive management and as defences against fragmentation and undesirable development. When the principles of exemption were introduced, I do not believe that anyone fully appreciated what the pos-itive benefits could be. Indeed, when I began on this study, I had not expected to find such a variety of situations in which estates were seen as being assets in planning terms.

The first example does not involve conditional exemption, but it shows how conservation thinking has developed. It is Heydon in Norfolk, where the saving of the Hall was considered on p. 37 (Figs 4 and 5). That was only part of the story, because the point of Heydon is as a whole (Figs 62 and 63), the village, most of which belongs to the Bulwer-Long family, with its fine church, the park, the Hall and sur-

62. Heydon, Norfolk, from the air in 1950. This shows the relationship of the village to the park with its avenues leading to the Hall (illustrated in Figs 4 and 5).

rounding estate. Some may remember the village from the film *The Go-Between*, while Norfolk planners think of it as Norfolk's first village conservation area, designated in 1971. That did not include the park or any of the estate, but in 1991 the whole estate was declared a conservation area by Broadland District Council. That made it eligible for a range of English Heritage and District repair grants and also grants for landscape work. All but two of the houses, one of which is the Old Rectory, and all the cottages belong to the estate, and over the last 30 years it has repaired and modernised the buildings in the village and the farmhouses and cottages. And the village flourishes with a pub, a shop that has a tea shop at the back, a hairdresser, a blacksmith and a village hall.

Captain Bulwer-Long was equally keen that the landscape should retain its traditional character, maintaining and renewing its planting and its hedges. So it was one fitting tribute to all he had achieved at Heydon that shortly before his death in 1996 he was given the Royal

63. The village green and church tower at Heydon in 1982. The restoration of the
house in the early 1970s has been followed by the successful conservation of the
village and the estate, the whole of which was designated a conservation area in
1991.

Agricultural Society's Bledisloe Award for Estate Management and a
second that John MacLachlan should have explained what William
Bulwer-Long had done in an article in *The Royal Agricultural Society of
England Journal* for 1996. He started out in 1964 with 160 acres in hand,
capital of £10 and an overdraft facility of £5000, and he built that up
into a modern farm of 1340 acres. In the 1950s and '60s, as is explained
in the article, the family had resisted requests from their farm tenants
for permission to remove hedges and plough up parkland and water
meadows, and as a result the farms taken back into hand 'had relatively
small fields, extensive areas of heavily tree'd parkland and inter-
connected stretches of water meadow.' He continued to resist advice to
change the landscape and in the last 12 years planted some 1½ miles of
hedge, mainly filling in existing gaps.

[315]

The article ends: 'Thanks to enthusiasm and foresight William Bulwer-Long succeeded in holding together an archetypal corner of England with its combination of a landscape attractive to wildlife and the human eye, an unspoilt village with a working community, a liveable country house in a satisfactory state of repair, supported only by 990 acres of let land, houses and cottages let at affordable rents and a modern 1300-acre farming business, conducted very much with the well-being of the landscape and wildlife in mind.' That explains why the local authority, through its Conservation Officer, welcomes the constructive relationship that they have built up with the Heydon estate and fully appreciates the role the estate plays in combining conservation planning with providing an economic framework for the community. Surely that is something hard to envisage writing 25 years ago?

Since many English houses like Heydon lie in parks, the elements are rarely as visually closely related as they are at Ripley near Harrogate (Figs 36 and 37). There the ancient settlement at the gates of the medieval manor house was transformed into a romantic model village in the early 19th century following the rebuilding of the manor house as a castle-style house in the late 18th century; slightly later came the formation of the lakes in the park and the creation of a latter-day Brownian landscape. The castle, which has grown from a medieval tower, is an oustanding building in its own right, and, while it provides the historical and visual key to the place, it is but one element in a remarkable picture whose quality can only be appreciated on foot but is suggested by a comparison of an aerial photograph with plans.

How vulnerable a picture it is can be seen from its recent history, to which reference was made on p. 219. Estate duty incurred in 1974 combined with a Capital Gains Tax liability incurred in settling the duty reduced the estate by 50%, from 3750 to 1850 acres. Only great determination and staying power on the part of Sir Thomas Ingilby and since 1984 of Lady Ingilby, combined with an essential element of luck of location 3½ miles from Harrogate with its conference centre opened in 1982, have enabled him to keep the picture intact. But Ripley is no longer primarily an agricultural estate and has had to develop a new economic base.

Survival is depending on adopting a fully commercial approach to the running of the castle and the opening in 1990 of the Boars Head Hotel in the centre of the village. That in turn has meant that the castle, hotel and estate now employ 100 people, which is six times as many as in 1974. It has also involved a realistic policy in the letting of houses in the village. While the estate has not been able to retain complete ownership in the village, having had to sell some plots for new building, it owns most of the properties facing the T-shaped layout. In the 1960s the rents were completely uneconomic, but since 1982 it has been possible to repair and modernise most of the buildings, often with grant aid from English Heritage, and produce a realistic return: at the same time the estate has a letting policy in favour of young couples with children who will attend the village school, so helping to keep a threatened institution open.

Thus it is very instructive to see how the area of historic landscape embracing the park and setting of the castle defined by English Heritage and the conservation area of the village overlap and how the historical, scenic and planning aspects now interlock with the new economic base, with its implications for employment and the community.

At present the balance is acceptable – just – but the physical demands on the castle itself and even more on the Ingilbys are too great to be sustained indefinitely, and the long-term survival of the entity must depend on reducing those demands while sustaining the alliance of the castle and the hotel. Any further loss of control in the village would be very regrettable, not only in social terms, because the houses would be bought up by professional people, but in terms of conservation planning because it would be exceedingly difficult for the local authority to provide the positive management that is provided quite naturally by the estate. The death of Sir Joslan in 1974, a matter of months before the transfer of the estate was complete and only two years before the introduction of exemption, illustrates all too clearly the point of exemption for the preservation of estates and how hard it is to achieve when the capital base is cut away so savagely.

At Rockingham, in Northamptonshire, the elements are similar, but their relationship is different because of the lie of the land (Figs 64 and 65). The castle commands a ridge with great views to the west over Leicestershire and the village climbs up the north-west slope of the hill from the plain towards the church and the castle, with the ancient park lying on the high ground to the south-west of the castle. It is an immensely ancient place, with the castle founded by William the Conqueror possibly occupying an Iron Age site and the park being essentially the royal deer park established by 1256, with its boundary scarcely altered since 1485. Thus if a modern plan is compared with the

64. Rockingham from the air in 1953. This shows the relationship of the village below the church with the castle commanding the top of the hill. In recent years Corby has come up to the belt of trees at the top of the picture.

earliest estate survey in 1615, the most substantial change is the alteration in the line of the road that was pushed away further from the castle in the 18th century. It is a place where views are very important, both of the castle and within the demesne but also out to the north-west and north, as can be seen on the map of land designated as heritage property for support by maintenance fund. Moreover while castle, park and village form a complete entity, that has developed an additional value,

[318]

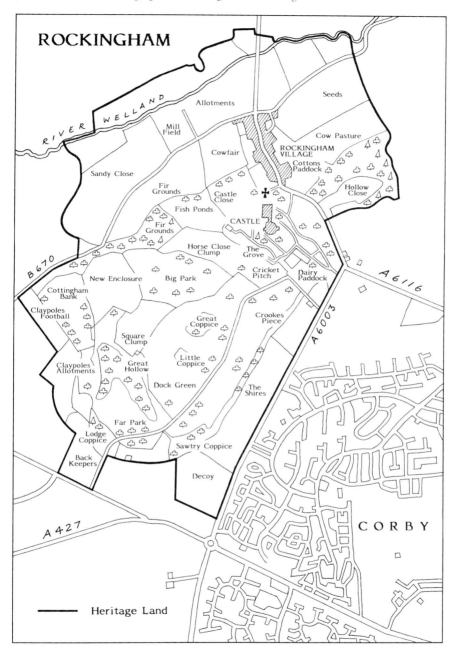

ROCKINGHAM

CORBY

—— Heritage Land

65. A plan showing the heritage land at Rockingham accepted for support by a
maintenance fund.

because the boundary of the Heritage Land is along the road that separates the estate from the new town of Corby, part of which was built on former Rockingham land. Thus the entity is a buffer against the town spreading and spoiling an area of outstanding importance.

The broader implications of exemption and planning can be clearly seen at Prideaux Place at Padstow on the north coast of Cornwall. Built by Nicholas Prideaux in 1592, the house (Fig. 66) has been long recognised as one of the principal historic houses of Cornwall, but in recent years more has been discovered about it that increases its interest and significance. First, the richly decorated barrel-vaulted ceiling of about 1640 in the Great Chamber (Fig. 26), which had been hidden by a later ceiling inserted when the room was subdivided, was revealed as one of

66. Prideaux Place at Padstow, Cornwall. The Elizabethan house overlooking its park and with its backdrop of trees protects the town.

the principal works attributable to the Abbotts, the dynasty of Barnstaple plasterers, and a smaller scale rival to the famous ceiling in the Long Gallery at Lanhydrock. A little later it was recognised that more of Edmund Prideaux's garden layout of the late 1730s survived and was an interesting essay in the manner of William Kent.

As a result of repairs carried out with the assistance of grant aid in the 1970s and early 1980s, the house was opened for the first time in 1987. The following year J.C.F. Prideaux-Brune died; as soon as his son, Peter Prideaux-Brune, succeeded, not only did he open the house more but his father's executors obtained conditional exemption from CTT on the house, contents and setting; also they put a substantial part of the estate into a maintenance fund to support the exempted property.

The significance of that series of decisions is much greater than might appear at first, because it has very positive benefits in terms of conservation planning. First, the setting of the house, with its deer park that runs down to the town, protects the town from development, providing a green backdrop to it, a situation whose reality is brought out by the contrast with that on the east side of the estuary, where there has been no unity of ownership and the land has been heavily built up.

The second important point about securing the future of Prideaux Place is that the estate also owns an important 3½ mile stretch of the coast that links up with the National Trust's Enterprise Neptune scheme.

Another significant point, albeit hard to evaluate, is the strength of local pride and interest in, indeed possessiveness about, Prideaux Place that has greatly increased since it has been open to the public. If opening has brought the house a new life, it has also made the house a focus for a wide range of cultural and social activities that extends far beyond the visitors who come on a day by day basis.

The estate at Squerryes Court, in Kent, represents another way in which estates are important for planned conservation, because it marches with two other estates which help hold together the Area of Outstanding Natural Beauty in the valley of the River Darent to the south of the North Downs between Oxted and Sevenoaks. The other estates are Titsey, now partly belonging to a charitable trust, and Chevening, a trust established by Act of Parliament. Going west out of Sevenoaks on the A25, there are a series of notable houses, first Chevening on the north side of the valley, then Brasted, a villa designed by Robert Adam, and Combe Bank, designed by Roger Morris for the future 4th Duke of Argyll, on the south side to the east of Westerham; then Quebec House in Westerham and just beyond the town Squerryes; and to the south of the latter Chartwell. Driving along the road the predominant feeling is of landscape and ancient communities under intense pressure from building accompanied by the constant pounding of the M25 in the background.

The garden at Squerryes is at present Grade 2 on the Register but it may be upgraded as a result of research into its history. The view from the entrance front has evolved gradually since the house was built in the late 17th century into an essentially 18th century composition with a backdrop on the north side of the valley provided by the Titsey woods. So here is an example of a house and garden not only providing the key to one estate, but being part of a larger jigsaw of positively managed landscape. It is the kind of point that would emerge if there was an application for conditional exemption, but there has not had to be one, and so its value may be taken for granted. However, it is part of a valuable pattern that exists all over the country, both in rural areas where the pressures are less intense and in those round cities and towns where they are always increasing and changing.

The protective role of estates in relation to a conurbation can be seen in the way the National Trust has acquired a string of properties that form a necklace round the south side of Manchester. That has never been the Trust's aim, but over the years it has acquired places for different reasons and under different circumstances, and these now fit together. The most westerly is the Dunham Massey estate of 3138 acres, which lies to the west of Altrincham. A few miles to the south of it and just north of Knutsford is the Tatton estate of 2087 acres. To the northeast of that and to the north-west of Wilmslow is the Style estate with Quarry Bank Mill, a property of 284 acres; and on the other side of Alderley Edge are two more properties, of 249 acres and 275 acres. Further east the National Trust has 1377 acres at Lyme. To the south of this necklace lie estates in other ownerships at Tabley, Peover, Capesthorne and Henbury.

Twenty-five years ago those concerned for the future of country houses but not involved with the business of estates were trying to understand the complexities of house and estate economics and making the case for the continuity of the relationship. But I do not think anyone involved at that time expected to witness not only the acceptance of that idea but also the growing emphasis on the significance of gardens, parks, landscapes and estates. The view of what is worth preserving has expanded in a most exciting and positive way, and thus country houses face the next century, and the next millennium, with a sense of appreciation that makes all the effort they involve worthwhile. Not all the entities that exist today will be there in 25 and 50 years' time and there is bound to be some continuation of the dispersal recorded by Michael Sayer, but what does seem likely is that houses will continue to challenge their occupants not to fail them, and families will find new ways of carrying out that challenge.

INDEX OF HOUSES AND GARDENS

Figures in italics refer to Plate and Illustration numbers

INDEX OF SUBJECTS